# Real-World Flutter

## by Tutorials

by Edson Bueno & Vid Palčar

# Real-World Flutter by Tutorials

Edson Bueno & Vid Palčar



## Notice of Rights



## Notice of Liability



## Trademarks



ISBN: 978-1-950325-76-4

# Table of Contents

# Book License

# Before You Begin

This section tells you a few things you need to know before you get started, such as what you'll need for hardware and software, where to find the project files for this book, and more.

# What You Need

To follow along with this book, you'll need the following:

- **Xcode 12.5.1 or later**. Xcode is iOS's main development tool, so you need it to build your Flutter app for iOS. You can download the latest version of Xcode from Apple's developer site here: https://apple.co/2asi58y or from the Mac App Store. Xcode 12.5.1 requires a Mac running macOS Big Sur (11) or later.

> **Note:** You also have the option of using Linux or Windows, but you won't be able to install Xcode or build apps for iOS on those platforms.

- **Cocoapods 1.10.2 or later**. Cocoapods is a dependency manager Flutter uses to run code on iOS.
- **Flutter SDK 3.3 or later**. You can download the Flutter SDK from the official Flutter site at https://docs.flutter.dev/get-started/install. Installing the Flutter SDK will also install the Dart SDK, which you need to compile the Dart code in your Flutter apps.
- **Android Studio 2020.3.1 or later**, available at https://developer.android.com/studio. This is the IDE in which you'll develop the sample code in this book. It also includes the Android SDK and the build system for running Flutter apps on Android.
- **Flutter Plugin for Android Studio 60.1.2 or later**, installed by going to Android Studio Preferences on macOS (or Settings on Windows/Linux) and choosing Plugins, then searching for "Flutter".

You have the option of using Visual Studio Code for your Flutter development environment instead of Android Studio. You'll still need to install Android Studio to have access to the Android SDK and an Android emulator. If you choose to use Visual Studio Code, follow the instructions on the official Flutter site at https://flutter.dev/docs/get-started/editor?tab=vscode to get set up.

Chapter 1, "Setting up Your Environment", explains more about Flutter history and architecture. You'll learn how to start using the Flutter SDK, and then you'll see how to use Android Studio and Xcode to build and run Flutter apps.

# Book Source Code & Forums

## Where to Download the Materials for This Book

The materials for this book can be cloned or downloaded from the GitHub book materials repository:

- https://github.com/raywenderlich/rwf-materials/tree/editions/1.0

## Forums

We've also set up an official forum for the book at https://forums.raywenderlich.com/c/books/real-world-flutter-by-tutorials. This is a great place to ask questions about the book or to submit any errors you may find.

"To my brother, Caio, who's the only person on this list who will actually read this book – because I'll make him. To my mom, Van, and my dad, Edson, for the unconditional love and support. To Will, my brother from another mother, and Paola, my sister from another mister, for being my partners in crime whenever I needed to decompress from this work. To Juanderson, my eternal roomie, who has always cheered for me. Lastly, to my teacher Kamila and my first employers, Ricardo and Tiago, without whom I'd probably be making my living doing something shameful to my family, like, I don't know, coding PHP."

*Edson Bueno*

"To my parents, Irena and Božidar, and my sister, Teja, who supported me growing up and shaped me into the person I am today. To my best friend Anej and his mobile app project, on which we worked as students. It was my first experience with Flutter and mobile development in general, and today this has grown into something I do for a living. To my friends, Albina and Jure, who always understood when I had to work instead of having fun with them. And to the co-author of this book, Edson, and the rest of the team that allowed me to learn from them while writing this book and being patient when I needed time."

*Vid Palčar*

# About the Authors

**Edson Bueno** is a tech lead who has been dedicated exclusively to mobile from the very first day of his career. Having always integrated consultancy firms, Edson has had the chance to collaborate on projects from the most diverse industries and experiment with all sorts of architectures. In the Flutter space, he has kept himself an active member of the community through article writing and being the proud creator of two viral packages on pub.dev, one of them elected by the Flutter Ecosystem Committee as a Flutter Favorite.

**Vid Palčar** is a software developer currently focusing on mobile development. He loves to seek new challenges by mainly focusing on work with start-ups and scale-ups. The projects he has been working on are solving everyday problems in the fields of smart homes and IoT, IPTV and video streaming, video and audio communication, sustainable/green mobility and logistics, and other mobile apps and games. In his free time, he takes every opportunity to explore new places, enjoy good food and attend great classical or jazz concerts.

# About the Editors

**Girish Maiya** is co-founder of SnapCommute Labs, which builds software products as well as provides software development service to the clients, especially in Flutter. Girish is a CA and a CISA with varied experience in audits, accounts, operations, finance, ERP implementation and testing as well as building innovative applications. He has worked in multinational organisations like GE, Infosys, Ernst and Young etc. in India as well as in US and UK and served clients like Yahoo, Cisco etc. He currently specialises in building plugins for Cordova, Ionic and Flutter.

**Emily Wydeven** is an avid scavenger of typos and grammatical errors. She has worked extensively in the tech industry and was managing editor of an online tech magazine for several years. She is a nerd for technology, cats, medical history, and comic books (among many other things). While her favorite comic book characters are Deadpool and Squirrel Girl, the character with whom Emily most closely identifies is Nancy Whitehead.

**Matthew Morey** is the final pass editor for this book. Matthew is an engineer, developer, hacker, creator, and tinkerer. As an active member of the mobile community and head of Emerging Technology at Valtech he has led numerous successful technology projects worldwide. When not developing apps he enjoys traveling, snowboarding, and surfing.

# Acknowledgments

Early ideation, book planning and draft chapters included significant work by **Prateek Sharma**. We're grateful for his help.

We would also like to thank Scott Gose of https://favqs.com for allowing us to use the FavQs API in this book.

# Introduction

Welcome to *Real-World Flutter by Tutorials*!

This book will teach you to build professional iOS and Android apps for the real world using Flutter. You'll gain all the foundations of mobile development you need to make the best decisions in your own codebase while addressing critical problems such as state management, user authentication and dynamic theming.

## How to Read This Book

After completing Chapter 1, "Setting up Your Environment", you're free to skip around chapters. You don't have to progress through this book linearly.

This book is split into 15 chapters:

1. **Setting up Your Environment** — This chapter welcomes you with an overview of what you'll build and how the book will work. It sets you up for success by teaching you everything you need to run the sample app.

2. **Mastering the Repository Pattern** — Get your data layer under control with the repository pattern. Learn how to properly handle exceptions, write clean mappers, support caching, pagination, different fetch policies and more.

3. **Managing State With Cubits & the Bloc Library** — This is your first step to becoming a BLoC wizard. Understand what state management is all about and why Blocs and Cubits are the best tools for the job.

**4. Validating Forms With Cubits** — Master Cubits before moving on to actual Blocs in the next chapter. Learn how to combine the bloc library with Formz to achieve first-class form validation in Flutter.

**5. Managing Complex State With Blocs** — This is your graduation to state management. Learn how Blocs are different from cubits, the reasons you'd pick one over another, and how to use Blocs to face complex challenges, such as pagination, search bars, filters and more.

**6. Authenticating Users** — Learn what user authentication is, how it works and how to best architect your application to support it.

**7. Routing & Navigating** — Learn everything you need to know about Navigator 2, how to set up a robust routing strategy, and how to connect your features in a decoupled way.

**8. Deep Linking** — Put your routing mechanism to the ultimate test by adding deep link support with the help of Firebase Dynamic Links.

**9. Internationalizing & Localizing** — Learn how to make your app accessible to other languages.

**10. Dynamic Theming & Dark Mode** — Learn how to use theming with dark mode in Flutter apps. Implement the light and dark themes in WonderWords by diving deep into inherited widgets.

**11. Creating Your Own Widget Catalog** — Learn about the need for a component library and storybook. Add platform-specific files to a package, make it runnable as a standalone app and use it to showcase widgets in that package. Also learn how to customize a storybook.

**12. Supporting the Development Lifecycle With Firebase** — Learn about monitoring app lifecycle with the help of Firebase Analytics and Firebase Crashlytics.

**13. Running Live Experiments With A/B Testing & Feature Flags** — Learn to test different app features and variations with Firebase Remote Config and Firebase A/B Testing tools.

**14. Automated Testing** — In this chapter, you'll learn about automated testing. You'll cover theory on the importance of automated testing, best practices and different test types, as well as see multiple examples.

**15. Automating Test Executions & Build Distributions** — This chapter covers automated test execution, project builds for Android and distribution of the builds to Firebase App Distribution.

## Feedback

Finally, for all readers, raywenderlich.com is committed to providing quality, up-to-date learning materials. We'd love to have your feedback. What parts of the book gave you one of those "aha" learning moments? Was some topic confusing? Did you spot a typo or an error? Let us know at https://forums.raywenderlich.com and look for the particular forum category for this book. We'll make an effort to take your comments into account in the next update of the book.

# Real-World Flutter by Tutorials

# Chapter 1: Setting up Your Environment

By Edson Bueno

Nothing fools you into thinking you're a great coder faster than a toy app. Any architecture looks robust in a TODO app; any state management approach looks revolutionary in a Counter app.

Example apps, toy apps, tutorial apps... They all play important roles in our learning path, but they don't always reflect the real world.

Fetching and displaying a list of items, for example, was probably one of the first things you learned how to do in Flutter. And you surely nailed it. The problem is, the real world wouldn't have stopped there; it would've kept pushing:

- "What if you add some tags to filter that list?"
- "What if you make it searchable?"
- "What if you allow the user to refresh the list by pulling it down?"
- "What if you cache the items in a local database?"
- "What if you refresh the list automatically when the user signs in?"
- "What if, instead of fetching the whole list at once, you fetch it in batches as the user scrolls?"

No problem. You'd certainly be capable of finding your way through these challenges on your own — Stack Overflow has your back. But then you'd have to ask: "Would your solution be the *best* way?" Would you still be able to look at your code and feel proud?

That's why this book exists: To be your survivors' guide to the real world — a cookbook full of recipes that demonstrate how professionals handle the most common problems in our industry.

This chapter will onboard you by explaining:

- What you'll build throughout the book.
- What an API key is and how to get yours.
- What compile-time variables are and how to specify them.
- What Firebase can do for you and how to set up its console.
- How to build and run the book's sample app. Because, yeah, not even *running* apps out in the wild is as simple as you might think.

"Welcome to the real world. It sucks. You're gonna love it." — Monica Geller, "Friends".

Throughout this chapter, you'll work on the **starter** project from this chapter's **assets** folder.

# Getting to Know the Sample App

Right out of the gate, you'll have the complete app in your hands. That means you won't have to wait until the last chapter to find out how the app or the codebase will look by the end of this book.

The second chapter's final project, for instance, is no different from the sixth chapter's. What changes is the starter project. Each chapter works as an isolated tutorial, starting from a different place to show you how each part of the app is built.

The app in question is **WonderWords**, an insightful quotes archive. Users can explore, upvote, downvote and mark their favorite quotes. And you thought closing the introduction with a quote was just a lazy cliché!

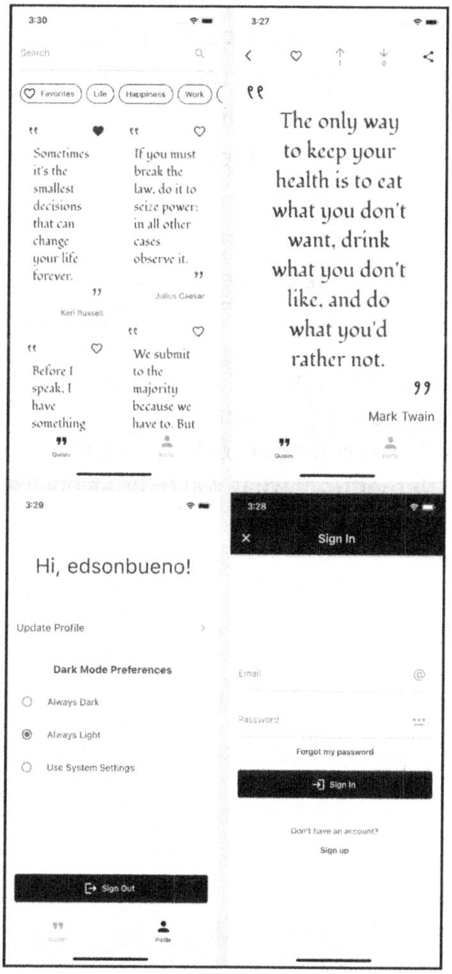

WonderWords has fought — and gracefully won — all the battles real-world apps have to go through: search, pagination, forms, authentication, deep links, internationalization, dark mode, analytics, feature flags, automated tests, CI/CD and more. Your interaction with it will start from the inside out.

## Overviewing the Architecture

"Talk is cheap. Show me the code," said the wise man. So kick things off by using your preferred IDE to open the starter project. Then, expand the **lib** folder.

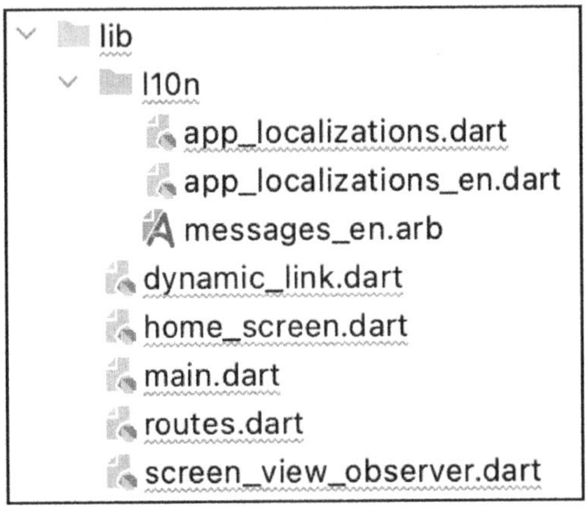


> **Note**: Ignore the errors for now; they'll go away as soon as you fetch the project's dependencies in the next section. Don't try to do that on your own just yet. **WonderWords** has some particularities that make fetching dependencies a bit different from what you're probably used to.

Considering this is the complete app, don't you find it odd that you see only seven Dart files under **lib**? The explanation lies in the **packages** folder, which is at the same level as **lib**. Expand it, and expand a few of its child directories.

Do you understand now why there were so few files before? The reason is you split the codebase into multiple local packages. Those packages are just like the ones you use from pub.dev, except these are internal to your project. Pretty cool, huh?

Some might think this is "too much" for a small app, or too complex for a less experienced team, but here's the truth:

- You never know how much an app will grow. It's extremely common for small apps to end up huge.
- Architecting an app like this makes even more sense for less mature teams. Isolated packages allow you to experiment, make mistakes and have total freedom regarding your patterns, architecture, state management approaches and more.

The list of advantages goes on and on:

- Finer-grained **dependency control**. Since each package has a separate **pubspec.yaml**, you don't have to depend on everything all the time anymore.
- Nice, **clean boundaries**. Your team has no choice but to be thoughtful about the public classes and functions they create.
- It's easier to avoid collisions and **merge conflicts**.
- Shorter **continuous integration (CI)** running time when changing packages individually. You'll learn more about this in Chapter 15, "Automating Test Executions & Build Distributions".

But, of course, it's not all sunshine and roses. Some routine procedures, like running unit tests, fetching dependencies or running `flutter clean`, now require you to do them once for each local package. The following section will show you how you can leverage some custom commands to automate those processes for you.

## Fetching Dependencies

If you're on Android Studio, open the terminal by clicking the bottom-left **Terminal** tab:

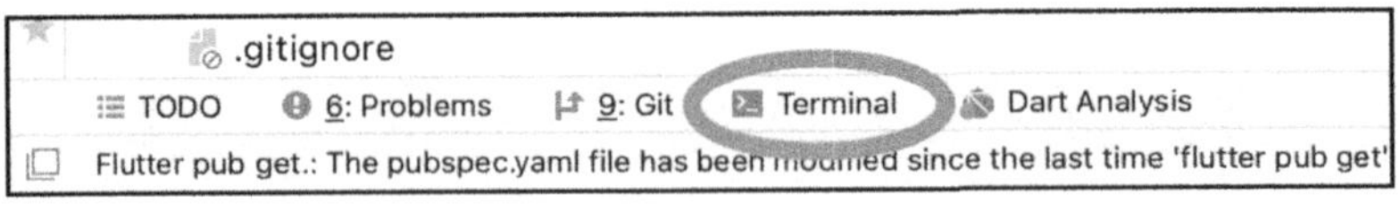

If you're using VS Code, you can do the same by clicking **View ▸ Terminal** on the toolbar.

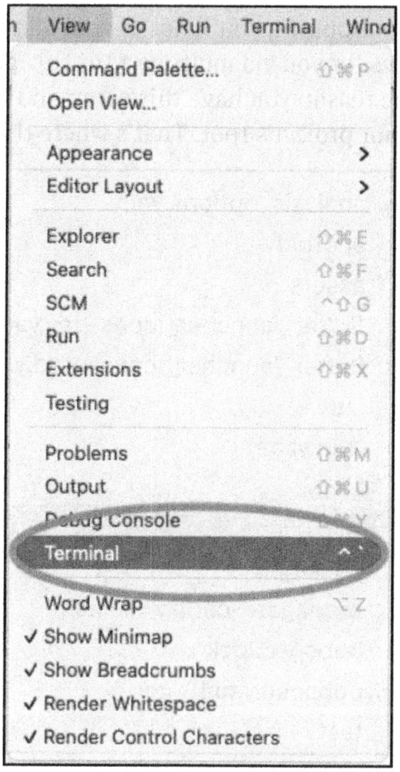


**Note**: You can always use your preferred standalone terminal app instead of the IDE-integrated one. If you do that, don't forget to use the cd command first to navigate to the root directory of your starter project.

Now, in the terminal tab you just opened, type `make get` and press **Enter**. Expect the command to take a while to finish executing.

If you look at your terminal's output, you'll notice that all `make get` does is fetch your project's dependencies for you via multiple `flutter pub get` commands, one for each local package. The reason you have this command available to you is the **makefile** file located in your project's root. That's where the command comes from.

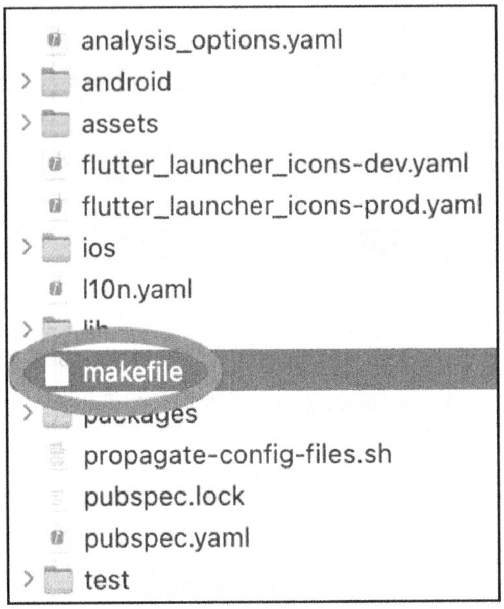


All **makefile** does is define a few custom commands that come in handy when working with multi-package projects. Feel free to copy-paste and adjust it to any future projects you work on using that same structure.

## Learning About Package Arrangement

The next thing to point out is *how* you're making this package arrangement. What are the criteria for deciding which files belong together? That topic transcends mobile development; the community has been debating it for a while in the old "package-by-layer versus package-by-feature" discussion.

> **Note**: This discussion is also called **folder-by-layer** versus **folder-by-feature**. That terminology is more relatable for teams who are either not using internal packages or are using programming languages that don't support packages.

## Package-by-layer

Using a package-by-layer structure means you group your files based on their technical aspects. So, for example, your database files get one package, your networking files get another, your widgets another and so on.

This is how WonderWords' package distribution would look with **package-by-layer**:

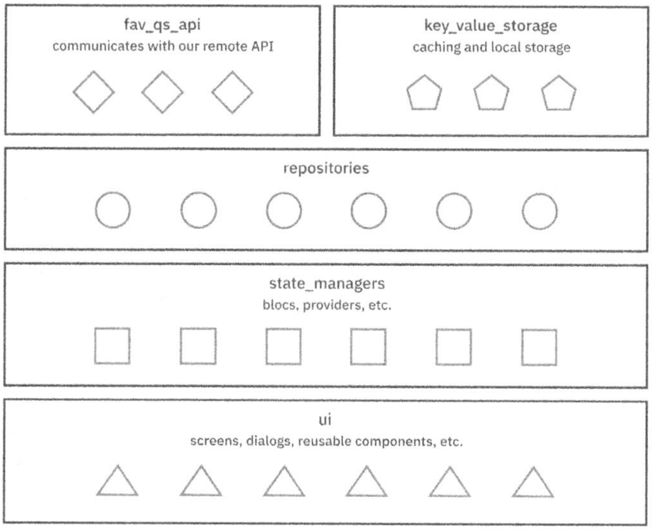


**Advantages**:

- For some reason, package-by-layer speaks to our nature; it's how our minds intuitively work. That makes the strongest argument in favor of this approach: there's a low learning curve.
- It encourages code reuse. Files belong to a layer and not to a feature of the app, so you don't think twice if you need to reuse a component even if the team originally created it to support another feature.
- Different projects end up having a similar (or even the same) structure. Curiously, that's also the first point on the list of disadvantages.

**Disadvantages**:

- The package-by-layer structure doesn't immediately convey the most interesting information about your app. When skimming through a codebase, it's unlikely that you want to know if it "has screens" more than you want to know which features it has.
- Everything is public. For example, every screen file can import all the state manager files, even though most screens use a single state manager. This makes it easier for inattentive developers to import files they're not supposed to.
- Developers have to jump around the file tree constantly. This is what happens when files that often change together are stored in different locations, such as screens and state managers. That goes against what Robert Cecil Martin, acclaimed author of "Clean Code", taught us about the Single Responsibility Principle: "Gather together the things that change for the same reasons."
- It doesn't scale well. As the number of files in your project grows, the number of packages stays the same. Whether your project has five or fifty screens, you still only have one **ui** package.
- It makes it hard to onboard new team members. You either know how all or none of the features work; there's no middle ground. You feel like you have to understand everything in order to help with anything.

## Package-by-feature

An alternative to grouping files based on their technical aspects is to group them by their domain affinity. For example, instead of having **quote_list_screen.dart** under **ui** and **quote_list_bloc.dart** under **state_managers**, you could have both under a **quote_list** package.

For WonderWords, using a **package-by-feature** approach would look like this:

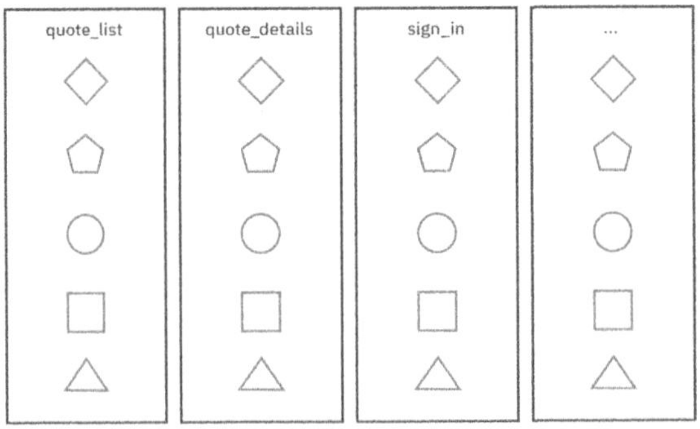

**Advantages**:

- With a package-by-feature approach, finding files is a breeze. The structure of your codebase now mimics the design of your app.
- It scales well. As the number of files grows, the number of packages grows accordingly.
- The codebase becomes self-documenting. At a glance, you have an idea of how big the app is and what it does.
- You have complete visibility control. For example, now **quote_list_bloc.dart** can only be visible inside the **quote_list** package.
- It offers smoother onboarding. You only have to understand the feature you're working on.
- You get clearer squad ownership. Each subteam knows exactly which packages it's responsible for.
- It's easy to conduct experiments and migrations. Want to try a new state management approach? No problem. Restrain it to a single feature package and no one else has to worry about it.

**Disadvantages**:

- It promotes the creation of the so-called **common package** — a package that developers usually create to hold all the code used by more than one feature. This might seem good in theory. In practice, the **common** package becomes a giant dumpster of files that are completely unrelated to one another.
- There's a higher risk of code duplication. If you need something that's already implemented in another feature, there's a chance you either don't know about it or don't want to take on the burden of moving it to the **common** package, so you just create another version.
- It demands a certain cognitive load when deciding where to place a file. "Should it be inside that package? Should I create another package for it? Should it be inside **common**?"

Now that you know how both package-by-layer and package-by-feature work, can you guess which one WonderWords uses?

Your answer is correct if you said neither... or both.

## Packaging by Convenience

As you've seen, both approaches have pros and cons. Package-by-layer works best for files that aren't tied to a single feature, like databases and networking stuff. In contrast, package-by-feature shines for files that are rarely reused, like screens and state managers.

So, why not mix both and create packages as you find convenient instead?

> **Note**: "Convenient" may sound sloppy but, as you'll see, that's the opposite direction of where you're heading.

Finally, this is how WonderWords' package distribution really is:

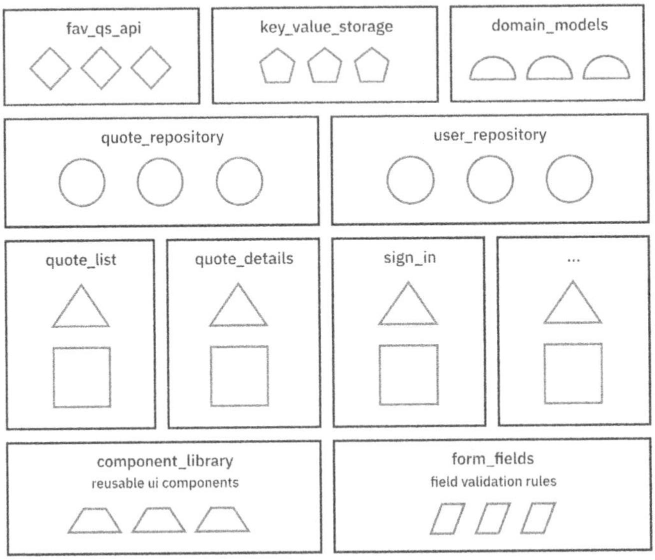


Notice that some packages are feature-based, like **quote_list**, **quote_details** and **sign_in**. In contrast, all the other packages represented above are layer-based, like **key_value_storage** and **component_library**.

These are the four commandments governing WonderWords' package distribution:

**1. Features get their own package**

For this command, you follow the package-by-feature approach. But what's a feature?

For some people, a feature is a screen; for others, it's a flow of related screens. Furthermore, formal definitions will tell you that a screen can gather many features, like a home screen. At the same time, a feature can span out across different screens, like an e-commerce checkout process. Sounds complex, right?

Luckily, you don't have to be that dogmatic. Here, you'll consider a feature to be either:

1. A screen.
2. A dialog that executes I/O calls, like networking and databases. WonderWords' **forgot_password** package falls into this category.

Other than that, if it's just a dummy UI component that you want to share between two or more screens, like a search bar, you should place it inside the **component_library** package.

**2. Features don't know about each other**

When screen A wants to open screen B, it doesn't import screen B and navigate to it directly. Instead, screen A's constructor receives a function that it can call when it wants to open screen B. In the end, the **main** application package will connect the wires.

To give you a concrete example from WonderWords, when the `QuoteListScreen` wants to open the `QuoteDetailsScreen`, it just calls the `onQuoteTap` callback it received in its constructor.

**3. Repositories also get their own package**

Chapter 2, "Mastering the Repository Pattern", will explain repositories in depth. For now, know that they're classes responsible for retrieving and sending data by coordinating different sources, like the network and a database.

For example, in WonderWords, **user_repository** coordinates between network and database calls to send and retrieve the user's information.

**4. No common package**

Repeat with me: **No common package**.

When you need to share something between two or more packages, you'll create a more specialized package to handle that. Five of your packages originated from this rule:

- **component_library**: Holds UI components that either are, or have the potential to be, reused across different screens.
- **fav_qs_api**: Since both **user_repository** and **quote_repository** talk to your remote API, it makes sense to create a separate package for it.
- **key_value_storage**: Same story as **fav_qs_api**, but this one wraps your local storage.
- **domain_models**: You can expect that repositories will need to start sharing models or custom exceptions at some point. Therefore, it's a good thing to have a separate package for your domain models right from the start.
- **form_fields**: Contains field validation logic that different features share.

Notice how you could have easily dumped these into a single **common** package, but instead, you ended up putting them into six different specialized packages.

> **Note**: Don't worry if you find all this overwhelming; the following chapters go through each of these commandments in detail.

Hopefully, that was enough to hype you up for what's yet to come. Now, you'll go through the steps you need to run the app for yourself.

# Learning About API Keys

WonderWords wouldn't be a real-world app if it didn't talk to a remote API. And, for a book that carries "real world" in its title, it couldn't just be any API. It needed one that offers features that are in demand: paginated listing, details, token-based authentication, sign up, the ability to favorite quotes and so on. That's how this book ended up with FavQs.com.

FavQs.com is an online quote repository with both web and mobile apps — and it also provides a completely free remote API.

> **Note**: A big shout-out to Scott Gose, the creator and maintainer of FavQs.com. His work has contributed to this book in more ways than he can imagine.

Even though FavQs.com is a free API that anyone can use, it needs a way to identify the apps that send them requests. That gives them a way to ban abusers — generally, people using bots to overload their servers with a massive number of requests.

Most public APIs, including FavQs.com, do that by asking developers to register on their website to get a code called an **API key**. Developers must then include that key in the header of any HTTP request they make. If, down the road, the API admins notice lousy behavior coming from that key, they can quickly ban it.

An API key is for your app what emails and passwords are for your users.

# Getting an API Key

To get your key, sign up at FavQs.com, then go to the API keys page (https://favqs.com/api_keys) and click **Generate API Key**. Copy the generated key and paste it wherever you can easily find it. You'll use it shortly.

## Storing the API Key

OK, now you not only know what an API key is, but you also have one in your hands. Your next step is knowing where to put it in the project.

Considering you have to send the key inside your HTTP headers, the first idea that might come to mind is to store it in the code itself. Something like this:

```
final appToken = 'YOUR_API_KEY';

options = BaseOptions(headers: {
  'Authorization': 'Token token=$appToken',
});
// Omitted code.
```

As it turns out, that approach has a crucial downside: Now, everyone who has access to your code can see what your key is — and can use it for malicious purposes. That risk becomes even more apparent if you use a public GitHub repository.

> **Note**: Crackers actually go the extra mile and set up bots that scan public repositories day and night. They can find keys within minutes of someone posting them.

Welcome to your first real-world problem: storing static sensitive keys. The solution? **Compile-time variables**.

## Storing Your API Key in a Compile-time Variable

Navigate to **packages/fav_qs_api/lib/src** and open **fav_qs_api.dart**.

> **Note**: You'll find two files with that name inside the package: one under **lib** and another under **src**. Make sure you open the one inside **src**.

Look at `setUpAuthHeaders` at the end of the file:

```
void setUpAuthHeaders(UserTokenSupplier userTokenSupplier) {
  final appToken = const String.fromEnvironment(
    _appTokenEnvironmentVariableKey,
  );
  options = BaseOptions(headers: {
    'Authorization': 'Token token=$appToken',
  });
  // Omitted code.
}
```

That's where you set up your headers. Focus on that `String.fromEnvironment()`. It's telling Dart to look up a value inside a compile-time variable called `fav-qs-app-token`.

Compile-time variables are nothing but values you have to pass to Dart when commanding it to run your app. You do that by specifying the `dart-define` parameter when using `flutter run` to run your app, like so:

```
flutter run --dart-define=fav-qs-app-token=YOUR_KEY
```

With that approach, everyone that wants to run your app has to provide their own key. The best part is that the code remains untouched. You can still share keys with your team, but they're not exposed in the code anymore.

But, you probably don't use the command line to run your app. Right? Don't worry. Next, you'll see how to configure your IDE to handle your `dart-defines` for you so you don't have to specify the key every time.

> **Note**: Follow the instructions below based on the IDE you use.

# Customizing Android Studio's Running Configs

At the top of your screen, click **main.dart**, then **Edit Configurations...**.

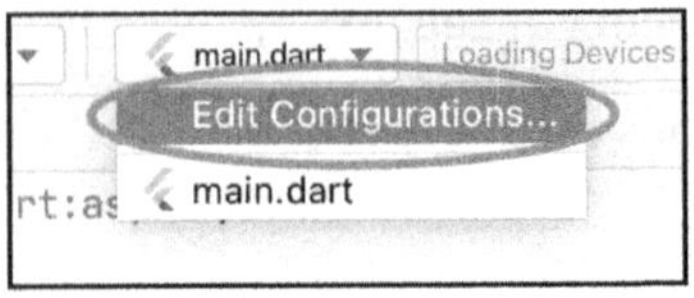


When you first open a project with Android Studio, it creates a default running configuration for you and calls it **main.dart** — because, well, it executes the **main.dart** file.

In the **Additional run args** field of this default configuration, enter `--dart-define=fav-qs-app-token=YOUR_API_KEY` — but replace **YOUR_API_KEY** with the actual key you got from FavQs.com. The result will look like this:

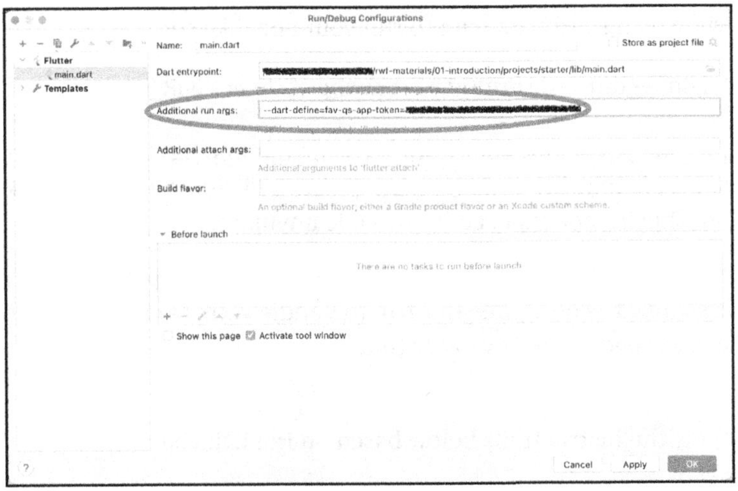


Finally, click **OK**.

# Customizing VS Code's Running Configs

Click **Run and Debug** on the left-side panel, then click **create a launch.json file**. Finally, select the **Dart & Flutter** environment.

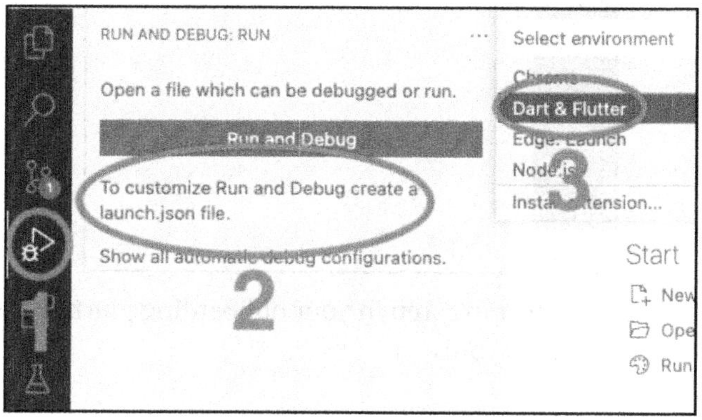


Notice that VS Code created and opened a **launch.json** file, which defines the different setups you can choose from when asking the IDE to build and run the app for you. Replace its contents with:

```
{
    "configurations": [
        {
            "name": "WonderWords",
            "request": "launch",
            "type": "dart",
            "program": "lib/main.dart",
            "args": [
                "--dart-define",
                "fav-qs-app-token=YOUR_API_KEY"
            ]
        }
    ]
}
```

Don't forget to replace **YOUR_API_KEY** with your actual key from FavQs.com.

Save the file. Notice that you now have a new configuration to pick when running the app.

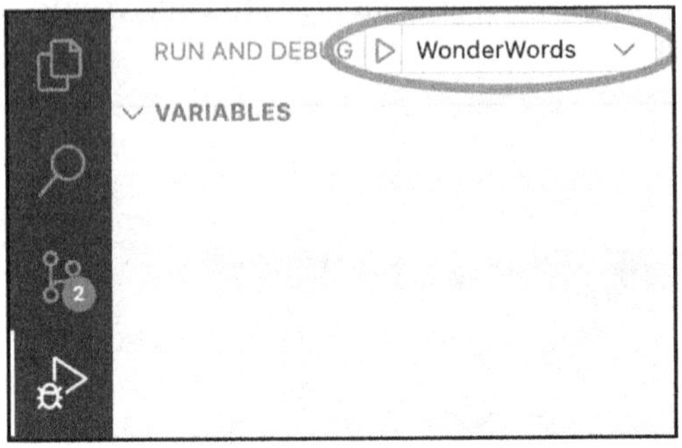


That's all for the API key. The next step in your onboarding journey is setting up Firebase's console for WonderWords.

> **Note**: Setting up Firebase's console is *mandatory* to run the app in all the following chapters. As tempting as it may sound, especially if you already know Firebase, please don't skip it.

## Configuring Firebase's Console

I'm probably not lucky enough to be the one introducing you to Firebase for the first time. But, just in case I am: Firebase is a platform from Google that pulls together a whole bunch of remote tools that make the app development life cycle smoother.

Firebase's useful capabilities range from equipping corporate apps with a device farm to execute tests all the way to helping front-end developers create remote APIs without writing back-end code. Nearly all professional apps use Firebase.

WonderWords relies on Firebase for all the typical use cases in mobile apps: dynamic links, analytics, crash reporting, feature flags and A/B tests. You'll cover these topics in later chapters, but since you need the configuration in place to run the app, you'll handle that part now.

## Creating a Firebase Project

Start by opening Firebase's console (https://console.firebase.google.com/) and signing in with a Google account. Then, click **Create a project** if you haven't used Firebase before, or **Add project** if you have.

For the project's name, enter **wonder-words.** If this is your first time using Firebase, make sure you check **I accept the Firebase terms**. Click **Continue**, then **Continue** again on the next screen.

Now, for the **Configure Google Analytics** screen, keep the default values. Select **I accept the Google Analytics terms**, then confirm by clicking **Create project**.

Once Firebase finishes creating your project, click **Continue** for the last time. If everything goes well, you'll see your project's dashboard. You'll visit this page a lot, so feel free to bookmark it.

The Firebase project you just created doesn't stand on its own; it serves only as a container for one or more Firebase *apps*, which you'll create next. For WonderWords, two apps are necessary: one for Android and another for iOS. Below, you'll find separate instructions for each. Be aware, though, following the Android instructions is optional if you'll only use iOS devices to run the app – or vice versa if you'll only use Android devices.

# Adding an iOS App

While still on your project's dashboard, click the **iOS** button near the center of the page. Then, for **iOS bundle ID**, enter **com.raywenderlich.wonderWords** and click **Register app**.

Firebase will now generate a configuration file for you. The Firebase SDK in your code will read that file later to know exactly where to point to for all of Firebase's services you decide to use in your app.

Download the file by clicking **Download GoogleService-Info.plist**. Then, click the **X** button at the top-left corner to skip the remaining steps and go back to the home page.

> **Note**: The other steps are instructions for setting up native apps. They don't fit your use case, so you'll strike out on your own.

Open **Xcode**, then click **File ▸ Open...** on the toolbar. Select the **Runner.xcworkspace** file in your project's **ios** folder. Finally, click **Open**.

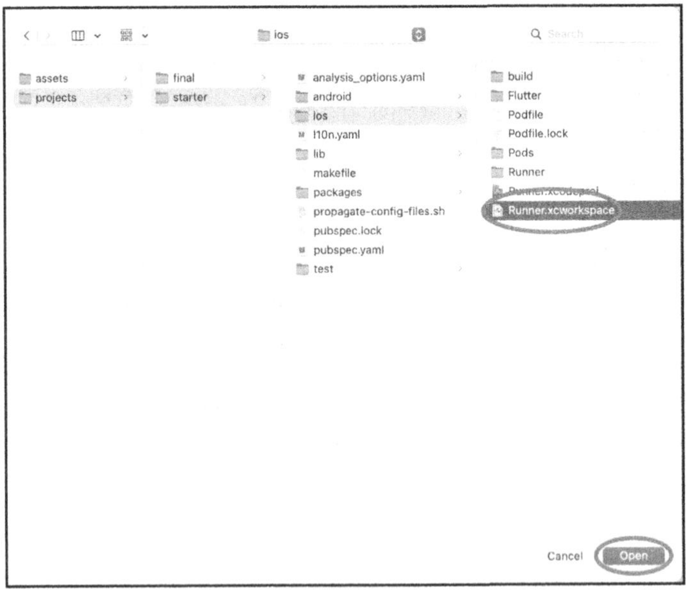

Once Xcode finishes opening, drag and drop your downloaded **GoogleService-Info.plist** into the **Runner** folder of your project in Xcode.

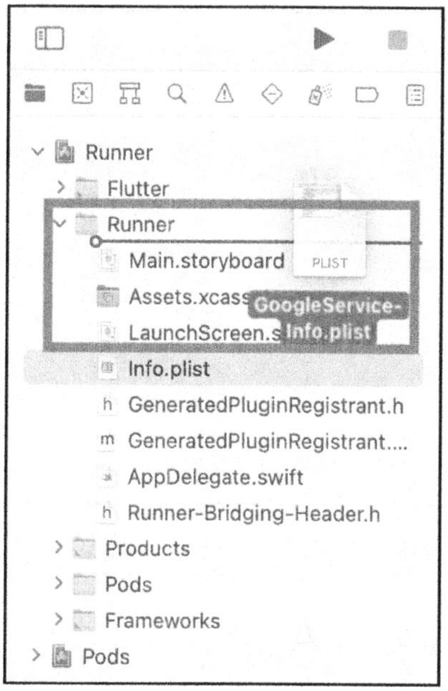


> **Note**: This has to be done through **Xcode** for it to change your project's configurations. Don't try to manually copy and paste the file using the **Finder** app.

In the window that pops up next, make sure you've selected **Copy items if needed** and click **Finish**.

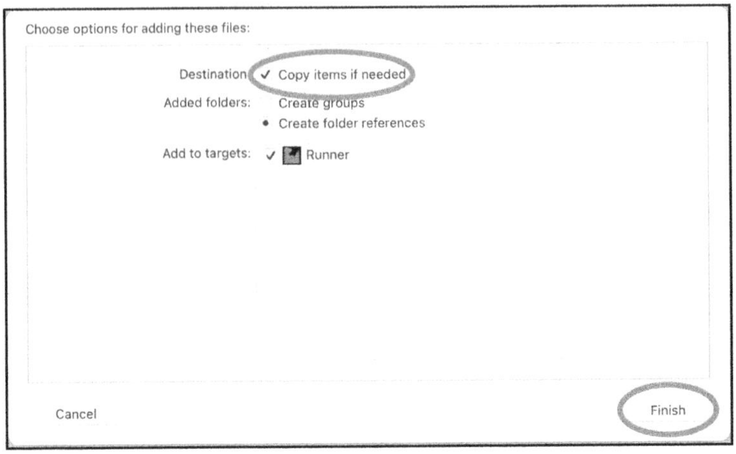


That was all! You can close **Xcode** now and get back to VS Code or Android Studio.

# Adding an Android App

Now, you'll handle the Android side of things. On Firebase's console home page, click **+ Add app** near the top of the page, then select the Android icon.

For the **Android package name**, enter **com.raywenderlich.wonder_words**. Then, click **Register app**.

Firebase will give you another configuration file: a **.json** file this time. Click **Download google-services.json** and, once again, skip the remaining steps. This time, paste the file in **android/app**.

# Running the App

It's party time! Use the custom running configuration you created a few sections ago to build and run your app. When you're done, you'll see something like this:

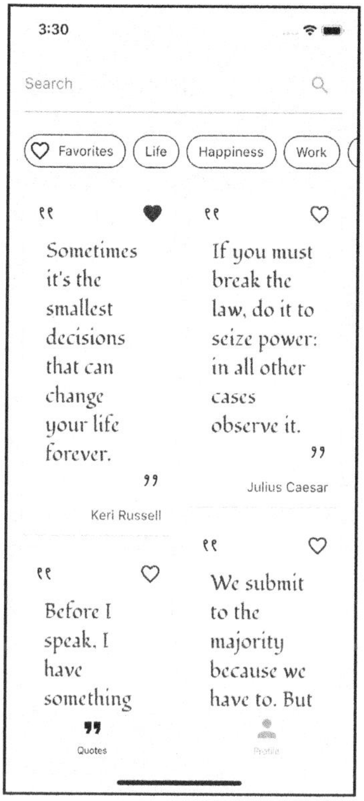


Spend some time getting familiar with WonderWords. You two have a long road ahead of you.

## Propagating the Configurations to the Following Chapters

As an outcome of this chapter, you added a few configuration files to your starter project:

- One or two Firebase configuration files, depending on whether you configured it for both platforms (Android and iOS).
- A `.idea` *or* `.vscode` hidden folder. Exactly which of these you have depends on the IDE you use. This folder is where the IDE generated your custom running configuration with the API key compile-time variable.

The problem is, you've only added these files to the *first* chapter's *starter* project, but you'll need them in place for all of the following chapters' starter *and* final projects as well. Without those files, you can't run the app.

You *could* just go ahead and manually copy-paste the files to their respective paths in all the other projects, but you're talking about at least two projects for each chapter in the book. The good news is you don't have to do that manually; your project contains a shell script that automates everything for you.

If you're on macOS or Linux, run the script by re-opening the **Terminal** tab in your IDE. From there, execute the following command: `sh propagate-config-files.sh`. If you're on Windows and don't know how to run shell scripts, you can follow this tutorial (https://www.thewindowsclub.com/how-to-run-sh-or-shell-script-file-in-windows-10).

The script assumes you haven't separated your starter project from the rest of the materials. If you did, you'll experience errors using it.

> **Note**: Propagating the configuration files, whether manually or by using the script, is a *mandatory* step. Without it, you won't be able to build and run the app in any of the following chapters.

Congratulations and welcome aboard!

# Key Points

- Splitting the codebase into **multiple local packages** is an incredible way to enforce separation of concerns, promote cleaner APIs, allow experiments, isolate mistakes, manage dependencies better, avoid merge conflicts and much more.
- You don't have to choose between the **feature-by-layer** and **feature-by-package** architectures; a mixed approach is often the best.
- Creating a **common package** is a bad practice. Create more specialized packages instead.
- An **API key** serves as your app's credentials for accessing a remote API, similar to a login and password.
- Don't store **API keys** in your code because anyone can read them. An alternative is using **compile-time variables**.

# Where to Go From Here?

This chapter included everything you could expect from a real-life onboarding: It presented the architecture, the app and the configurations you need to run it.

Before you proceed, make sure you get to know WonderWords very well as a user. Also, feel free to spend some time getting familiar with the general pieces of the architecture — but be careful not to get frustrated if you don't grasp how something works right away. Starting from the next chapter, you'll learn everything you need to know about these topics, building the confidence you need to apply any of these patterns like they're second nature to you.

Have fun!

# Chapter 2: Mastering the Repository Pattern

By Edson Bueno

The purpose of this book is to arm you with recipes to solve real-world problems in the most elegant fashion. By the end of the book, you'll have recipes for form validation, list pagination, routing, dark mode and more. This chapter covers the most universal of them: a recipe for manipulating data.

Fetching and sending data is basically all you do as a mobile developer. Think about it: You're either showing the user what came from the server or sending what came from the user to the server.

You might already be familiar with the not-so-secret ingredient behind this recipe: the **repository pattern**. By the end of this chapter, you'll not only have mastered repositories, but you'll also have learned:

- How to handle **class dependencies** in WonderWords' architecture.
- What a **barrel file** is and how to create one.
- What **pagination** is.
- What **streams** are.
- What a **fetch policy** is.
- What **domain models** are.
- How to approach **exceptions**.
- What **mappers** are.

That's a lot to learn, so get ready to dive right in! While going through this chapter, you'll work on the **starter** project from this chapter's **assets** folder.

# Learning About Repositories

Almost every app, from the simplest to the most complex, contains these two elements in its architecture:

- **State managers**: Blocs, Cubits, Providers, ViewModels and so on.
- **Data sources**: Classes that interact directly with the database or network client to fetch responses and return them as parsed models.

> **Note**: You're probably used to seeing these under different names. Developers usually suffix state managers with `Bloc` or `Provider` instead of `StateManager`. Similarly, data sources' names don't have to end in `DataSource`; in WonderWords, for example, `FavQsApi` is a data source.

More often than not, state managers talk directly to data sources. So, for instance, a state manager like `QuoteListBloc` gets the data it needs by interacting directly with `FavQsApi` — a data source.

Connecting a state manager directly to a data source works great — as long as there's only one data source in that relationship. Things get messy when there's more than one, such as when apps need to cache data.

**Caching** means backing up your API results in a local database. Doing this allows you to retrieve that data later, even if the network fails. It's also useful when you want to respond faster and save bandwidth the next time the user opens that screen.

When you're caching results for a certain screen and your state managers are in charge of talking directly to the data sources, your state managers accumulate another huge responsibility: coordinating between two data sources — the database's and the network's.

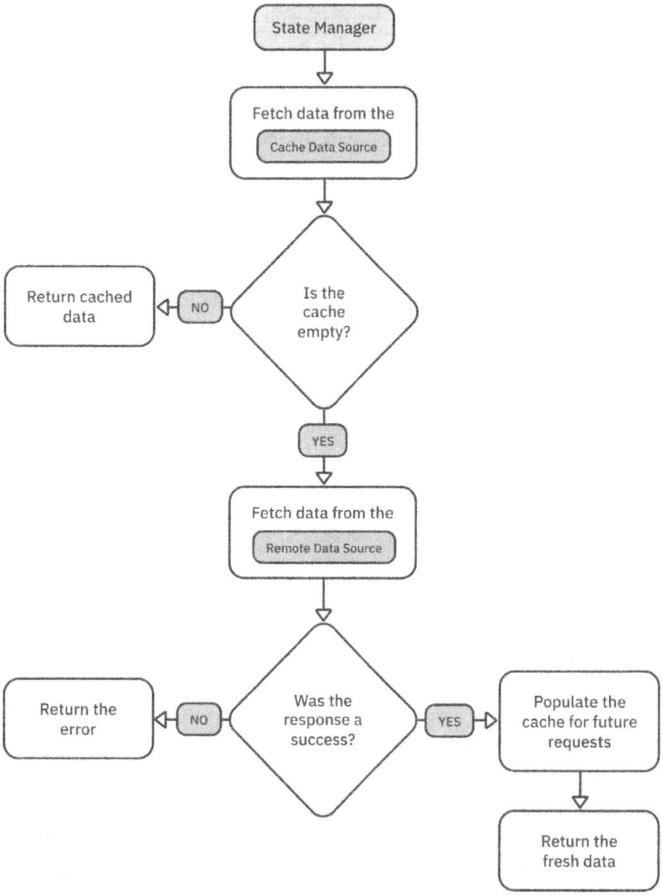

This is where repositories come to the rescue.

The **repository pattern** consists of creating a class, the repository, that sits in the middle of your state managers and data sources and takes all the coordination effort away from your state managers. In other words, your state managers won't have to care where the data comes from anymore.

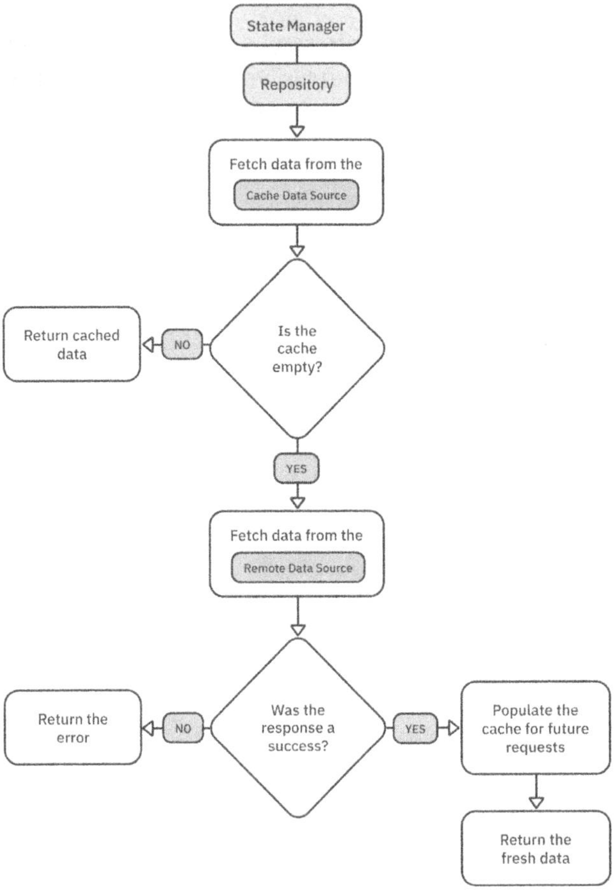


Notice that repositories also allow you to share coordination logic between different state managers in the future.

That's really all there is to it. In fact, the repository pattern is so simple and brings so much value to your codebase that if you had to choose a single pattern to take away from the book, this should be it.

Let all that knowledge sink in for a minute while you learn about another concept that's just as important: **class dependencies**.

# Introducing Class Dependencies

A **class dependency** is any class that another class depends upon to do its work. For example, if `QuoteRepository` relies on `FavQsApi` to fetch its data, that makes `FavQsApi` a class dependency of `QuoteRepository`. Simple, right?

Now, there are two ways a class can get an instance of one of its class dependencies:

1. **Instantiating it by itself**: You can do this inside the constructor, in the property's declaration, just before using it in a function or anywhere else you want. An extremely minimal example would be:

```
class QuoteRepository {
  final FavQsApi _favQsApi = FavQsApi();

  // Omitted code.
}
```

2. **Requiring an instance to be passed in its constructor**: For example:

```
class QuoteRepository {
  const QuoteRepository(
    this.favQsApi,
  );

  final FavQsApi favQsApi;

  // Omitted code.
}
```

Both approaches have pros and cons.

The first one has the benefit that you don't expose your inner dependencies to users of your class, which makes your classes more self-contained. For example, users of `QuoteRepository` don't have to know it depends on `FavQsApi`. The downside is if other repositories in your code also depend on `FavQsApi`, you won't be able to share the same instance between them because each of them creates its own. Another con is that you'll need to repeat that instantiation logic everywhere you need it.

> **Note**: Keep in mind the snippet above is just a minimal example. Instantiating classes is often not as simple as calling `FavQsApi()`. In the real world, your dependencies also have their own dependencies and other parameters they expect to receive in the constructor. That's why replicating that instantiation logic is problematic.

On the other hand, the second approach, asking for the dependency in the constructor, just flips the pros and cons of the first one. It's good because you can share instances of the dependencies between different classes... and bad because your classes aren't self-contained anymore. The dependencies are now exposed in the constructor, and the class's users need to take care of them.

Which one is best? As always, it depends on the situation. You'll put both these ideas into practice throughout this chapter.

## Handling Class Dependencies in WonderWords

If you think back to the architecture rules from Chapter 1, "Setting up Your Environment", you'll remember that each repository gets a separate internal package. But why?

Repositories are often used by multiple features. That alone makes it impossible for you to put them inside a feature package because features shouldn't depend on one another — therefore, you wouldn't be able to use a repository in more than one feature.

An alternative would be to have a single **repositories** package that all your features could depend on to access all the repositories. But packages are supposed to group stuff that's often used together, and it's improbable that a single feature would end up needing all repositories.

That leaves you with one right choice: having one package for each repository.

To save you some time, this chapter already has a **quote_repository** package under the **packages** folder of the starter project. Open the project in your preferred IDE. Then, fetch the project's dependencies by using the terminal to run `make get` from the root directory. Wait until the command finishes executing; ignore all the errors in the code for now.

Expand the **lib** folder of this **quote_repository** package, and, under **src**, open **quote_repository.dart**:

Kick off the work by replacing `// TODO: Add constructor and data sources properties.` with:

```
QuoteRepository({
  required KeyValueStorage keyValueStorage,
  required this.remoteApi,
  @visibleForTesting QuoteLocalStorage? localStorage,
}) : _localStorage = localStorage ??
          QuoteLocalStorage(
            keyValueStorage: keyValueStorage,
          );

final FavQsApi remoteApi;
final QuoteLocalStorage _localStorage;
```

There are a couple of things to note in there:

First, take a look at the two `final` properties. As mentioned, repositories orchestrate multiple data sources. In this case, you have two:

1. **FavQsApi**: Retrieves and sends data to your remote API. `FavQsApi` comes from another internal package of this project: **fav_qs_api**.

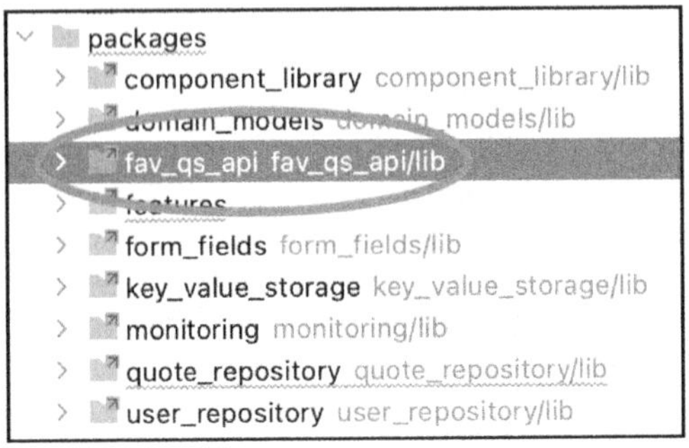


2. **QuoteLocalStorage**: Retrieves and stores quotes in the device's local storage. `QuoteLocalStorage` does *not* come from a separate package. It's defined inside this same folder you're working on.

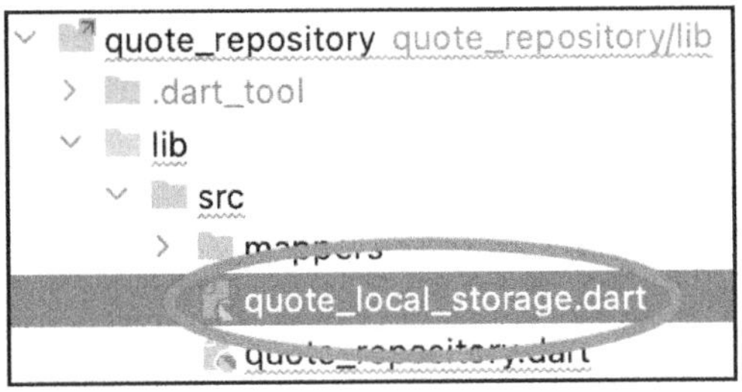

The first question you might have is: Why does `FavQsApi` have its own package while `QuoteLocalStorage` doesn't?

`QuoteLocalStorage` is more specialized because it only deals with quotes. Therefore, it has no utility outside the **quote_repository** package.

`FavQsApi`, on the other hand, is more generic because it handles both quotes and authentication calls. That makes it suitable for the **user_repository** package as well, which you'll cover in Chapter 6, "Authenticating Users". As you know, when you need to share code between two packages — in this case, two repositories — you have to create a third one. In this case, that's **fav_qs_api**.

Although `QuoteLocalStorage` doesn't come from a separate package, it depends on `KeyValueStorage`, which *does* come from the separate **key_value_storage** package.

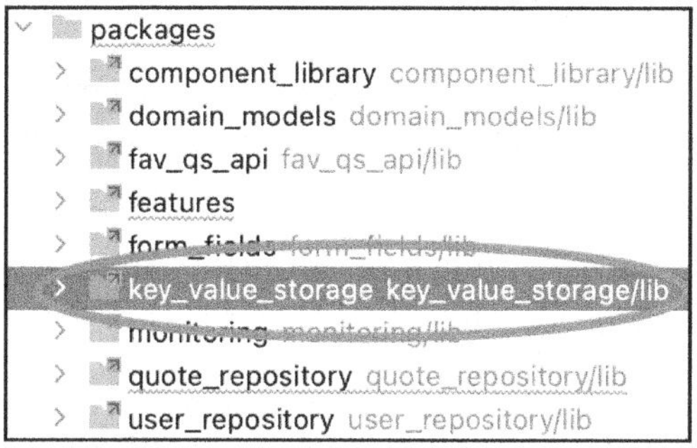


Think of `KeyValueStorage` as WonderWords' local database. It's a wrapper around the popular Hive (https://pub.dev/packages/hive) package. It had to become an internal package of its own to concentrate all of the Hive configuration in a single place.

> **Note**: If you navigate to `KeyValueStorage` by Command-clicking it inside the constructor you just created, you can look at the doc comments in there to become more familiar with the way it works.

Now, getting back to your constructor, notice it has three parameters: two required and one optional.

```
QuoteRepository({
  required KeyValueStorage keyValueStorage,
  required this.remoteApi,
  @visibleForTesting QuoteLocalStorage? localStorage
}) : _localStorage = localStorage ??
          QuoteLocalStorage(
            keyValueStorage: keyValueStorage,
          );
```

The answer to the previous question about whether you should *require* class dependencies in the constructor or instantiate them by yourself inside the class is: It depends. Here's how you decide:

- Class dependencies whose files are situated *inside* the same package you're working on should be instantiated *inside* the constructor. This is the case for `QuoteLocalStorage`.
- Class dependencies that come from *other* internal packages, like `KeyValueStorage` and `FavQsApi`, *must* be received in the constructor.

Why is that? If a class comes from another package, like `FavQsApi`, it's likely that it's used by another internal package as well — **user_repository**, for example. That means that requiring the dependency to be passed in the constructor, rather than instantiating it inside the dependent class, is the best choice because it allows you to share the same instance across all places that use it.

> **Note**: These shared instances still have to be created somewhere. That's the main application package's job because it's the one responsible for integrating all the other packages. You'll learn more about this in Chapter 7, "Routing & Navigating".

On the other hand, when the class dependency is defined inside the same package you're working on, like `QuoteLocalStorage`, you know for sure there's no other package using it. Therefore, there's no reason to expose it, and instantiating it inside the dependent class makes the most sense.

Notice that even though `QuoteLocalStorage` is instantiated inside `QuoteRepository`'s constructor, as it should be, you still *allowed* it to be received in the constructor via the optional parameter. The intent behind this optional parameter isn't to expose the class dependency to users of `QuoteRepository`. Instead, it only exists to allow you to provide a mock instance in automated testing, which is why you annotated it with `@visibleForTesting`. You'll learn more about this in Chapter 14, "Automated Testing".

# Creating a Barrel File

Adding the constructor to `QuoteRepository` wasn't enough to make the errors disappear; your starter project still doesn't compile.

The issue is that your state managers cannot import `QuoteRepository`, even though the feature packages they're on have already listed **quote_repository** as a package dependency in their **pubspec.yaml**.

That's happening because `QuoteRepository` is inside an **src** folder, and Dart considers all files under **src** to be private.

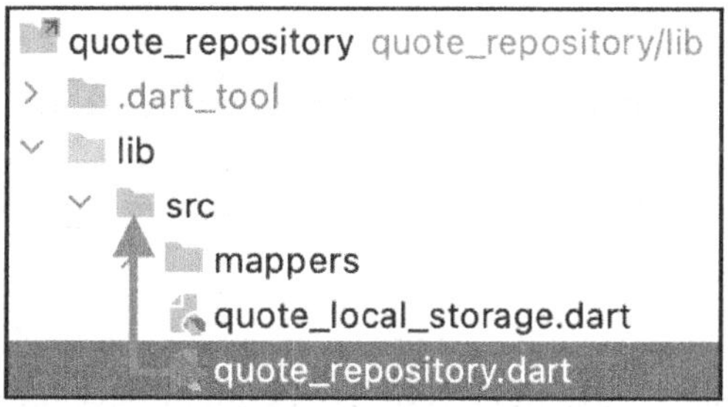


> **Note**: Having an **src** folder isn't mandatory; you could just have everything under **lib**. But then you'd be automatically exposing every file, even the ones that are supposed to be internal, like **quote_local_storage.dart**.

The Dart package layout conventions (https://dart.dev/tools/pub/package-layout) recommend that you put everything under an **src** folder, like you just did, but then consciously expose the files you want exposed by exporting them from an "exporter" file that you place directly under **lib**. This exporter file is known as a **barrel file**. Part of the convention is to give the barrel file the same name as the package.

To see this in practice, create a second **quote_repository.dart** file, but put this one directly under the **lib** folder.

Then, insert the following line in that file:

```
export 'src/quote_repository.dart';
```

That's all! All you did was create a public file to export your private ones. Since the state managers in the starter project were already importing this public barrel file, all the errors have now disappeared.

Observe that this barrel file works as a proxy, allowing you to change the internal structure of your package without affecting dependent packages. For example, if you move any of your **src** files to an **src/any/folder/you/want** directory, other packages wouldn't even have to know about the move because they just import the barrel file.

Also, say you wanted to expose **quote_local_storage.dart** as well (which you don't). All you'd have to do is add another `export` line to that barrel file.

To make sure everything works, build and run using the custom running configuration you created in the previous chapter. Since `getQuoteListPage()` in `QuoteRepository` just throws an exception for now, expect to see an error screen:

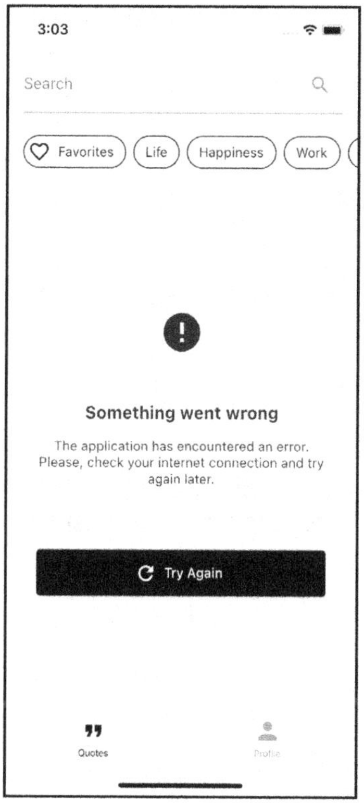


> **Note**: If you're having trouble running the app, it's because you forgot to propagate the configurations you did in the first chapter's starter project to the following chapters' materials. If that's the case, please revisit Chapter 1, "Setting up Your Environment".

# Learning About Pagination

Next on your plate is adding a real implementation to that `getQuoteListPage()` in `QuoteRepository`. Doing this will teach you everything you need to understand how all the other functions work. Start by observing the function's definition; there are three things worth pointing out in there:

1. The **page** word in the function's name.
2. The first parameter: `pageNumber`.
3. The return type: `Stream<QuoteListPage>`. For now, just stick with `QuoteListPage`; you'll learn about the `Stream` part in the next section.

These are all indicators that you're about to deal with something called **pagination**.

Pagination, or **paging**, happens when an API splits a list of results into batches — the so-called **pages**. It then expects you to request these batches individually, as you need to show them to the user. That allows users to start interacting with the app faster since they don't need to wait for the entire list to load. It also reduces the risk of wasting cellular data by fetching items the user might not even get to see.

Imagine how much time and data it would take if Google delivered all the bazillion pages of your search results to you at once!

Pagination explains why `getQuoteListPage()` returns a `QuoteListPage` instead of some sort of `List<Quote>`. `QuoteListPage` contains two properties:

1. **quoteList**: The items on that page.
2. **isLastPage**: Indicates whether that page is the last one, so the state managers know when to stop asking for more pages. You'll see this property in use in Chapter 5, "Managing Complex State With Blocs".

Now for the `Stream` part...

# Learning About Streams

Two types characterize asynchronous programming in Dart: `Future` and `Stream`.

`Futures` represent values that you can't access immediately. For example, when `getQuote()` returns `Future<Quote>` instead of just `Quote`, it's saying that it can't return that `Quote` *immediately* because it will take some time to get it. So, instead of making the caller of the function wait for the actual `Quote`, the function immediately returns a channel — the `Future` — to the caller. It'll send the actual data through that channel later, when the fetching succeeds.

A `Stream` is just the plural form of a `Future`. A `Future` emits *one* value at a time; a `Stream` can emit *multiple* values.

The reason `getQuoteListPage()` returns a `Stream` and not a `Future` has absolutely nothing to do with pagination and the fact that it could be emitting a sequence of pages. The actual reason lies in the `fetchPolicy` parameter of `getQuoteListPage()`. You'll dive into that now.

# Learning About Fetch Policies

As soon as you decide to cache results from a network call, you need to make a decision about the policy you want to follow when delivering those results later:

- Will you always return the cached items? What if they become stale?
- Will you continue to fetch items from the server every time and use the cached ones only as a fallback if the request fails? If so, will the frequent loading times upset the user? Assuming the data doesn't change often, won't you just be wasting cellular data by making unnecessary network calls?

There's no definitive answer to these questions; you have to take each situation into account. How frequently does the data become stale? Should you prioritize speediness or accurateness in this scenario?

So, it's time to be more specific and decide what the best decision for WonderWords' home screen is.

When users open WonderWords, they probably want to see fresh quotes every time. If they like a quote so much they want to see it again, they can always favorite that quote.

Up to this point, it would be safe to assume the best policy would be to fetch quotes from the server every time and not worry about caching. But then, what if the network call fails? In that case, it would be great to have cached items to show as a fallback.

OK, you have a policy now. You'll continue fetching quotes from the server every time, but then cache those quotes so you can use them in the future if the network call fails.

Your new strategy is pretty solid, but still has a huge flaw: Fetching items from the API every time means frequent — and long — loading times for the user. When a user opens an app, they want to start interacting with it as soon as possible.

Well... You can't make the server return your items faster. But, now that you're caching quotes anyway, there's a master move you can make: Instead of showing a loading screen every time the user opens the app, you can show the cached quotes instead, using them as a placeholder to entertain the user while you fetch fresh quotes under the hood. Problem solved!

> **Note**: Notice that with this new policy, returning a `Future` from your repository is no longer enough. When the state manager asks for the first page, you'll emit the cached one (if any) *first* and *then* the one from the API, when it arrives. As you now know, you need to use a `Stream` when you're working with multiple emissions.

Cool! The good news is that you now have a custom-tailored strategy for Wonder Words' home screen. The bad news is that, even when considering just the home screen, the policy you designed still isn't the best for *every* situation. Well, you wanted a *real-world* book, didn't you?

## Considering Additional Scenarios

Consider these edge scenarios:

- What if the user wants to purposefully refresh the list by pulling it down? In that case, you can't return the "old" data first. Also, the user won't mind seeing a loading screen; after all, they consciously requested fresh data.
- What if the user searches for a specific quote, but then clears out the search box so they can get back to the ones they saw previously? In that case, just showing the cached data is best. You don't need to emit fresh items later, because the user just wants to go back to the previous state.

The moral of the story is: Depending on how complex a screen is, a *single* fetch policy might not be enough. When that's the case, the best thing you can do is let the state manager decide the best policy for each step of the user experience journey. That's the whole reason why `getQuoteListPage()` has that `fetchPolicy` parameter.

`fetchPolicy` is of type `QuoteListPageFetchPolicy`, which is the `enum` at the end of the file you're working on. These are the enum's values:

- **cacheAndNetwork**: Emit cached quotes first, if any, followed by quotes from the server, if the HTTP call succeeds. Useful for when the user first opens the app.
- **networkOnly**: Don't use the cache in any situation. If the server request fails, let the user know. Useful for when the user consciously refreshes the list.
- **networkPreferably**: Prefer using the server. If the request fails, try using the cache. If there isn't anything in the cache, then let the user know an error occurred. Useful for when the user requests a subsequent page.
- **cachePreferably**: Prefer using the cache. If there isn't anything in the cache, try using the server. Useful for when the user clears a tag or the search box.

> **Note**: Notice that if it weren't for the **cacheAndNetwork** policy, which is the only one that can emit twice, having a `Future` as the return type would suffice.

Enough theory! It's time to get back to coding...

# Populating the Cache

Each of the four supported policies might need data from the server at one point in time; after all, there's no **cacheOnly** policy. So, your first step will be to create a utility function that fetches data from the server and populates the cache with it. That way, you can reuse that function inside the main `getQuoteListPage()` for all policies.

Open **lib/quote_repository/src/quote_repository.dart** and find the function that begins with `Stream<QuoteListPage> getQuoteListPage(....` After this function, insert this new function:

```
// 1
Future<QuoteListPage> _getQuoteListPageFromNetwork(int
pageNumber, {
  Tag? tag,
  String searchTerm = '',
  String? favoritedByUsername,
}) async {
  try {
    // 2
    final apiPage = await remoteApi.getQuoteListPage(
      pageNumber,
      tag: tag?.toRemoteModel(),
      searchTerm: searchTerm,
      favoritedByUsername: favoritedByUsername,
    );

    final isFiltering = tag != null || searchTerm.isNotEmpty;
    final favoritesOnly = favoritedByUsername != null;

    final shouldStoreOnCache = !isFiltering;
    // 3
    if (shouldStoreOnCache) {
      // 4
      final shouldEmptyCache = pageNumber == 1;
      if (shouldEmptyCache) {
        await
_localStorage.clearQuoteListPageList(favoritesOnly);
      }

      final cachePage = apiPage.toCacheModel();
      await _localStorage.upsertQuoteListPage(
        pageNumber,
        cachePage,
        favoritesOnly,
      );
    }
```

```
      final domainPage = apiPage.toDomainModel();
      return domainPage;
    } on EmptySearchResultFavQsException catch (_) {
      throw EmptySearchResultException();
    }
  }
```

A lot's going on in there:

1. Unlike `getQuoteListPage()`, this function can only emit one value — either the server list or an error. Therefore, having a `Future` as the return type is enough.
2. Gets a new page from the remote API.
3. You shouldn't cache filtered results. If you tried to cache all the searches the user could possibly perform, you'd quickly fill up the device's storage. Plus, users are willing to wait longer for searches.
4. Every time you get a fresh *first* page, you have to remove all the subsequent ones you had previously stored from the cache. That forces those following pages to be fetched from the network in the future, so you don't risk mixing updated and outdated pages. Not doing this can introduce problems; for example, if a quote that used to be on the second page moved to the first page, you'd risk showing that quote twice if you mixed cached and fresh pages.

Even though there are no visual changes to the app, build and run to make sure everything still works.

There are still two unexplained things: that `catch` block and the `toRemoteModel()`, `toCacheModel()`, and `toDomainModel()` calls. You'll dive into those now.

# Learning About Model Separation

Notice the object you get from the API by calling `remoteApi.getQuoteListPage()` is a `QuoteListPageRM`; **RM** stands for **remote model**. But, then, when you cache that result with `_localStorage.upsertQuoteListPage()`, the expected object is actually a `QuoteListPageCM`, where **CM** stands for **cache model**.

The types don't match.

To make things even more interesting, the object you have to ultimately return at the end of your repository's `getQuoteListPage()` is a `QuoteListPage` — so, neither of the two types above. Why is that?

Each layer of your app has its own specifications when it comes to its models. Your remote models, for example, replicate the structure of the JSONs and is full of JSON parsing annotations. On the other hand, your cache models are full of database stuff, which varies depending on the database package you're using. Not to mention that some property types can also be different; for example, something that's a `String` for the API could be an `enum` for the database.

Lastly, since your repository's data comes from the database at some times and from the network at others, you need a neutral, impartial model to return to your repository's users. This is called the **domain model**, which is represented in this case by the pure `QuoteListPage`.

In other words, domain models are models that are agnostic to the source they're coming from.

WonderWords defines domain models inside the separate **domain_models** package, which all the repositories' packages depend on. Doing this allows different repositories to share the same domain models.

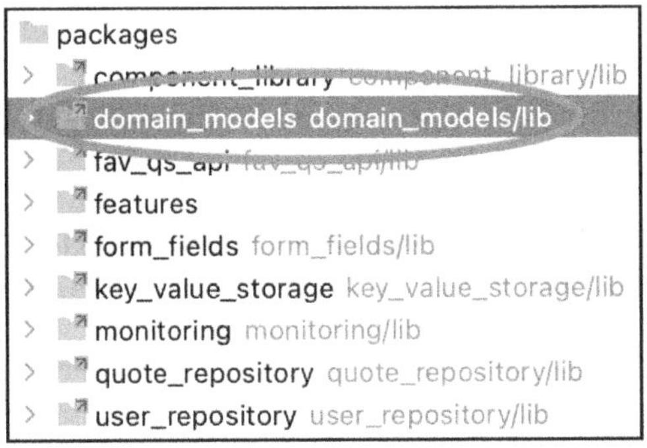


WonderWords follows another good practice, as well: In addition to domain models, it also defines **domain exceptions** in that same package. The same way you return neutral/domain models when everything goes right, you can throw neutral/domain exceptions when things go wrong.

You can see this happening inside that `catch` block you just wrote; whenever you catch an `EmptySearchResultFavQsException`, which comes from the **fav_qs_api** package, you replace it with an `EmptySearchResultException`, which comes from **domain_models**.

Having these domain exceptions may seem unnecessary, but that's the only way your state managers can execute custom logic depending on the exception that occurred. For example, since the **quote_list** feature doesn't depend on the **fav_qs_api** package, `QuoteListBloc` can't check whether an exception is an

`EmptySearchResultFavQsException`, simply because it doesn't know that type. But, since the **quote_list** package *does* depend on **domain_models**, `QuoteListBloc` has no problems verifying if an exception is an `EmptySearchResultException` and using that to show a custom message to the user.

# Learning About Mappers

OK, now you understand why you need different models for each data source and a neutral one to ultimately return from the repositories. But, how do you go from one model type to another? You might have guessed that you need some kind of converter. These converters are called **mappers**.

Mappers are just functions that take an object from one model and return an object from another. Any necessary conversion logic takes place in the middle. For example:

```
Quote mapCacheModelToDomainModel(QuoteCM cacheQuote) {
  return Quote(
    id: cacheQuote.id,
    body: cacheQuote.body,
    author: cacheQuote.author,
    favoritesCount: cacheQuote.favoritesCount,
    upvotesCount: cacheQuote.upvotesCount,
    downvotesCount: cacheQuote.downvotesCount,
    isUpvoted: cacheQuote.isUpvoted,
    isDownvoted: cacheQuote.isDownvoted,
    isFavorite: cacheQuote.isFavorite,
  );
}
```

All you're doing is instantiating a new `Quote` object using the values from the `QuoteCM` object you received.

Then, to use this mapper function, you'd just have to do this:

```
final domainQuote = mapCacheModelToDomainModel(cacheQuote);
```

Alternatively, you can make your mappers look prettier using Dart extension functions (https://dart.dev/guides/language/extension-methods):

```
extension QuoteCMtoDomain on QuoteCM {
  Quote toDomainModel() {
    return Quote(
      id: id,
      body: body,
```

```
      author: author,
      favoritesCount: favoritesCount,
      upvotesCount: upvotesCount,
      downvotesCount: downvotesCount,
      isUpvoted: isUpvoted,
      isDownvoted: isDownvoted,
      isFavorite: isFavorite,
    );
  }
}
```

Now you don't have to receive a `QuoteCM` anymore; using Dart extension functions allowed you to create a function that works just as if you declared it inside of `QuoteCM`. Notice you can just type `id`, or `body`, for example, to access the properties inside `QuoteCM`. Mind-blowing, right?

Calling that mapper now becomes:

```
final domainQuote = cacheQuote.toDomainModel();
```

Much better, right?

Mappers are so simple, they're almost tedious. That's why we went ahead and created all of them for you inside the **mapper** directory of your **quote_repository** package. Look at the files in there to get a feeling for the overall structure.

# Supporting Different Fetch Policies

Since you finally understand everything going on in `_getQuoteListPageFromNetwork()`, you're ready for the main act.

Go to the upper `getQuoteListPage()` and replace `throw UnimplementedError();` with:

```
final isFilteringByTag = tag != null;
final isSearching = searchTerm.isNotEmpty;
final isFetchPolicyNetworkOnly =
    fetchPolicy == QuoteListPageFetchPolicy.networkOnly;
// 1
final shouldSkipCacheLookup =
    isFilteringByTag || isSearching ||
isFetchPolicyNetworkOnly;

if (shouldSkipCacheLookup) {
  // 2
  final freshPage = await _getQuoteListPageFromNetwork(
```

```
      pageNumber,
      tag: tag,
      searchTerm: searchTerm,
      favoritedByUsername: favoritedByUsername,
    );

    // 3
    yield freshPage;
  } else {
    // TODO: Cover other fetch policies.
  }
```

Here's what's happening:

1. There are three situations in which you want to skip the cache lookup and return data straight from the network: If the user has a tag selected, if they're searching or if the caller of the function explicitly specified the `networkOnly` policy.
2. This uses the function you created a few sections earlier.
3. The easiest way to generate a `Stream` in a Dart function is by adding `async*` to the function's header and then using the `yield` keyword whenever you want to emit a new item. You can take a deep dive on the subject here: Creating streams in Dart (https://dart.dev/articles/libraries/creating-streams).

You've now covered all the scenarios where you don't need the cache lookup — which is when the user has a filter or when the policy is `networkOnly`. Now, you'll work on the scenarios where the cache lookup is mandatory.

Replace `// TODO: Cover other fetch policies.` with:

```
final isFilteringByFavorites = favoritedByUsername != null;

final cachedPage = await _localStorage.getQuoteListPage(
  pageNumber,
  // 1
  isFilteringByFavorites,
);

final isFetchPolicyCacheAndNetwork =
    fetchPolicy == QuoteListPageFetchPolicy.cacheAndNetwork;

final isFetchPolicyCachePreferably =
    fetchPolicy == QuoteListPageFetchPolicy.cachePreferably;

// 2
final shouldEmitCachedPageInAdvance =
    isFetchPolicyCachePreferably ||
isFetchPolicyCacheAndNetwork;
```

```
if (shouldEmitCachedPageInAdvance && cachedPage != null) {
  // 3
  yield cachedPage.toDomainModel();
  // 4
  if (isFetchPolicyCachePreferably) {
    return;
  }
}

// TODO: Call the remote API.
```

Here's what you just did:

1. Your local storage keeps the favorite list in a separate bucket, so you have to specify whether you're storing the general or the favorites list.
2. Whether `fetchPolicy` is `cacheAndNetwork` or `cachePreferably`, you have to emit the cached page. The difference between the two policies is that, for `cacheAndNetwork`, you'll also emit the server page later on.
3. To return the cached page, which is a `QuoteListPageCM`, you have to call the mapper function to convert it to the domain `QuoteListPage`.
4. If the policy is `cachePreferably` and you've emitted the cached page successfully, there's nothing else to do. You can just `return` and close the `Stream` here.

Your next step is to fetch the page from the API to complete the three remaining scenarios:

1. When the policy is `cacheAndNetwork`. You've already covered the **cache** part, but the **AndNetwork** is still missing.
2. When the policy is `cachePreferably` and you couldn't get a page from the cache.
3. When the policy is `networkPreferably`.

To do this, replace `// TODO: Call the remote API.` with:

```
try {
  final freshPage = await _getQuoteListPageFromNetwork(
    pageNumber,
    favoritedByUsername: favoritedByUsername,
  );

  yield freshPage;
} catch (_) {
  // 1
  final isFetchPolicyNetworkPreferably =
      fetchPolicy == QuoteListPageFetchPolicy.networkPreferably;
  if (cachedPage != null && isFetchPolicyNetworkPreferably) {
    yield cachedPage.toDomainModel();
    return;
  }

  // 2
  rethrow;
}
```

There's nothing too fancy going on here:

1. If the policy is `networkPreferably` and you got an error trying to fetch a page from the network, you try to revert the error by emitting the cached page instead — if there is one.
2. If the policy is `cacheAndNetwork` or `cachePreferably`, you've already emitted the cached page a few lines earlier, so your only option now is to `rethrow` the error if the network call fails. That way, your state manager can handle it properly by showing the user an error.

That's all for this chapter! Build and run to make sure everything works as intended. The last time you did this, you saw an error screen. Now, expect to see this:

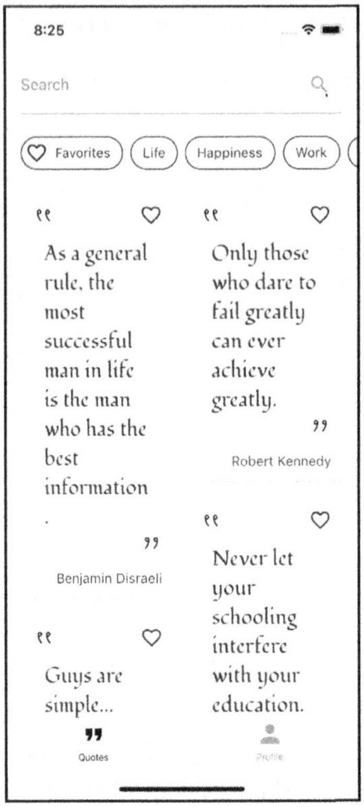


Play with the app on your device and notice how it leverages the different fetch policies. For example, when you refresh the list by pulling it down, it takes longer to load the screen; that's the `networkOnly` policy in use. When you add a tag and then remove it, the app comes back to the previous state pretty quickly; that's due to the `cachePreferably` policy. When you close the app and reopen it, data loads almost instantly, but then you can see how it's swapped out after a few seconds; that's `cacheAndNetwork` in action.

# Key Points

- Repositories become indispensable when you have more than one data source involved in the same operation. The most common situation where that happens is when you cache API results.
- **Caching** improves the user experience by allowing your app to respond faster and without an internet connection. It also saves data consumption by avoiding unnecessary round-trips to the server.
- A **repository** is an orchestrator of **data sources**. It abstracts the actual source of the data away from your state managers.
- When a **class dependency** is defined in the same package you're working on, you should instantiate it inside the dependent class. Alternatively, if a class dependency comes from another internal package, you should require it to be passed in the constructor.
- Structuring a package with an **src** folder and a **barrel file** allows you to cherry-pick the files you want to export and hide your package's internal structure.
- **Pagination** minimizes the risk of fetching data unnecessarily.
- **Streams** are just **Futures** that can emit multiple results.
- A **fetch policy** is the strategy you use to fetch some piece of data. Sometimes having a *single* policy is not good enough, so you should allow the caller of the function to decide the most appropriate policy for each moment.
- Each source of data in your app needs its own model classes. Ultimately, **mapper functions** will convert these source-specific models into neutral/domain models to avoid leaking implementation details throughout your codebase.

## Where to Go From Here?

This chapter took some effort, but keep in mind that this is as complex as repositories get. Supporting different fetch policies is quite an accomplishment.

While all the concepts are still fresh in your mind, explore how the other functions in `QuoteRepository` work. For instance, see how we used Dart extension functions (https://dart.dev/guides/language/extension-methods) to avoid code repetition and achieve a better code design in the functions that modify the quotes, like `favoriteQuote()` and `upvoteQuote()`.

The following chapters will show you how the other side of all this works. You'll learn how to consume repositories by building state managers powered by the Bloc library (https://bloclibrary.dev/#/).

# Chapter 3: Managing State With Cubits & the Bloc Library

By Edson Bueno

Spend five minutes on FlutterDev (https://www.reddit.com/r/FlutterDev/), the largest Flutter online forum, and you'll notice a curse-like phenomenon: Once every three days, someone *has* to come in and ask: "What's the best state management approach?" or "Should I learn BLoC or Riverpod?"

The community's obsession with **state management** has gotten to a state — no pun intended — where people have started believing it's a Flutter issue rather than a computer science one. The truth is, state management is part of programmers' lives from the moment they start turning bits on and off — most people just use other names for it.

State management is the price you pay for interactivity. If your app responds to user input, you're managing state.

**State** is the condition of your app at any given moment. When the user taps a button that takes them to another screen, your app is in a different condition — that is, a different state. If the screen has an empty text field, typing something into that field takes your app to a different state.

The question is, then, "What's the best approach to manage all those state transitions in your code?" And the curse has struck again...

The commonsense answer to that question is: "It depends on your needs", or "There isn't a single best approach for *every* situation". This book has already used the "It depends on the situation" card a few times, but this is *not* solid advice when it comes to state management. It implies you'd have to learn several approaches so you could build the necessary judgment to pick the best one for each situation. And while that would be awesome, it's just not realistic. It's not *real-world*.

This book gets off the fence and advocates for the **BLoC pattern**. Now, this doesn't mean it's the best approach for *every* situation — there really isn't such a thing. That part of the advice above checks out. This book advocates for the BLoC pattern because it's been pretty darn good for all the situations the authors have experienced, and that's more than one could ask for.

The top complaint on the internet about BLoC is its alleged "high learning curve". But then, even if that's true, isn't *learning* the whole reason you're here?

This chapter is the first of a three-chapter journey that will give you expert-level knowledge about implementing the BLoC pattern using the Bloc Library (https://bloclibrary.dev). You'll start by building a Cubit, which is a simplified version of a Bloc. Along the way, you'll also learn:

- What BLoC really is.
- Which problem it solves.
- How it solves that problem.
- The difference between a Bloc and a Cubit.
- How to model your screens' states.
- How to fetch and send data using a Cubit.

While going through this chapter, you'll work on the **starter** project from this chapter's **assets** folder.

# Defining BLoC

BLoC stands for business logic components and is a design pattern introduced by Google in 2018 (https://www.youtube.com/watch?v=PLHln7wHgPE). It first came out as *the* state management solution that enabled code sharing between Flutter (mobile) and Angular (web) back before Flutter web was a thing. Since then, the community has proven the pattern to be way more powerful than that.

To be clear, BLoC is a **design pattern**, not a package — contrary to what many think. Any packages you may stumble upon that contain the word "bloc" in their names are there just to *help you implement* the pattern, and you can choose to use them or not. It's similar to how **dependency injection** is just a pattern, and you can choose whether or not to use a package to implement it.

The reason many people think BLoC is a package instead of a pattern is that a package named bloc (https://pub.dev/packages/bloc) has stood out in the community to the point where it's as popular as the pattern itself. That recognition is well deserved — the package is fantastic.

The bloc package is also more properly referred to as the Bloc Library. Strictly speaking, Bloc Library is a broader term that encompasses both the bloc package and some satellite packages that originated from it.

> **Note**: Notice the different names and casing conventions: **BLoC** is the pattern. **Bloc Library** is the family of packages that help you implement the pattern. **bloc** is the core package of that family. **Bloc** is the entity in your code – the classes you create – as in "the Bloc that manages that screen".

It's rare for a Flutter app to use the bloc package directly. Typically, you'd use it through one of its children packages. In WonderWords, for example, you'll use bloc through flutter_bloc (https://pub.dev/packages/flutter_bloc) and bloc_test (https://pub.dev/packages/bloc_test).

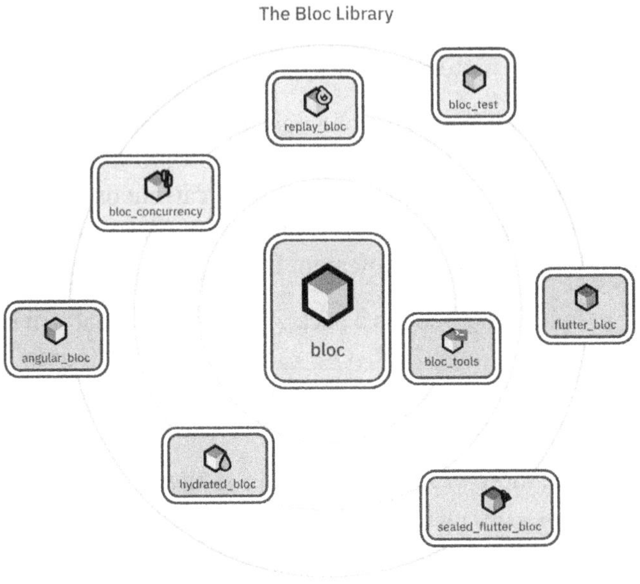


You were just reading about how you don't *need* any packages to work with the BLoC pattern, so why does WonderWords use the Bloc Library?

- For the many amenities it provides, like testing tools.
- For the community support you gain from it. A quick search in their repo's issues (https://github.com/felangel/bloc/issues) can get you multiple answers to any problem you might run into in the future.

Now, you know what the BLoC pattern is, what it isn't, and which tools you'll use to work with it. So now, take a step back and consider why you actually need BLoC at all.

## Positioning BLoC in a Codebase

The mechanics of *all* user-facing apps boil down to three steps:

1. **Take user input**. For example, taps on a button or insertions into a text field.
2. **Do magic in the middle**, known as **business logic**. After you receive some user input, you'll want to do something in reaction to it, right? That something usually involves talking to an external source or validating the text field's value.
3. **Render the new state of the app**. In other words, show something different to the user after you've processed their input.

> **Note**: In Flutter, the *middle* part is the only one where you have total freedom regarding where you can put your code. Step one *has to happen* in the widget layer — from a widget's `onTap` or `onChange` callback, for example. Step three also *has to happen* in the widget layer, this time by returning the appropriate widgets from the `build()` function. On the other hand, step two's code is a breeze. You can keep it in the widget layer — inside a `StatefulWidget` — or you can place it anywhere else, like inside a state manager, for example. How you end up handling it is what defines your app's **architecture**.

The BLoC pattern is nothing but a proposal about *how* to structure that middle part.

BLoC stands for **B**usiness **Lo**gic **C**omponent. Replace "component" with "class" and, combined with what you just learned, you have: A class to delegate anything *that is not* taking user input and rendering the output.

> **Note**: To be fair, that's essentially what all state management approaches are. What usually changes from one approach to another are the rules behind that communication between the **widget** and the **state manager**.

# Speaking and Listening to a Bloc

In the BLoC world, user inputs are called **events.** For illustrative purposes only — *don't insert this anywhere* — this is how a widget would forward an event to a Bloc *or* a Cubit, which is just a simplified Bloc:

```
// 1
UpvoteIconButton(
  // 2
  onTap: () {
    // 3
    bloc.add(
      QuoteUpvoted(),
    );

    // OR

    // 4
    cubit.upvoteQuote();
  },
)
```

Here's the complete breakdown:

1. `UpvoteIconButton` is a widget from WonderWords that will serve as a model here.
2. You provide an `onTap` callback to `UpvoteIconButton` to capture the user input.
3. You then forward that event to a bloc by calling `add()` on it and passing an object to it. Don't worry about the details for now. From here on, you'll work exclusively with Cubits - the simplified Blocs - and leave the actual Blocs for Chapter 5, "Managing Complex State with Blocs".
4. Can you see how just forwarding an event to a Cubit is already simpler than doing the same to a Bloc? Starting with Cubits will help you build the confidence to move on to complex Blocs in Chapter 5, "Managing Complex State With Blocs".

The Cubit then receives that event and processes it — by talking to a repository, for example. Then, it sends an object — the state — back to the widget layer. The state object contains all the information the UI needs to rebuild itself and reflect the new app's state to the user.

This is how you listen to the states coming out of a Cubit:

```
@override
```

```
Widget build(BuildContext context) {
  return BlocBuilder<QuoteDetailsCubit, QuoteDetailsState>(
    builder: (context, state) {
      if (state is QuoteDetailsSuccess) {
        return _Quote(
          quote: state.quote,
        );
      } else if (state is QuoteDetailsFailure) {
        return ExceptionIndicator();
      } else {
        return CenteredCircularProgressIndicator();
      }
    },
  );
}
```

Notice how `BlocBuilder` doesn't care if you're using a Cubit or a Bloc. In fact, a Cubit *is* a Bloc, just a simplified one.

`BlocBuilder` is a widget that comes from the **flutter_bloc** package. **flutter_bloc** is the member of the Bloc Library that makes the bridge between the base bloc package, which you could use in a pure Dart project, and the Flutter world, with all the widget-related stuff.

All `BlocBuilder` does is call the `builder` function for you whenever the Cubit — or Bloc — emits a new state object. You'll get your chance to play with it in a couple of sections. For now, just start forming a picture in your head of how the big pieces connect.

Next, it's time to get your hands dirty.

# Creating the State Class

If you've done state management in the past with `StatefulWidget` and `setState`, or even `Provider` and `ChangeNotifier`, you're probably used to having your screen's state spread around multiple variables. For example:

```
class _QuoteDetailsScreenState extends State<QuoteDetailsScreen>
{
  bool _isLoading = true;
  Quote? _quote;
  dynamic _error;

  @override
  Widget build(BuildContext context) {
    if (_isLoading) {
```

```
        return CenteredCircularProgressIndicator();
      } else if (_error != null) {
        return ExceptionIndicator();
      } else {
        return _Quote(
          quote: _quote!,
        );
      }
    }
  }
```

Your state here is determined by a combination of the `_isLoading`, `_quote` and `_error` properties. The problem with that is that it's very easy to update one variable and forget to reset another, like:

```
Future<void> _fetchQuoteDetails() async {
  setState(() {
    _isLoading = true;
  });
  try {
    final quote = await
quoteRepository.getQuoteDetails(quoteId);
    setState(() {
      _isLoading = false;
      _quote = quote;
      _error = null;
    });
  } catch (error) {
    setState(() {
      _quote = null;
      _error = error;
    });
  }
}
```

Can you spot what's wrong with the code above? You forgot to set `_isLoading` to `false` in case an error happens. Should the UI, then, display a progress indicator, since `_isLoading` is `true`, or an exception indicator, since `_error` isn't `null`?

That problem is known as a **logical dependency**. You *know* `isLoading` should be `false` if `_error` isn't `null`. But nothing is physically preventing you from *unintentionally* breaking that rule and sending an ambiguous message.

With Blocs and Cubits, whenever you want to update your UI, you do so by emitting *one* object with all the information the UI needs to know to rebuild itself properly. In practice, that just means you have to get all your state variables together in a single class. For example:

```
class QuoteDetailsState {
  QuoteDetailsState({
    required this.isLoading,
    required this.quote,
    required this.error,
  });

  final bool isLoading;
  final Quote? quote;
  final dynamic error;
}
```

But still, the logical dependency issue remains — you can still have a non-null `error` while `isLoading` is set to `true`. Not for long, though. You're about to learn an easy fix for this.

## Using Inheritance to Solve the Logical Dependency Issue

Open the starter project and use the terminal to run `make get` from the root folder. Wait for the command to finish, then navigate to the **quote_details** feature package: **packages/features/quote_details**.

> **Note**: Ignore the errors on **quote_details_screen.dart** for now.

Open **quote_details_state.dart** in the **lib/src** folder. You'll notice a `part of` directive at the top of the file. Leave that on hold until the next section.

Now, replace `// TODO: Create models for all possible screen states.` with:

```
// 1
abstract class QuoteDetailsState extends Equatable {
  const QuoteDetailsState();
}

// 2
class QuoteDetailsInProgress extends QuoteDetailsState {
  const QuoteDetailsInProgress();

  // 3
  @override
  List<Object?> get props => [];
}

class QuoteDetailsSuccess extends QuoteDetailsState {
  const QuoteDetailsSuccess({
    required this.quote,
    // TODO: Receive new property.
  });

  // 4
  final Quote quote;
  // TODO: Add new property.

  @override
  List<Object?> get props => [
        quote,
        // TODO: List new property.
      ];
}

class QuoteDetailsFailure extends QuoteDetailsState {
  const QuoteDetailsFailure();

  @override
  List<Object?> get props => [];
}
```

Watch how this simple pattern solves the logical dependency issue you saw in the previous code snippet. Instead of having `QuoteDetailsState` hold the three variables, you made it an `abstract` class and broke it down into three separate concrete classes. Both approaches do the same thing, but now the logical dependencies have become *physical*. For example, you can't have a `Quote` if the state is `QuoteDetailsFailure`.

Now, analyze the code above step by step:

1. You defined a **base** `QuoteDetailsState`, which is `abstract`, meaning you can't instantiate it. It just serves as a common ancestor to the subsequent classes.
2. You then created three concrete children for `QuoteDetailsState` from the previous step: `QuoteDetailsInProgress`, `QuoteDetailsSuccess` and `QuoteDetailsFailure`.
3. You had to override `props` in all the children classes because the parent `QuoteDetailsState` extends `Equatable`. You'll learn more about this in the next section.
4. `QuoteDetailsSuccess` is the only class where having a `quote` property makes sense.

Breaking your state down into multiple classes means there's no room for ambiguity when you want to send a new state from your Cubit to your UI. You continue to have one state type, `QuoteDetailsState`, but now you have to use `QuoteDetailsInProgress`, `QuoteDetailsSuccess` or `QuoteDetailsFailure` to instantiate it.

That approach works like an `enum` on steroids. With it, your "enum values" — `InProgress`, `Success` and `Failure` — can have properties of their own, as happens for `QuoteDetailsSuccess` and the `quote` property.

> **Note**: The suffixes in the classes' names — `InProgress`, `Success` and `Failure` — follow the Bloc Library's naming convention (https://bloclibrary.dev/#/blocnamingconventions?id=naming-conventions).

Now, there are only two things left for you to understand everything going on in the snippet above:

- The `Equatable` class you're extending from `QuoteDetailsState`.
- That `props` property you're overriding in `QuoteDetailsState` and `QuoteDetailsSuccess`.

Next, you'll dive into that.

# Comparing Objects in Dart

When you check if two objects are equal in Dart, as in `bookA == bookB`, the only thing you're actually comparing by default is whether the two objects are the same instance, *not* if their properties have the same value. For example:

```
final bookA = Book(title: 'Real-World Flutter by Tutorials');
final bookB = Book(title: 'Real-World Flutter by Tutorials');

print(bookA == bookB); // prints false
```

If you wanted to make a *real* comparison where the output for the above is `true`, you'd have to implement two functions inside the `Book` class: == and `hashCode`. The problem is, overriding these functions is way more complex than it sounds.

The equatable (https://pub.dev/packages/equatable) package offers you a way out. With it, all you have to do is extend `Equatable` and then list the properties you want to include in the comparison by overriding `props`, just like you did in your code for `QuoteDetailsState`.

But why are you using `Equatable` in your Cubit's state classes? Why would you need *real comparisons* in there? For two reasons:

- Later, when you write your unit tests in Chapter 14, "Automated Testing", you'll want to be able to determine if the objects your cubit emits are what you expect them to be.
- If, for any reason, you end up emitting two equal objects in a row from your Cubit's code, the Bloc Library will be able to internally disregard any duplicates and avoid unnecessary widget rebuilds.

Now that you've properly modeled your state classes, it's time to jump into the Cubit's code.

# Creating a Cubit

Still in that same **src** directory, open **quote_details_cubit.dart**. Then, replace `// TODO: Create the Cubit.` with:

```
// 1
class QuoteDetailsCubit extends Cubit<QuoteDetailsState> {
  QuoteDetailsCubit({
    required this.quoteId,
    required this.quoteRepository,
  }) : super(
          // 2
          const QuoteDetailsInProgress(),
        ) {
    _fetchQuoteDetails();
  }

  final int quoteId;
  // 3
  final QuoteRepository quoteRepository;

  void _fetchQuoteDetails() async {
    // TODO: Fetch data from QuoteRepository.
  }

  void refetch() async {
    // TODO: Add a body to refetch().
  }

  void upvoteQuote() async {
    // TODO: Add a body to upvoteQuote().
  }

  void downvoteQuote() async {
    // TODO: Challenge.
  }

  void unvoteQuote() async {
    // TODO: Challenge.
  }

  void favoriteQuote() async {
    // TODO: Challenge.
  }

  void unfavoriteQuote() async {
    // TODO: Challenge.
  }
}
```

Except for leaving a bunch of `TODO`s for later, here's what you just did:

1. To create a Cubit, you have to extend `Cubit` and specify your *base* state class as the generic type. The only reason you're able to import the `Cubit` class in this file is because this **quote_details** package's **pubspec.yaml** lists **flutter_bloc** as a dependency.
2. When extending `Cubit`, you *have* to call the `super` constructor and pass an instance of your initial state to it. This value is what the Cubit will provide to the UI when the screen first opens.
3. You'll use the `QuoteRepository` you created in the previous chapter.

> **Note**: Remember the `part of` directive you had at the top of the previous **quote_details_state.dart**? This file now corroborates that with a `part` also at the top.
>
> The `part` and `part of` combination is a Dart tool that enables you to treat **quote_details_state.dart** as a continuation of this **quote_details_cubit.dart** file. Notice that, although you use `Equatable` in the state file, its `import` line is actually here in this one. Having files that extend one another like this has two significant advantages:
>
> 1.) Any files importing **quote_details_cubit.dart** immediately get access to everything in **quote_details_state.dart**.
>
> 2.) These two files can share private members, such as properties, classes and functions.

The entire backbone of your Cubit is ready. From now on, you'll work on adding some meat to it.

# Fetching Data

Continuing on your Cubit's file, it's time to give some love to that first `_fetchQuoteDetails()`. Replace `// TODO: Fetch data from QuoteRepository.` with:

```
try {
  // 1
  final quote = await quoteRepository.getQuoteDetails(quoteId);
  // 2
  emit(
    QuoteDetailsSuccess(quote: quote),
  );
} catch (error) {
  emit(
    const QuoteDetailsFailure(),
  );
}
```

Here, you just:

1. Used the `quoteId` received in the constructor to fetch the entire `Quote` object from `QuoteRepository`. If you're not familiar with the `async`/`await` syntax from Dart, you can read more about it in Dart's documentation (https://dart.dev/codelabs/async-await#working-with-futures-async-and-await).

2. Called `emit()` from within a Cubit, which is how you send new state objects to your widget layer. You'll learn how to react to those from the UI side in the next section.

Notice you're calling this `_fetchQuoteDetails()` from your constructor. That will cause your Cubit to fetch this data as soon as you open the screen.

> **Note**: You didn't have to `emit()` a `QuoteDetailsInProgress` at the beginning of the function because you already defined it as your initial state using the `super` constructor.

# Responding to User Input

If you get an error from `QuoteRepository` when trying to fetch a quote, the code you just wrote handles that error by emitting a `QuoteDetailsFailure` state. Your UI will then reflect that state by showing a classic "Something went wrong" widget:

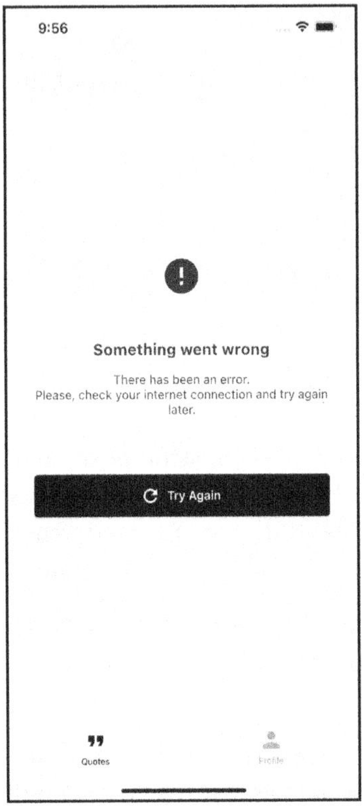


As you can see, this widget has a **Try Again** button that the user can use to try fetching the quote again. If the user taps that button, its `onTap` callback is set to call `refetch()`, which you declared in your Cubit. That's a perfect example of a **user input** — or an **event**, in BLoC terminology — being forwarded to a Cubit.

The only problem is, right now, `refetch()` doesn't do anything. Change this by replacing `// TODO: Add a body to refetch().` with:

```
// 1
emit(
  const QuoteDetailsInProgress(),
);

// 2
_fetchQuoteDetails();
```

That's all. You just had to:

1. Reset your Cubit to its initial state, `QuoteDetailsInProgress`, so the UI shows the progress indicator again.
2. Recall the function you created in the previous section to fetch the quote from `QuoteRepository`.

Now, it's time to step to the other side of the curtain and see how to handle those state emissions from your widgets.

# Consuming a Cubit

Still in the same folder as your Cubit, open **quote_details_screen.dart** and scroll down to the `QuoteDetailsView` widget. Inside the `build()` function, replace:

```
return StyledStatusBar.dark(
  child: Placeholder(),
);
```

With:

```
return StyledStatusBar.dark(
  child: BlocBuilder<QuoteDetailsCubit, QuoteDetailsState>(
    builder: (context, state) {
      return const Placeholder();
    },
  ),
);
```

This is how you listen to the states coming out of a Cubit. Again, notice there's no `CubitBuilder`, only `BlocBuilder`. Never forget: A Cubit *is* a Bloc.

In your `BlocBuilder` above, you used the angle brackets — <> — to specify two generic types:

- The type of the Cubit you want to listen to: `QuoteDetailsCubit`.
- The type of the state objects coming out of that Cubit: `QuoteDetailsState`.

Next, you passed in a function to the `builder` property. That function will run every time your Cubit emits a new state. You'll use the provided `state` object to infer the current state and then return the widget that correctly portrays that state.

Right now, you're just returning a `Placeholder`, regardless of what the current state is. Change that by replacing that `return const Placeholder();` with:

```
return WillPopScope(
  onWillPop: () async {
    // 1
    final displayedQuote =
        state is QuoteDetailsSuccess ? state.quote : null;
    Navigator.of(context).pop(displayedQuote);
    return false;
  },
  child: Scaffold(
    // 2
    appBar: state is QuoteDetailsSuccess
        ? _QuoteActionsAppBar(
            quote: state.quote,
            shareableLinkGenerator: shareableLinkGenerator,
          )
        : null,
    body: SafeArea(
      child: Padding(
        padding: EdgeInsets.all(
          WonderTheme.of(context).screenMargin,
        ),
        // 3
        child: state is QuoteDetailsSuccess
            ? _Quote(
                quote: state.quote,
              )
            : state is QuoteDetailsFailure
                ? ExceptionIndicator(
                    onTryAgain: () {
                      // 4
                      final cubit =
context.read<QuoteDetailsCubit>();
                      cubit.refetch();
                    },
                  )
                // 5
                : const CenteredCircularProgressIndicator(),
```

```
          ),
        ),
      ),
    );
```

Now that was something! Going over it step by step:

1. The `WillPopScope` widget allows you to intercept when the user tries to navigate back from the screen. You're using that to send the current quote back to the home screen if the current state is a `QuoteDetailsSuccess`. That's necessary so the previous screen can check whether the user has favorited or unfavorited that quote and use that to also reflect that change accordingly. None of that has to do with BLoC specifically; it's just how WonderWords' inter-screen communication works. More on this in Chapter 7, "Routing & Navigating".
2. Here, you're inspecting the `state` object to update your UI accordingly. If the `state` is anything other than a success, you don't show the app bar.
3. You're doing the same thing you did in the previous step, but now for the bulk of the screen's content.
4. `BlocBuilder` gives you that `state` object inside the `builder`, but it doesn't give you the *actual Cubit* in case you want to call a function — send an event — on it. Using this `context.read<YourCubitType>()` is how you get the instance of your Cubit to call functions on it.
5. If the state is neither a `QuoteDetailsSuccess` nor a `QuoteDetailsFailure`, you know for sure it's a `QuoteDetailsInProgress`.

You're almost there! You just need to perform one last step before building and running your project.

# Providing a Cubit

You'd get an error if you tried building and running your project now. That's because your `BlocBuilder<QuoteDetailsCubit, ...>` doesn't have an actual `QuoteDetailsCubit` instance to work with yet; specifying it as the generic type isn't enough.

You *could* solve this by simply passing an instance of your Cubit to the `BlocBuilder`'s `bloc` property, but there's a better way. The official recommendation is to place a `BlocProvider` widget anywhere above your `BlocBuilder` in the widget tree. By doing this, you'll leverage the widget tree to make the Cubit instance available *internally*.

To see how this looks in practice, jump up to the `QuoteDetailsScreen` widget in the same **quote_details_screen.dart** file. Inside the `build()` function, replace:

```
return QuoteDetailsView(
  onAuthenticationError: onAuthenticationError,
  shareableLinkGenerator: shareableLinkGenerator,
);
```

With:

```
return BlocProvider<QuoteDetailsCubit>(
  create: (_) => QuoteDetailsCubit(
    quoteId: quoteId,
    quoteRepository: quoteRepository,
  ),
  child: QuoteDetailsView(
    onAuthenticationError: onAuthenticationError,
    shareableLinkGenerator: shareableLinkGenerator,
  ),
);
```

Done! That will make not only your `BlocBuilder` work, but also the `context.read<QuoteDetailsCubit>()` calls you have down below in your code. In fact, what `BlocBuilder` uses internally is exactly a `context.read()` call just like yours.

> **Note**: That strategy of using a special type of widget to make an object available internally through the `BuildContext` is a pattern that's used a lot in Flutter: `Theme.of(context)`,`Navigator.of(context)`, etc. Chapter 10, "Dynamic Theming & Dark Mode", will go deep into that pattern.

Build and run the project using the custom running configuration you created in the first chapter. Tap any quote on the home screen and make sure your quote shows up as intended.

**Note**: The app bar buttons won't work just yet. That's next on your list.

**Note**: If you're having trouble running the app, you might have forgotten to propagate the configurations you did in the first chapter's starter project to the following chapters' materials. If that's the case, please revisit Chapter 1, "Setting up Your Environment".

Since the home screen caches the quotes locally, the quote details screen works even without internet. That makes it hard for you to reproduce an eventual error and see how this screen's error state looks. The easiest way to force this is to, on **quote_details_cubit.dart**, add the following two lines at the beginning of the `_fetchQuoteDetails()` function:

```
emit(
  const QuoteDetailsFailure(),
);
return;
```

This is what you'll see when you try that:

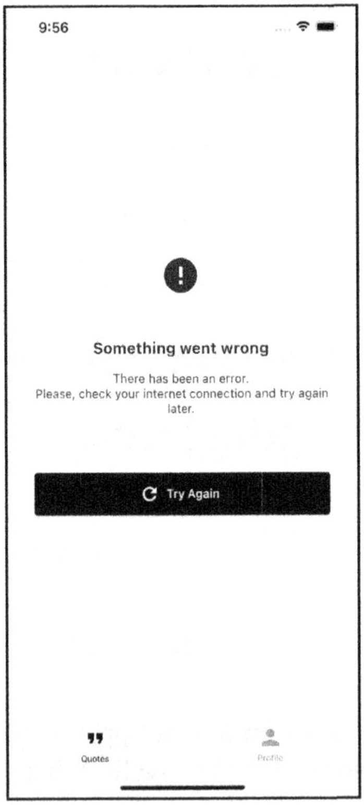


**Note**: If you decide to try this, don't forget to remove the added lines after you're done seeing the error.

# Sending Data

The reason your app bar buttons don't work yet couldn't be simpler: You haven't implemented those functionalities. Change this by going back to your Cubit's file and replacing `// TODO: Add a body to upvoteQuote().` with:

```
try {
  final updatedQuote = await
quoteRepository.upvoteQuote(quoteId);
  emit(
    QuoteDetailsSuccess(
      quote: updatedQuote,
    ),
  );
} catch (error) {
  // TODO: Handle error.
}
```

So far, so good, right? When the user is signed in, and you ask your Repository to upvote a quote, it returns a new `Quote` object with the updated votes count. The only thing you have to do, then, is emit a new `QuoteDetailsSuccess` with that new quote. You either can or cannot emit a `QuoteDetailsInProgress` at the beginning of this function. As of now, you're not doing this so the user can continue seeing the quote while the request loads.

Now for the not-so-straightforward part. If the upvote request fails — because there's no internet connection, for example — how do you want to present that error to the user? Do you want to remove the entire quote from the screen and present that same error state from the previous screenshot? Probably not. If the problem is only with *upvoting* that quote, there's no reason to deprive the user of even seeing the quote.

Most mobile apps handle this kind of scenario, where you have all the information you need but just can't *send* something to the server, by using an alert dialog (https://www.material.io/components/dialogs) or a snackbar (https://material.io/components/snackbars) to present the error to the user.

For example:

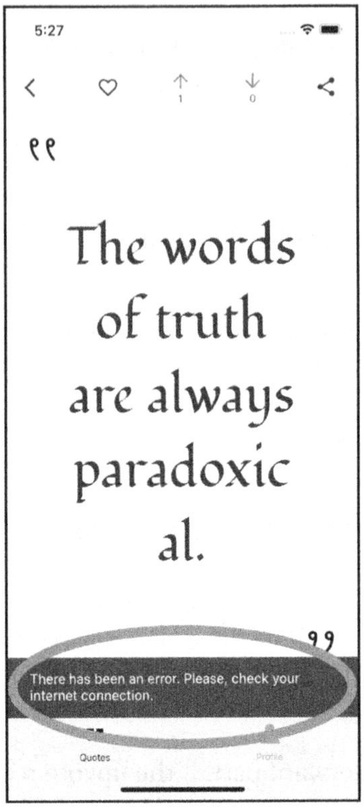


Notice the user is still in the *success* state, but you now show a snackbar on top if an error happened updating that quote. To support this in your code, you have to add a new property to the `QuoteDetailsSuccess` state. Do this by going back to the **quote_details_state.dart** file and replacing:

1. `// TODO: Receive new property.` with `this.quoteUpdateError,`.
2. `// TODO: Add new property.` with `final dynamic quoteUpdateError;`.
3. `// TODO: List new property.` with `quoteUpdateError,`.

> **Note**: You're calling this property `quoteUpdateError` instead of `quoteUpvoteError` so you can use the same property for the other app bar actions, such as favoriting and downvoting.

Now, you just have to use that property, first by populating it and then by consuming it from your UI's code. For the first part, open **quote_details_cubit.dart** and replace the `// TODO: Handle error.` with:

```
// 1
final lastState = state;
// 2
if (lastState is QuoteDetailsSuccess) {
  // 3
  emit(
    QuoteDetailsSuccess(
      quote: lastState.quote,
      quoteUpdateError: error,
    ),
  );
}
```

Here's what's going on:

1. The `state` property of a Cubit contains the last state you emitted. Here, you're assigning `state` to a local variable, so you're able to leverage Dart's type promotion inside the `if` block below. Type promotion just means Dart will automatically convert `lastState`'s type from `QuoteDetailsState` to `QuoteDetailsSuccess` if it passes that `if` condition. You can learn more about why this only works with local variables in Dart's documentation (https://dart.dev/tools/non-promotion-reasons#property-or-this).

2. You know for sure `state` will be a `QuoteDetailsSuccess` since the upvote button doesn't even appear in the other states.

3. You're basically re-emitting the previous state, but now with an error in the `quoteUpdateError` property.

Now, it's up to your UI to inspect that `quoteUpdateError` property and display a snackbar if needed.

## Displaying a Snackbar

This is trickier than it sounds. Your first instinct might be: Just check whether the new state is a `QuoteDetailsSuccess` and show a snackbar in addition to returning the appropriate widget if the `quoteUpdateError` property isn't `null`. Something like this:

```
BlocBuilder<QuoteDetailsCubit, QuoteDetailsState>(
  builder: (context, state) {
    final hasQuoteUpdateError =
      state is QuoteDetailsSuccess ? state.quoteUpdateError :
null;

    if (hasQuoteUpdateError != null) {
      // You'd have to schedule this for the next frame because
you can't command Flutter
      // to display something else while it's already working on
building a layout.
      WidgetsBinding.instance?.addPostFrameCallback((_) {
        ScaffoldMessenger.of(context)
          ..hideCurrentSnackBar()
          ..showSnackBar(const GenericErrorSnackBar());
      });
    }

    return WillPopScope(
      // Omitted code. Nothing would change in here.
    );
  },
)
```

The above wouldn't work. Here's why: The `builder` function might rerun a few times per state, and that would cause your snackbar to pop up more than once for the same error.

Think about this scenario:

1. The user tries to upvote a quote without internet.
2. You show them a snackbar.
3. Some time passes with the user taking no action whatsoever.
4. Suddenly, Flutter reruns your `builder`, and the same snackbar pops up again, even though the user hasn't tried to upvote the quote again.

Weird, right?

Reasons that can cause your `builder` function to re-execute are often changes in configurations, such as the device's rotation, theming, localization, etc. That's no problem if all you do in your `builder` function is return widgets; Flutter is quite smart in figuring out if anything has changed in your widget tree before repainting the UI. On the other hand, if you try using your `builder` to *execute actions*, such as displaying a snackbar, a dialog, or navigating to another screen, you might end up in trouble. The purpose of `builder` is to return widgets; anything other than that, you should consider as a side effect.

The way the Bloc Library enables you to *execute those actions* instead of *returning widgets* is with the `BlocListener` widget. A `BlocListener` is incredibly similar to a `BlocBuilder`, except it takes a `listener` function instead of a `builder` one. That `listener` function also gives you a `context` and a `state`, but it doesn't expect you to return anything from it since you're not *building* any widgets.

Since you already have a `BlocBuilder` on the screen, adding a `BlocListener` widget would mean adding yet another level of indentation to your code. For example:

```
BlocListener<QuoteDetailsCubit, QuoteDetailsState>(
  listener: (context, state) {
    // Show the snackbar if the state is QuoteDetailsSuccess and
has a
    // quoteUpdateError.
  },
  child: BlocBuilder<QuoteDetailsCubit, QuoteDetailsState>(
    builder: (context, state) {
      return WillPopScope(
        // Omitted code. Nothing would change in here.
      );
    },
  ),
)
```

Luckily, the Bloc Library has thought of everything. The `BlocConsumer` widget solves the indentation issue by working as a combination of `BlocBuilder` and `BlocListener`, which takes in both a `listener` and a `builder`.

Open **quote_details_screen.dart** and replace the term `BlocBuilder` in your code with `BlocConsumer`. Now, specify this new `listener` property above the `builder` inside your `BlocConsumer`:

```
listener: (context, state) {
  final quoteUpdateError =
    state is QuoteDetailsSuccess ? state.quoteUpdateError :
null;
  if (quoteUpdateError != null) {
    // 1
    final snackBar =
      quoteUpdateError is UserAuthenticationRequiredException
        ? const AuthenticationRequiredErrorSnackBar()
        : const GenericErrorSnackBar();

    ScaffoldMessenger.of(context)
      ..hideCurrentSnackBar()
      ..showSnackBar(snackBar);

    // 2
    if (quoteUpdateError is UserAuthenticationRequiredException)
{
      onAuthenticationError();
    }
  }
},
```

The biggest driver here is the fact that the user has to be signed in to vote or favorite a quote in WonderWords. So, if the cause of the error is the user not being signed in, you're:

1. Showing them a more specific snackbar.
2. Sending them over to the sign-in screen. Actually, you're just calling the `onAuthenticationError` callback you received in the constructor; the **main** application package will handle the actual navigation for you. The purpose of that is to prevent feature packages from depending on one another — more in Chapter 7, "Routing & Navigating".

> **Note**: `AuthenticationRequiredErrorSnackBar` and `GenericErrorSnackBar` are custom classes defined in your **component_library** internal package.

That was all for this chapter. Now, build and rerun your project.

Tap a quote on the home screen, and you should see nothing different from the last time. But now, when you tap the **upvote** button (up arrow in the app bar), you'll see this:

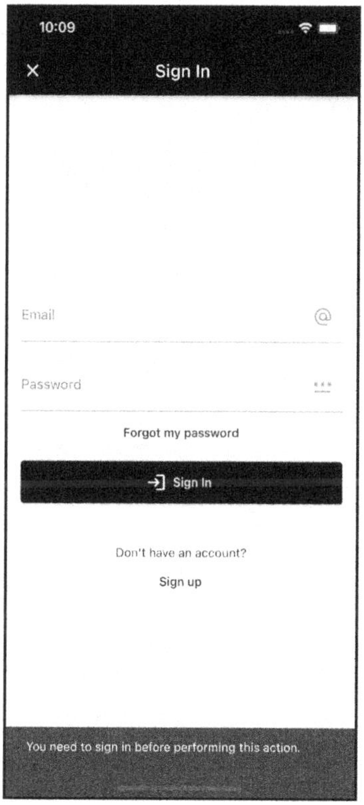


If you want to see the upvote button working free of errors, create a FavQs.com account by tapping the **Sign Up** button you can see on the screenshot above – or sign in with your account if you already have one. After doing this, try upvoting a quote again, and it will work just fine.

## Challenge 1: Downvoting, Unvoting, Favoriting and Unfavoriting

You did a fantastic job with the upvoting functionality, but you can't say you didn't have any help. How about putting your knowledge to the test and implementing all remaining actions in the app bar on your own? That includes downvoting, unvoting, favoriting and unfavoriting.

You won't need to write any UI code. All you have to do is replace each `// TODO: Challenge.` in your Cubit with actual code. All functions should have the same structure as the `upvoteQuote` function, the difference being they'll call different functions of `QuoteRepository`.

In the end, you'll notice your functions will somewhat be copies of one another. Can you think of a smart way to avoid that repetition? There are numerous possible solutions. Check out the challenge project to see the solution.

Good luck!

# Key Points

- A **Bloc** or **Cubit** is a class you use to take away from your widget code everything that's not *capturing user input* or *building other widgets*.
- A Cubit is a stripped-down version of a Bloc. The only difference is how they receive user-driven events. Between the two, one isn't any better than the other. As you'll learn in Chapter 5, "Managing Complex State With Blocs", a Bloc just allows for more complex use cases at the cost of a little more boilerplate.
- Use `Equatable` in your **state classes** to better unit test your code and also avoid unnecessary widget rebuilds.
- Use the `BlocBuilder` widget to rebuild your UI in response to changes in state.
- As a UX rule of thumb, use an "error state" widget to display errors that happened when *retrieving* information, and a **snackbar** or **dialog** to display errors when *sending* information.
- You *shouldn't* use a `BlocBuilder` to display a snackbar or dialog or to navigate to another screen. Use a `BlocListener` instead.
- If you end up with both a `BlocBuilder` and a `BlocListener` in your code, it's better to combine both into a single `BlocConsumer` widget.
- Your widgets send an event to a Cubit by calling a function on it. For example: `cubit.upvoteQuote()`.
- You get an instance of your Cubit to call functions on it by calling `context.read<context.read<YourCubitType>()>`.
- Use a `BlocProvider` widget to make your Cubit available internally through the widget tree.

# Chapter 4: Validating Forms With Cubits

By Edson Bueno

When developing mobile apps, you'll notice your screen types usually fall under one of these three buckets:

- **Details**
- **Forms**
- **Master** or **list**

The previous chapter taught you how to use Cubits to manage the state of the first type: the details screen. That was bloc library (https://bloclibrary.dev/) level one. The *next* chapter, aka level three, handles the third type: the master screen. This chapter is level two, where you tackle **forms**.

Managing the state of forms puts you in front of a whole different set of challenges. For example, this time, you won't need to *fetch* data like you did for the details screen; your job is now to *send* whatever the user types to the server. Well, not quite *whatever* the user types: What if they enter an email in an invalid format?

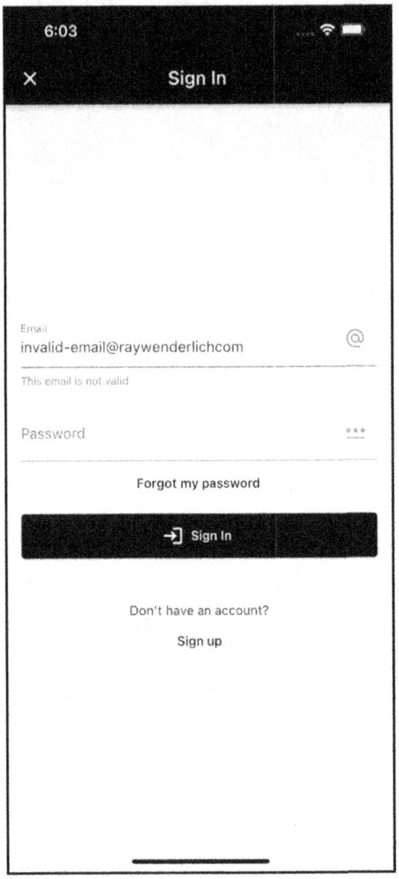

In fact, that's where the bulk of the struggle comes from for screens: You have to keep track of what the user types, occasionally run some logic to make sure it's in the expected format — a step known as **validation** — and meanwhile keep the user posted on the latest validation status of each field on the screen.

Validating what the user types before sending it to the server serves at least two purposes:

- Making sure the user doesn't flood the database with invalid data.
- Avoiding unnecessary calls to the server if the data isn't valid, which would cause delays and unnecessary data consumption.

WonderWords has a few different forms: the sign-in page, the sign-up page, the forgot password dialog and the update profile page. They're pretty much the same as far as their code goes, but since sign-in screens are the ones users see most, this is the one you'll focus on for this chapter. During that process, you'll learn how to:

- Create model state classes for forms.
- Create reusable abstractions for your form fields.
- Manage the state of forms.
- Create a form that responds to different types of user interaction.

While going through this chapter, you'll work on the **starter** project from this chapter's **assets** folder.

# Designing State Classes for Forms

Quick recap of the previous chapter: You create the **state class** to pack all the information your Cubit has to emit to your widgets, so they can rebuild themselves and reflect the new user state.

For example, the details screen you worked on in the last chapter had a few mutually exclusive types of state:

The screen was loading, showing an error or showing the quote — but *never* more than one at a time. You used a class hierarchy to model this in an enum-like way:

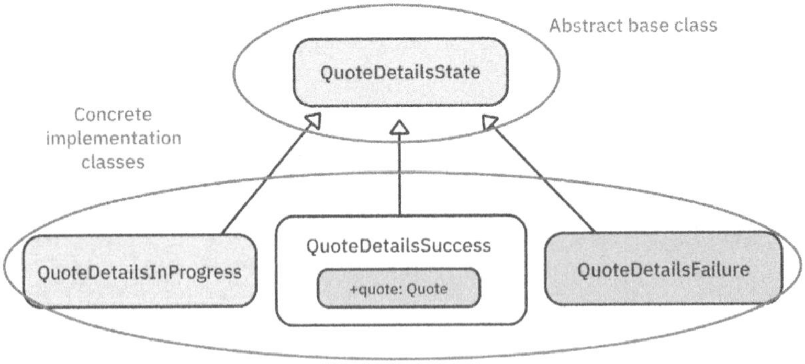

Now, for the sign-in screen, this will be very different — and a bit simpler:

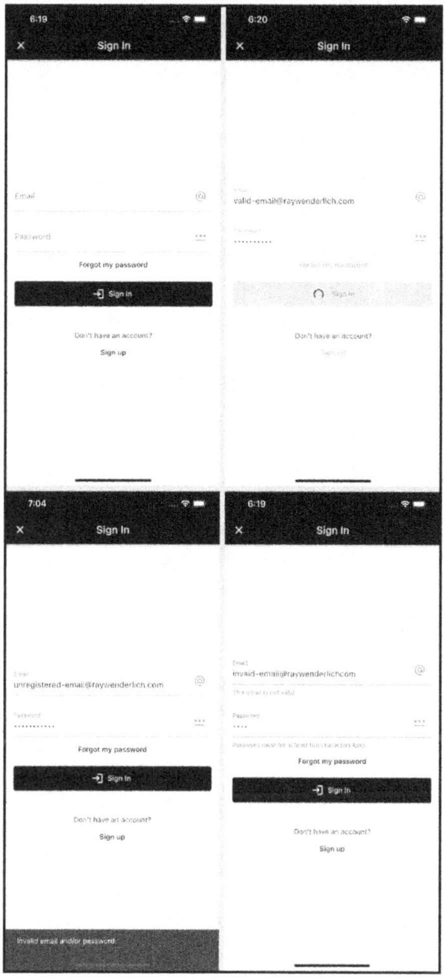


The screen contains only one *type* of state: It's always showing the form. Sometimes it shows the form *with* a loading indicator; sometimes it shows the form *with* a snackbar; sometimes it shows the form *with* one or two invalid fields. Nonetheless, it's *always* showing the form, so a single class is enough to model this.

To see this in practice, open the starter project and fetch the dependencies using the terminal to run the `make get` command from the root directory. Wait for the command to finish executing, and just ignore the errors in the project's files for now. Some work will be necessary before you can build the app.

Now, open the **sign_in_state.dart** file under **packages/features/sign_in/lib/src**.

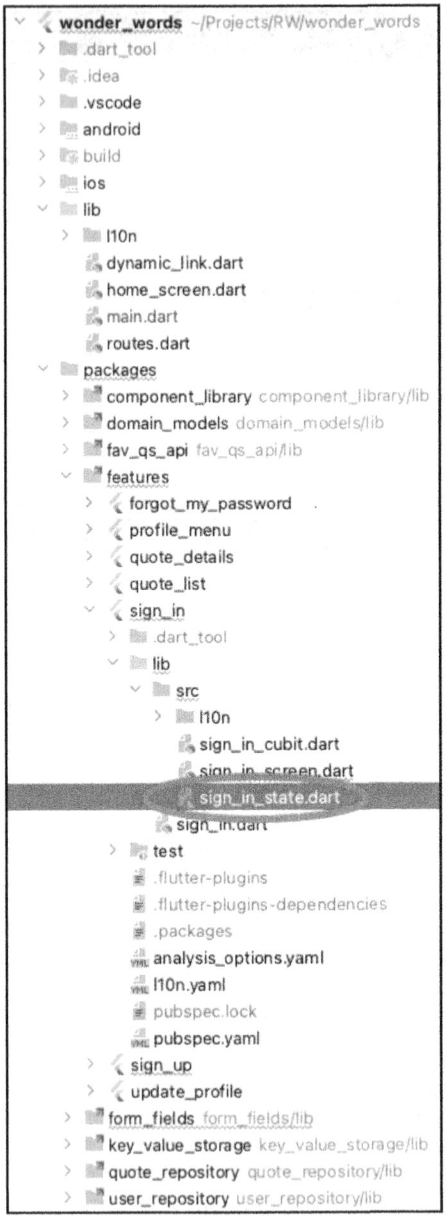

Replace `// TODO: Create your state class.` with:

```
class SignInState extends Equatable {
  const SignInState({
    // 1
    this.email = const Email.unvalidated(),
    this.password = const Password.unvalidated(),
    // 2
    this.submissionStatus,
  });

  final Email email;
  final Password password;
  final SubmissionStatus? submissionStatus;

  // 3
  SignInState copyWith({
    Email? email,
    Password? password,
    SubmissionStatus? submissionStatus,
  }) {
    return SignInState(
      email: email ?? this.email,
      password: password ?? this.password,
      submissionStatus: submissionStatus,
    );
  }

  // 4
  @override
  List<Object?> get props => [
        email,
        password,
        submissionStatus,
  ];
}
```

Here's what's going on in the code above:

1. You need a separate property to hold the state of each field on the screen. You'll dive into these `Email` and `Password` classes in the next section.

2. This enum property will serve to inform your UI on the state of the latest *submission* try. If it's `null`, it means the user hasn't tried to submit the form just yet. The property's type is `SubmissionStatus`, an enum at the bottom of this same file. Take a look at it.

3. Creating a `copyWith` function is a simple pattern that's used a lot in Flutter. The only thing it does is instantiate a *copy* of the current object by changing just the properties you choose to pass on to the function when calling it. For example, if you call `oldSignInState.copyWith(password: newPassword)`, you'll get a *new* `SignInState` object that holds the *same* values as `oldSignInState`, except for the `password` property, which will use the `newPassword` value instead. You can learn more about it in `copyWith()`this article on (https://developer.school/tutorials/dart-flutter-what-does-copywith-do). This function will come in handy when coding the Cubit later.

4. You learned all about `Equatable` and this `props` property in the last chapter. Check out `Equatable`this overview of (https://pub.dev/packages/equatable#overview) if you need a refresher.

That's all for the state class. You'll now dig down one more level and dive into these field-specific classes. `Email` is already complete, but `Password` just contains a placeholder implementation and needs your help to start working.

# Abstracting Form Fields With Formz

Still on the same **sign_in_state.dart** file, **Command-click** the `Password` class if you're on macOS, or **Control-click** it if you're on Windows. Alternatively, you can simply open the **password.dart** file under **packages/form_fields/lib/src**.

Notice that, by opening this new file, you stepped away from the **sign_in** package for a bit and are now on **form_fields**. The reason for that is the work you'll do next will be shared among multiple features in the app. As you might remember, anything that's shared between two or more feature packages needs to be in a third, independent package since features shouldn't depend on one another.

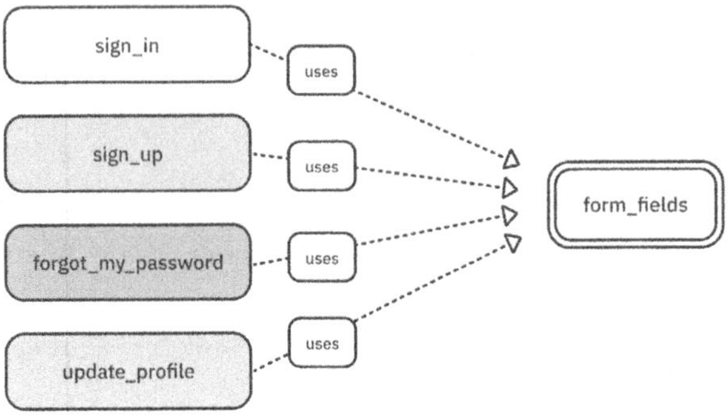


Now, back to work. Delete *everything* in **password.dart**, and insert this instead:

```
// 1
import 'package:formz/formz.dart';

// 2
class Password extends FormzInput<String,
PasswordValidationError> {
  // TODO: Add the constructors.

  // TODO: Add the validator function.
}

enum PasswordValidationError {
  empty,
  invalid,
}
```

Disregard any errors for now. So far, you just:

1. Added an `import` to the Formz (https://pub.dev/packages/formz) package, which is already listed as a dependency in this package's **pubspec.yaml**. Formz helps you create classes to represent your fields' states in a way that's generic enough for you to reuse them for different screens. Although Formz isn't part of the bloc library, both are from the same creator and work exceptionally well together.

2. This is how you create a class to encapsulate both the state and the validation rules of a form field in Formz. You just had to declare a class and extend `FormzInput` from it. You'll use `Password` for all password fields in WonderWords.

When extending `FormzInput`, you had to specify two generic types within the angle brackets (<>):

- **String**: This indicates the type of `value` this field can hold. For example, in the case of a *quantity* field in a shopping cart, this could be an `int`. Since this will actually hold a password typed by the user, `String` is the obvious choice.
- **PasswordValidationError**: This is the type that distinguishes the different ways in which this field can be invalid. The common practice is to create a dedicated enum for each `FormzInput` you create, as you did with `PasswordValidationError` at the bottom of this file.

Now, replace `// TODO: Add the constructors.` with:

```
const Password.unvalidated([String value = '']) :
super.pure(value);

const Password.validated([String value = '']) :
super.dirty(value);
```

The first thing that might've jumped out at you is this lesser-known `[String value = '']` syntax in the constructors. That one is easy: This is how you define a *positional* but at the same time *optional* parameter in Dart. You can check out Dart's documentation on parameters (https://dart.dev/guides/language/language-tour#parameters) if you want to know more about it.

The second thing is the fact that you've declared *two* constructors:

- `unvalidated`, which calls the `pure` constructor of the `super` class.
- `validated`, which calls `dirty` — what a naughty constructor!

What's happening here is that every time you create a `FormzInput`, you have to implement two constructors: `pure` and `dirty`. So, that's what you did, except you added your own seasoning to it by giving these two constructors *different* names under your `Password` class: `validated` and `unvalidated`.

The reason for choosing these different names is just that they're more aligned with the way you'll be using them shortly.

Just a little about this in advance: You use the `unvalidated` constructor when you don't want to validate your field's `value` just yet — **un**validated doesn't mean **in**validated. For example, the `SignInState` class you created in the previous section uses this `unvalidated` constructor for its initial state. This allows you to have an empty value for both fields on the screen when you first open it — that is, without accusing any validation errors prematurely — since emails and passwords shouldn't be empty.

> **Note**: Don't expect to fully grasp this just yet. It'll all become clearer when you create your Cubit in the next section.

Lastly, remove `// TODO: Add the validator function.` from your code and add this instead:

```
@override
PasswordValidationError? validator(String value) {
  if (value.isEmpty) {
    return PasswordValidationError.empty;
  } else if (value.length < 5 || value.length > 120) {
    return PasswordValidationError.invalid;
  } else {
    return null;
  }
}
```

This is the function Formz runs every time you check if a `Password` is `valid` or `invalid`.

To implement your `validator()` function, all you have to do is execute your validation logic and return an error if the field is invalid — or `null` if it's valid. Notice you're also differentiating an `empty` field from an `invalid` field, even though you still treat them both as errors. This allows you to show a more descriptive error message that differentiates an empty value from one that's in an invalid format.

As you can see, the only rule for passwords in WonderWords is that they should have more than five characters and fewer than 120. Also, notice the error you return must be of the same type you specified as the second generic argument when extending `FormzInput` – `PasswordValidationError`, in this case.

Great job! You're now ready for the main act. Go back to the **sign_in** package, and this time open the **sign_in_cubit.dart** file.

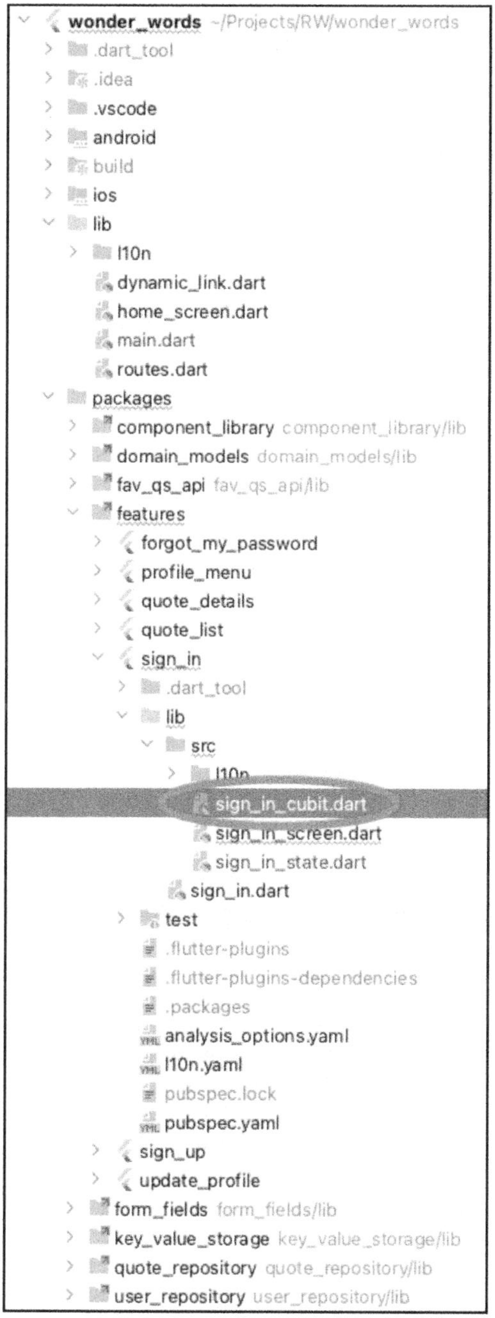

## Creating the Cubit

Replace `// TODO: Create the Cubit.` with:

```
// 1
class SignInCubit extends Cubit<SignInState> {
  SignInCubit({
    // 2
    required this.userRepository,
  }) : super(
          // 3
          const SignInState(),
        );

  final UserRepository userRepository;

  // TODO: Take in UI events.
}
```

There isn't much going on yet. You just:

1. Created a new Cubit by creating a class that extends `Cubit` and has `SignInState` specified as the state type. `SignInState` is the class you created two sections ago.
2. Requested a `UserRepository` to be passed through your constructor. `UserRepository` is the class you'll use to ultimately send the sign-in request to the server. Don't worry about the internals of `UserRepository` yet — that's for Chapter 6, "Authenticating Users".
3. Instantiated a `SignInState` using all the default values as your Cubit's initial state.

Now, to finish your Cubit's backbone, replace `// TODO: Take in UI events.` with:

```
void onEmailChanged(String newValue) {
  final previousScreenState = state;
  final previousEmailState = previousScreenState.email;
  final shouldValidate = previousEmailState.invalid;
  final newEmailState = shouldValidate
      ? Email.validated(
          newValue,
        )
      : Email.unvalidated(
          newValue,
        );

  final newScreenState = state.copyWith(
    email: newEmailState,
```

```
    );

    emit(newScreenState);
  }

  void onEmailUnfocused() {
    final previousScreenState = state;
    final previousEmailState = previousScreenState.email;
    final previousEmailValue = previousEmailState.value;

    final newEmailState = Email.validated(
      previousEmailValue,
    );
    final newScreenState = previousScreenState.copyWith(
      email: newEmailState,
    );
    emit(newScreenState);
  }


  void onPasswordChanged(String newValue) {
    // TODO: Handle the user changing the value of the password
field.
  }

  void onPasswordUnfocused() {
    // TODO: Handle the user taking the focus out of the password
field.
  }

  void onSubmit() async {
    // TODO: Handle the submit button's tap.
  }
```

These are all public functions you're creating, so you can call them from your widgets when specific user interactions happen. For example: When the user indicates they're done editing the email field by tapping elsewhere on the screen, you'll call the `onEmailUnfocused()` function to kick-off the validation process. For now, don't worry about the implementations of `onEmailChanged()` and `onEmailUnfocused()`; those are there just to save you some time. You'll understand everything that's going on when you implement `onPasswordChanged()` and `onPasswordUnfocused()`.

You've still got plenty of work to do, but at least now the errors are all gone. Before you continue, build and run your app to make sure you're on the right track. To open the sign-in screen, tap the **Profile** tab and then **Sign In** at the top of the screen.

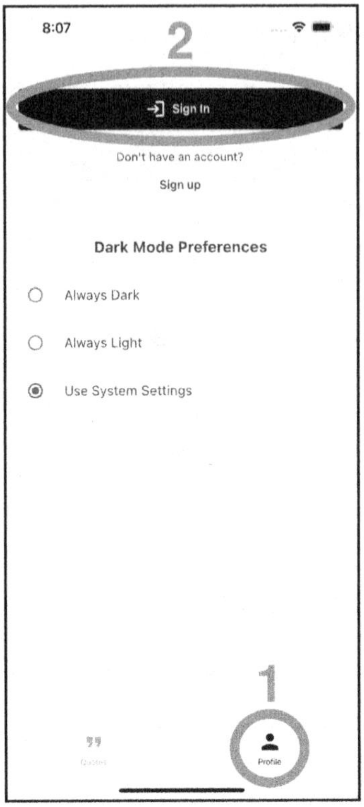


> **Note**: If you're having trouble running the app, it's because you forgot to propagate the configurations you did in the first chapter's starter project to the following chapters' materials. If that's the case, please revisit Chapter 1, "Setting up Your Environment".

Your screen still won't behave as expected, but it should open just fine and look like this:

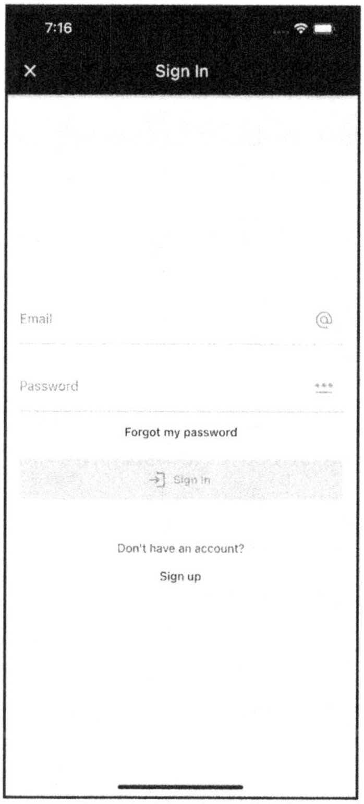


# Responding to User Interaction

Time to add some meat to some of the functions you've just declared in your Cubit. Start inside `onPasswordChanged()` by replacing `// TODO: Handle the user changing the value of the password field.` with:

```
// 1
final previousScreenState = state;
// 2
final previousPasswordState = previousScreenState.password;

final shouldValidate = previousPasswordState.invalid;
// 3
final newPasswordState = shouldValidate
    ? Password.validated(
      newValue,
```

```
        )
      : Password.unvalidated(
          newValue,
        );

  // TODO: Emit the new state.
```

In the near future, you'll make your UI call this `onPasswordChanged()` function whenever the user changes what's in the password field. When that happens, the code you just wrote will:

1. Grab your Cubit's `state` property and assign it a more meaningful name within this function.
2. Use the `previousScreenState` variable to retrieve the previous state of the `password` field.
3. Recreate the state of the password field using the `newValue` received in the function parameter.

Lastly, do you remember the `validated` and `unvalidated` constructors you created a few sections ago? You're using them here to add some motion to the screen:

- You use the `validated` constructor to force the validation to kick in *while the user is still typing* only if you were already showing a validation error for that field.
- Otherwise, if the previous value in that field hasn't been validated yet — or if it has been validated and considered valid — you'll wait until the user takes the focus out of that field to validate it.

> **Note**: The reason you don't *always* validate the field *as the user types* is because that would cause errors to be shown before the user is done typing. Think about how annoying it would be if the user started typing an email with the letter "a", and you immediately showed an error since "a" isn't a valid email.

Wow, that was a lot! If it's any comfort, it only gets easier from here. As proof, replace `// TODO: Emit the new state.` with:

```
// 1
final newScreenState = state.copyWith(
  password: newPasswordState,
);

// 2
emit(newScreenState);
```

See? Easier! Here, you just:

1. Used the `copyWith` function from the beginning of the chapter to create a copy of the screen state, changing only the `password` property.
2. Emitted the new screen's state.

That's all for `onPasswordChanged()`. Now, before jumping into the widgets side of things, you need to take care of that `onPasswordUnfocused()` function too. Do this by replacing `// TODO: Handle the user taking the focus out of the password field.` with:

```
final previousScreenState = state;
final previousPasswordState = previousScreenState.password;
// 1
final previousPasswordValue = previousPasswordState.value;

// 2
final newPasswordState = Password.validated(
  previousPasswordValue,
);

// 3
final newScreenState = previousScreenState.copyWith(
  password: newPasswordState,
);
emit(newScreenState);
```

This is simpler than what you did for `onPasswordChanged()`. You didn't need a `newValue` parameter this time since the user hasn't inserted new data; they've just taken the focus out of the field. So, you:

1. Grabbed the latest value of the password field.
2. Recreated the state of the password field by using the `validated` constructor to force validation of the latest value.
3. Re-emitted the screen's state with the new/validated password state.

Well done! Now, to the widgets side of the curtain...

# Hooking up the UI

Still in the same folder you've been working on, open **sign_in_screen.dart**, and scroll down to the `_SignInFormState` class. Replace `// TODO: Create the FocusNodes.` with:

```
// 1
final _emailFocusNode = FocusNode();
final _passwordFocusNode = FocusNode();

@override
void initState() {
  super.initState();
  // 2
  final cubit = context.read<SignInCubit>();
  _emailFocusNode.addListener(() {
    // 3
    if (!_emailFocusNode.hasFocus) {
      // 4
      cubit.onEmailUnfocused();
    }
  });
  _passwordFocusNode.addListener(() {
    if (!_passwordFocusNode.hasFocus) {
      cubit.onPasswordUnfocused();
    }
  });
}

@override
void dispose() {
  // 5
  _emailFocusNode.dispose();
  _passwordFocusNode.dispose();
  super.dispose();
}
```

Just ignore the `TODO`s for now. Here's what's happening in the snippet above:

1. You created two `FocusNode`s: One for the email field and one for the password field. `FocusNode`s are objects you can attach to your `TextField`s to listen to and control a field's focus.
2. This is how you get an instance of a Cubit to call functions on it. This `context.read()` call only works because the topmost widget in this file has a `BlocProvider`. Revisit the previous chapter if you need a refresher on all that.
3. You then added listeners to your `FocusNode`s. These listeners run every time the respective field gains *or* loses focus. Since you're only interested in knowing when the focus is *lost*, you added this `if` statement to distinguish between the two events.
4. Within each listener's code, you call the corresponding function you just implemented in your Cubit.
5. You have to dispose of `FocusNode`s.

So far, so good, but still... None of this will work unless you attach these `FocusNodes` to their corresponding `TextFields`.

Scroll down to the `build()` function, and locate `// TODO: Attach _emailFocusNode.`. Replace it with:

```
focusNode: _emailFocusNode,
```

Now do the same for the password field by replacing `// TODO: Attach _passwordFocusNode.` with:

```
focusNode: _passwordFocusNode,
```

Done! You're now properly notifying your Cubit of when your fields lose focus.

There are still two other things left:

- You also have to notify your Cubit when the user changes the value in those fields.
- Your fields have to rebuild themselves when your Cubit emits a new state; that's how you *show* or *clear* a validation error. Don't forget this is a two-way street: You have to both notify *and* listen to a Cubit.

The good news is that, to save you some time, the above is already done for the email field; you'll learn how to do it by practicing on the password field.

## Forwarding Change Events to the Cubit

Continuing on your password's `TextField`, this time replace `// TODO: Forward password change events to the Cubit.` with:

```
onChanged: cubit.onPasswordChanged,
```

> **Note**: Check out Dart's documentation (https://dart.dev/guides/language/effective-dart/usage#dont-create-a-lambda-when-a-tear-off-will-do) if you don't know why you didn't have to write the line above as `onChanged: (newValue) => cubit.onPasswordChanged(newValue)`.

Perfect! There's nothing left for you to *send* to your Cubit anymore. Now is finally the time to start *consuming* the Cubit too.

## Consuming the Cubit

Scroll up a bit and find `// TODO: Check for errors in the password state.`. Replace it with:

```
final passwordError =
            state.password.invalid ? state.password.error :
null;
```

Yet another one-liner. Here, you're checking if the password's field status is invalid, and if it is, you grab the error type.

> **Note**: As counterintuitive as it may seem, you can't access the `error` property directly without first checking if the field is `invalid`. The reason is the `error` property doesn't take into account if the field is `validated` or `unvalidated`. If a field is `unvalidated`, you shouldn't present any errors to the user.

Now, back in your password `TextField`, replace `// TODO: Display the password validation error if any.` with:

```
// 1
errorText: passwordError == null
    // 2
    ? null
    // 3
    : (passwordError == PasswordValidationError.empty
        // 4
        ? l10n.passwordTextFieldEmptyErrorMessage
        : l10n.passwordTextFieldInvalidErrorMessage),
```

Going over it step by step:

1. You're using the `errorText` property of the `TextField` class to display a validation error.
2. If `passwordError` is `null`, you set `errorText` to `null`, which will cause your field to display as valid. `passwordError` is the property you created in the last step.
3. Otherwise, if `passwordError` isn't `null`, you return a different `String` depending on whether the error is `PasswordValidationError.empty` or `PasswordValidationError.invalid`.
4. This `l10n.whatever` syntax is how you retrieve custom internationalized messages in WonderWords. You'll learn all about this in Chapter 9, "Internationalizing & Localizing".

What a section! But there's only one way to make sure it actually works: Build and run your app.

Open the sign-in screen and play with the fields for a bit. For example, insert two characters on the password field, then tap outside of it. Does it show any errors? Awesome! Now, empty the field. Did the error change? Expect to see something like this:

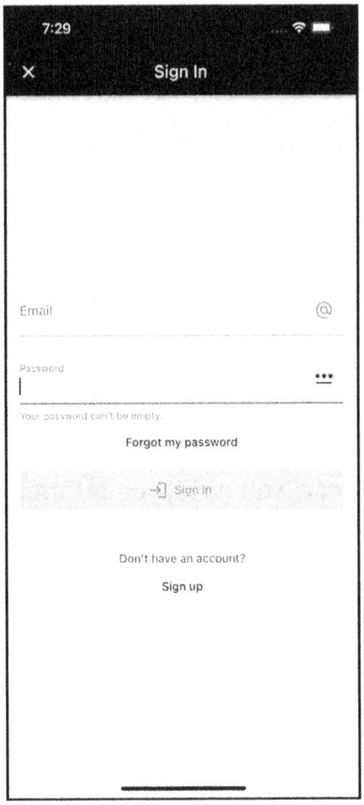


Time for the icing on the cake: the **Sign In** button.

# Submitting the Form

Open the Cubit's file. Replace `// TODO: Handle the submit button's tap.` with:

```
// 1
final email = Email.validated(state.email.value);
final password = Password.validated(state.password.value);

// 2
final isFormValid = Formz.validate([
  email,
  password,
```

```
]).isValid;

// 3
final newState = state.copyWith(
  email: email,
  password: password,
  // 4
  submissionStatus: isFormValid ? SubmissionStatus.inProgress :
null,
);

// 5
emit(newState);

// TODO: Submit the data.
```

This is what you're doing here:

1. When the user taps the **Sign In** button, you want to validate the two fields no matter what — even if the user hasn't touched the fields at all and tapping the button is their first action after opening the screen.
2. This is an alternative way of checking if all fields are valid. You could've used `email.valid && password.valid` instead, but the way you did it here scales better — it's easier to add and remove fields.
3. You then create a new state for the screen using the updated fields. Emitting this new state in step five is what will cause any errors to show up in the `TextFields`.
4. If the form is valid, you'll change the `submissionStatus` to `SubmissionStatus.inProgress` so you can use that information in your widgets to display a loading indicator.
5. You're emitting a new state even though you *still have work left to do* in this function. You're doing this so your screen updates the fields and puts the loading indicator before you send the actual request to the server.

Now, to finish your work in this Cubit for good, remove `// TODO: Submit the data.` and insert this:

```
// 1
if (isFormValid) {
  try {
    // 2
    await userRepository.signIn(
      email.value,
      password.value,
    );
```

```
      // 3
      final newState = state.copyWith(
        submissionStatus: SubmissionStatus.success,
      );

      emit(newState);
    } catch (error) {
      final newState = state.copyWith(
        // 4
        submissionStatus: error is InvalidCredentialsException
            ? SubmissionStatus.invalidCredentialsError
            : SubmissionStatus.genericError,
      );

      emit(newState);
    }
  }
```

Here's the explanation for the code above:

1. Notice this `if` has no corresponding `else` statement. If the fields aren't valid, you don't need to do anything else. You've already emitted the new state from the code in the previous snippet, and at this point, the screen will already show the errors on the fields.
2. Finally, if the values inserted by the user *are* valid, send them to the server.
3. If your code gets to this line, it means the server returned a successful response. `UserRepository` will take care of storing the user information locally and refreshing the other screens for you — details in Chapter 6, "Authenticating Users". All you have to do here is set your `submissionStatus` to `SubmissionStatus.success` so you can use that information in your widget shortly to close the screen.
4. On the other hand, if you get an error from the server, you change your `submissionStatus` to `SubmissionStatus.invalidCredentialsError` if the cause is missing their credentials or `SubmissionStatus.genericError` if the cause is anything else — lack of internet connectivity, for example.

That's all for the Cubit! Now, similar to what you did for the field validations, your next step is to go back to your UI and hook it up to this new code by:

- Calling this `onSubmit()` function from the appropriate places.
- Executing logic based on the `submissionStatus` property.

You're close...

## Forwarding the Submit Event

Go back to the **sign_in_screen.dart** file. Close to the bottom of the file, replace `// TODO: Forward the onTap event to the Cubit.` with:

```
onTap: cubit.onSubmit,
```

Easy peasy, right? Now, scroll up just a bit and replace `// TODO: Forward the onEditingComplete to the Cubit.` with:

```
onEditingComplete: cubit.onSubmit,
```

Here, you're giving the `onEditingComplete` event of the password `TextField` the same treatment you gave to taps on the **Sign In** button. The `onEditingComplete` callback is how Flutter lets you know the user has tapped the **done** button on the keyboard:

You're done *sending* stuff to the Cubit; now you just have to finish *consuming* it too.

## Listening to Changes in the Submission Status

First, you'll want to disable the **Sign In** button if a submission is already in progress. That way, you protect yourself from sending multiple requests to the server if the user is impatient and keeps tapping the button.

Still in **sign_in_screen.dart**, find the `final isSubmissionInProgress = false;` line, and give it a real value by completely replacing it with:

```
final isSubmissionInProgress =
    state.submissionStatus == SubmissionStatus.inProgress;
```

This is getting too easy...

Notice this `isSubmissionInProgress` variable is used in a few different places below to disable the `TextFields` and display an *in-progress* version of the **Sign In** button, which does nothing when pressed.

Now, for your last bit of challenge, scroll up to `// TODO: Execute one-off actions based on state changes.`. Before replacing that `TODO` with some actual code, notice where it's located: inside the `listener` callback of the `BlocConsumer` widget. If you don't recall that part from the previous chapter, here's a quick recap:

1. A `BlocConsumer` widget is a combination of two widgets:

- `BlocBuilder`, which gives you the `builder` callback.
- `BlocListener`, which provides the `listener` callback.

2. The `listener` callback differs from the `builder` in the sense that it doesn't expect you to return any widgets from it and is guaranteed to run *once per state change*.
3. That *once per state change* feature is crucial when you need to *execute one-off actions*, such as navigating to another screen, displaying a dialog, displaying a snackbar, etc. In other words, it's crucial when you want to *do* something instead of *return* something.

Back to the action. Finally, replace `// TODO: Execute one-off actions based on state changes.` with:

```
if (state.submissionStatus == SubmissionStatus.success) {
 // 1
 widget.onSignInSuccess();
 return;
}

final hasSubmissionError = state.submissionStatus ==
       SubmissionStatus.genericError ||
   state.submissionStatus ==
SubmissionStatus.invalidCredentialsError;

// 2
if (hasSubmissionError) {
 ScaffoldMessenger.of(context)
   ..hideCurrentSnackBar()
   ..showSnackBar(
     // 3
     state.submissionStatus ==
SubmissionStatus.invalidCredentialsError
         ? SnackBar(
             content: Text(
               l10n.invalidCredentialsErrorMessage,
             ),
           )
         : const GenericErrorSnackBar(),
   );
}
```

Here's what's going on in there:

1. If the submission is a success, you call the `onSignInSuccess` callback you received in the screen's constructor. Ultimately, that will lead to the **main** app package closing this screen and getting back to whatever screen opened it. The sign-in screen can open on a few different occasions, such as when a signed-out user tries to favorite a quote.
2. Check if the current `submissionStatus` contains an error.
3. If yes, display a different snackbar with a more descriptive message, depending on what that error is.

> **Note**: Please refer to the previous chapter if you need a refresher on `BlocBuilder`, `BlocListener`, `builder`, `listener`, etc.

That's all for this chapter. You did it! Build and run your app one last time to check on your final product.

Please, keep in mind your sign-in screen will only work as intended if you either completed the previous **Exercise** unit or continued following along from the challenge project.

To make sure your last snippet of code works, open the sign-in screen and try inserting an unregistered email and password. You should expect to see a snackbar indicating the error at the bottom.

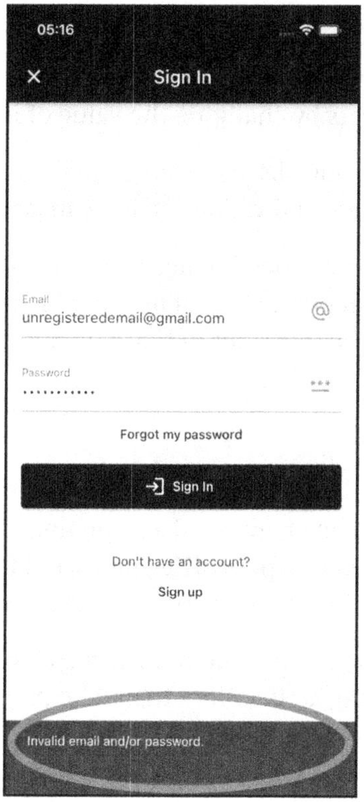

# Key Points

- **Validating** values entered by the user can save unnecessary calls to the server and also ensures you won't contaminate your database with faulty data.
- Adding a `copyWith()` function to your data classes allows you to easily create copies of that class's objects by changing the value of just one or two properties.
- The **Formz** package helps you abstract your form fields by creating classes that gather both that field's state and validation logic in a single place.
- When working with forms, you need to decide what user events you'll use as triggers for your validation process. A robust approach is to validate them whenever the user takes the focus out of that field or taps the **Submit** button.

# Where to Go From Here?

Before you move on to the next chapter, take some time to study the other form screens on **WonderWords**: **sign_up**, **profile_menu** and **forgot_my_password**. The differences from the sign-in screen are subtle, but they exist.

When you're done with that, you'll be more than ready for your ultimate state management challenge: using actual Blocs to handle pagination, search, filters and more — all at once. Good luck!

# Chapter 5: Managing Complex State With Blocs

By Edson Bueno

Two chapters ago, you embarked on a journey to master state management with the bloc library (https://bloclibrary.dev). You started by using a Cubit — a simplified Bloc — to manage the quote details screen. Then, in the previous chapter, you consolidated that knowledge and demonstrated how far one could go with Cubits. You learned how to use Cubits to handle what's perhaps the most common challenge in app development: form validation. Finally, this chapter is where you step up to the real thing: Blocs.

Now, if you think of Cubits as *worse* than Blocs, that's actually not the case at all: Cubits can do 95% of what Blocs can do at 60% of the complexity — numbers taken from the same source that revealed 73.6% of all numbers are made up on the spot.

The point is: You don't stop using Cubits once you know Blocs. If this was a shooter game, Cubits would be your handguns: lighter and easier to use, thus more effective for close combat. Yet, sometimes you just need a ~~Bloc~~ sniper rifle and don't care about carrying the extra weight. But that's enough metaphors for a "real-world" book...

In this chapter, you'll learn how to:

- Understand the difference between Cubits and Blocs, and what that looks like in the code.
- Communicate with a Bloc.
- Create a Bloc.
- Generate, manipulate and consume `Streams`.
- Implement a full-fledged search bar with advanced techniques such as debouncing.
- Determine the exact situations where you should pick Blocs over Cubits.

While going through this chapter, you'll work on the **starter** project from this chapter's **assets** folder.

# Differentiating Between Cubits and Blocs

Both Cubits and Blocs do only two things:

- Take in events.
- Emit states.

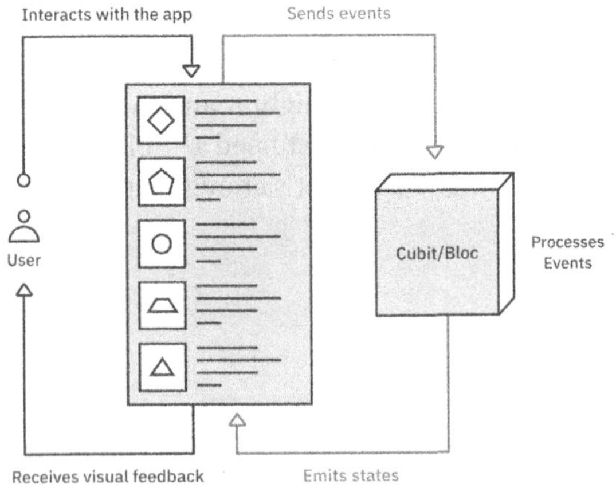


Events come in, and states go out. Nothing new so far, right?
Now, get this tattooed on your brain: The *only* difference between Cubits and Blocs is how they *take in* those UI events. Nothing else.

As you've seen from the last two chapters, Cubits take in events through functions you define inside them and then call from your widgets. For example:

```
UpvoteIconButton(
  onTap: () {
    if (quote.isUpvoted == true) {
      cubit.unvoteQuote();
    } else {
      cubit.upvoteQuote();
    }
  },
  // Omitted code.
)
```

Blocs, on the other hand, come pre-baked with an `add()` function you have to use for *all events*. For example:

```
UpvoteIconButton(
  onTap: () {
    if (quote.isUpvoted == true) {
      bloc.add(QuoteDetailsUnvoted());
    } else {
      bloc.add(QuoteDetailsUpvoted());
    }
  },
  // Omitted code.
)
```

Since you have to use *one* function for *all* your events, you differentiate between the events through the object you pass in as the `add()` function's argument. You specify the type of these objects when you define the Bloc, as in:

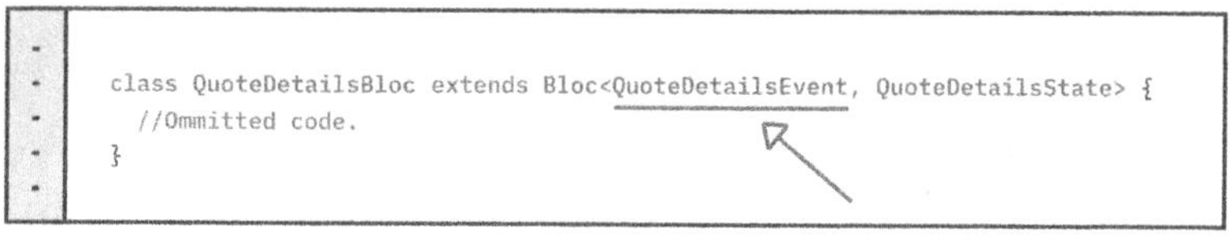


vs.

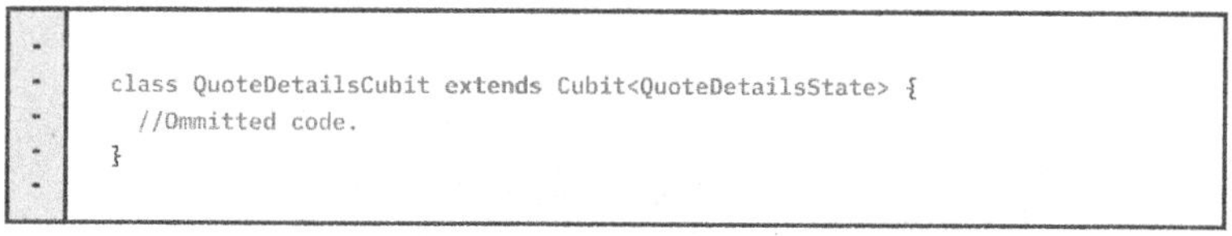


This means that when using Blocs, besides having to create a *state class* — as you do for Cubits — you now have one extra level of complexity: creating an **event class**.

Throughout this chapter, though, you'll see that this extra cost of using Blocs doesn't come without benefits. Having all your events coming in through a *single* function gives you a whole lot more control over how to process these events. As a general rule, screens with search bars can benefit a lot from that.

For WonderWords specifically, the home screen is the ideal candidate for Blocs — lots of different events *and* a search bar — so that's where your focus will be for the rest of this chapter.

Having gone through the last two chapters, creating state classes should no longer be a mystery to you. So, you'll skip that part and dive right into the unknown territory: the **event classes**.

# Creating Event Classes

Open the starter project and fetch the dependencies by running the `make get` command from the root directory. Ignore any errors in the code for now and open **quote_list_event.dart** inside the **quote_list** feature package.

You're about to create *nineteen* classes within this file, so take a deep breath. Keep in mind that creating event classes is one of the few things that differentiates Blocs from Cubits, so you have to make sure this becomes second nature to you.

Kick off the work by replacing `// TODO: Create the event classes.` with:

```
// 1
abstract class QuoteListEvent extends Equatable {
  const QuoteListEvent();

  @override
  List<Object?> get props => [];
}

// 2
class QuoteListFilterByFavoritesToggled extends QuoteListEvent {
  const QuoteListFilterByFavoritesToggled();
}

// 3
class QuoteListTagChanged extends QuoteListEvent {
  const QuoteListTagChanged(
    this.tag,
  );

  final Tag? tag;

  @override
  List<Object?> get props => [
        tag,
      ];
}

// 4
class QuoteListSearchTermChanged extends QuoteListEvent {
  const QuoteListSearchTermChanged(
    this.searchTerm,
  );

  final String searchTerm;

  @override
  List<Object?> get props => [
        searchTerm,
      ];
}

// 5
class QuoteListRefreshed extends QuoteListEvent {
  const QuoteListRefreshed();
}
```

Does this look familiar to you? Creating event classes is very similar to creating state classes in that enum-like format you used for the **quote_details** feature in Chapter 3, "Managing State With Cubits & the Bloc Library". In the code above, you just:

1. Defined an abstract `QuoteListEvent` class to use as a common ancestral for all subsequent classes in this file. In **quote_list_bloc.dart**, you specify this class as your Bloc's event type when declaring it.

```
class QuoteListBloc extends Bloc<QuoteListEvent, QuoteListState> {
  //Ommitted code.
}
```

2. Created a `QuoteListFilterByFavoritesToggled` subclass to send to the Bloc when the user turns the favorites filter on or off.

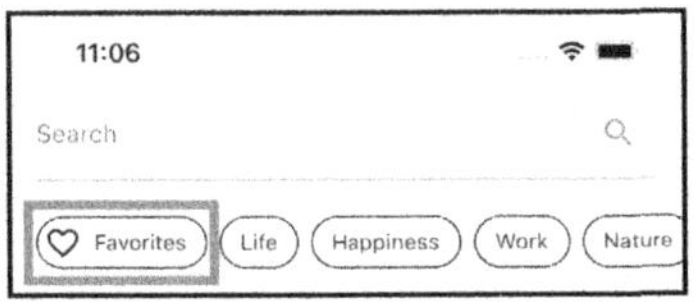


3. Created `QuoteListTagChanged` for when the user selects a new tag. The `tag` property is optional because the event can also be the user *clearing* a previously selected tag, in which case you'll use `null` for the value.

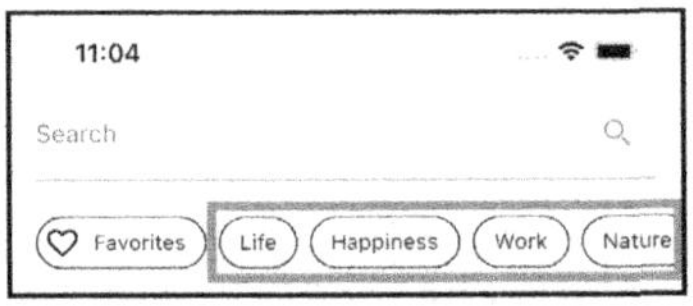


4. Created `QuoteListSearchTermChanged` for when the user changes the content in the search bar.

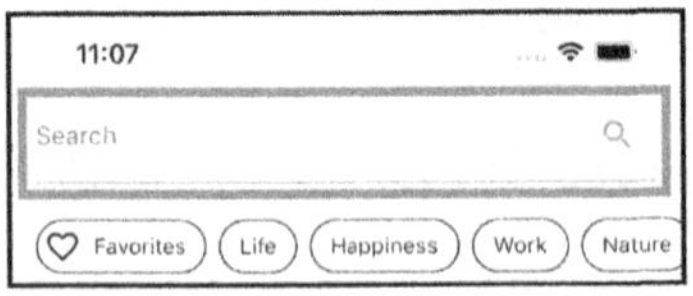

5. Created `QuoteListRefreshed` for when the user pulls the list down to force it to refresh.

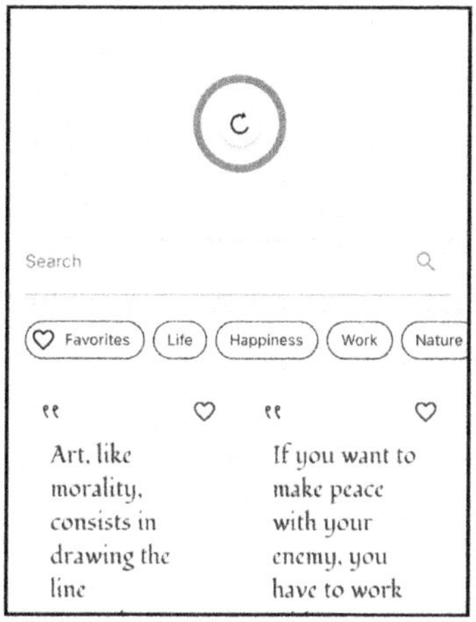


There are still some events left. Keep the ball rolling by appending this to the bottom of the file:

```
class QuoteListNextPageRequested extends QuoteListEvent {
  const QuoteListNextPageRequested({
    required this.pageNumber,
  });

  final int pageNumber;
}
```

You'll use this `QuoteListNextPageRequested` class on two occasions:

- When the user is scrolling down and nears the bottom of the page.

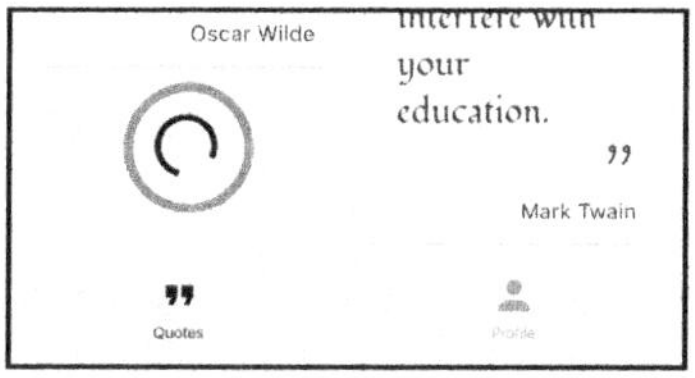

- If fetching a new page fails and the user taps the "try again" widget.

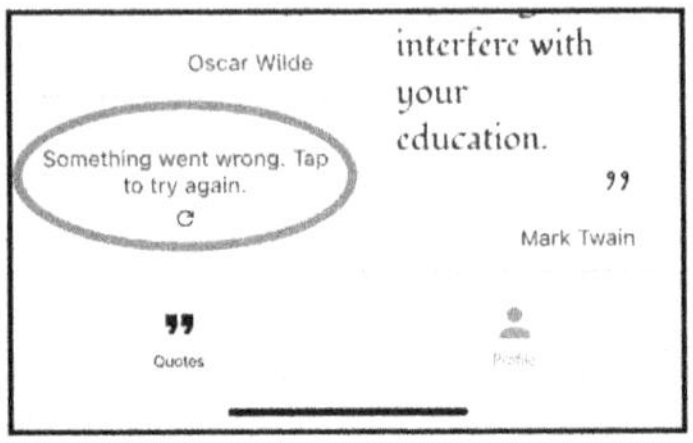


You've got five more events left. Cross out two others by now appending the following to the bottom of the file:

```
abstract class QuoteListItemFavoriteToggled extends
QuoteListEvent {
  const QuoteListItemFavoriteToggled(
    this.id,
  );

  final int id;
}

class QuoteListItemFavorited extends
QuoteListItemFavoriteToggled {
  const QuoteListItemFavorited(
    int id,
  ) : super(id);
}

class QuoteListItemUnfavorited extends
QuoteListItemFavoriteToggled {
  const QuoteListItemUnfavorited(
    int id,
  ) : super(id);
}
```

This one is a bit different. Notice that you added one more level to your class hierarchy by creating a new abstract class, `QuoteListItemFavoriteToggled`. This extends the previous class, `QuoteListEvent`.

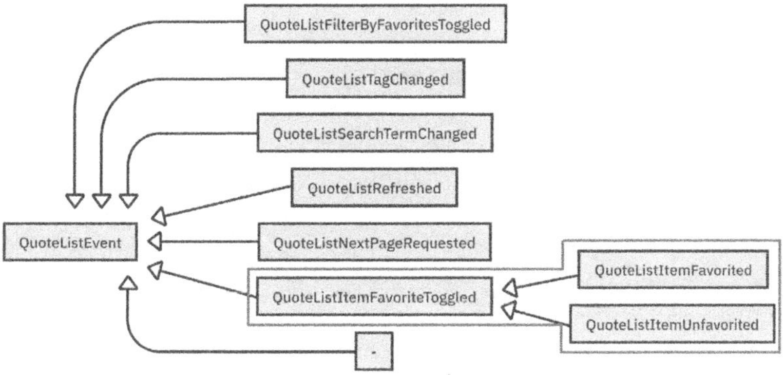


Having this base `QuoteListItemFavoriteToggled` class allows you to share some logic between `QuoteListItemFavorited` and `QuoteListItemUnfavorited` when coding the Bloc later. You'll use these two concrete classes to represent the taps on the favorite button of a quote card:

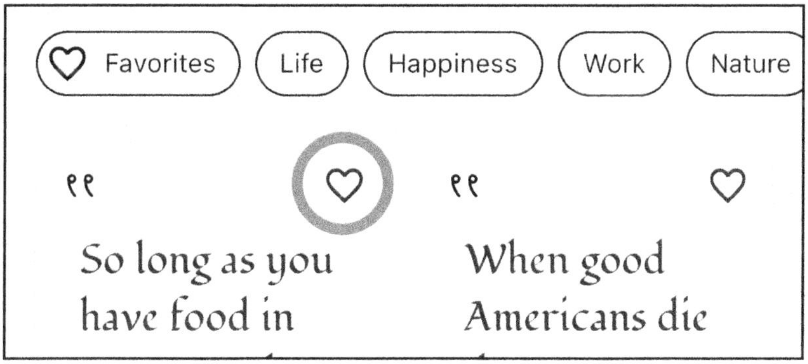

Finally, add these last three classes to the bottom of the file:

```
class QuoteListFailedFetchRetried extends QuoteListEvent {
  const QuoteListFailedFetchRetried();
}

class QuoteListUsernameObtained extends QuoteListEvent {
  const QuoteListUsernameObtained();
}

class QuoteListItemUpdated extends QuoteListEvent {
  const QuoteListItemUpdated(
    this.updatedQuote,
  );

  final Quote updatedQuote;
}
```

Those are the least intuitive ones. You'll go through a quick explanation of how to use each of them, but don't worry about fully grasping it for now; it'll all get clearer when you use them in a few sections. Here's what these classes do:

1. **QuoteListFailedFetchRetried**: Used when the user taps the main **Try Again** button, which appears when an error occurs while trying to fetch the first page.

2. **QuoteListUsernameObtained**: Used to trigger the data fetching when the screen first opens and you've obtained the signed-in user's username. It'll also be used to refresh the list when the user signs in or out of the app at a later time. It's vital to refresh the list when the user's authentication status changes, so you reflect that user's favorites accordingly.

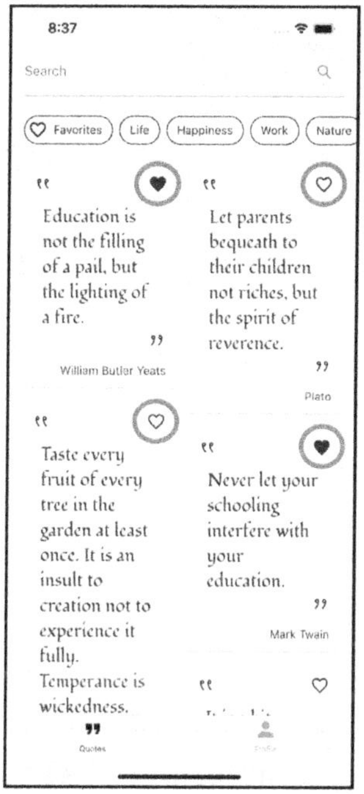


3. **QuoteListItemUpdated**: Used when the user taps a quote and modifies it on that quote's details screen — favoriting it, unfavoriting, upvoting, etc. You need this event so you can reflect that change on the home screen as well.

Nineteen classes and ten events later, you're finally done. And you still wonder why "Complex" is in the chapter's name...

> **Note**: Everything you've done so far could also be accomplished with a simple Cubit. In fact, this will be true until almost the end of the chapter, when you start the **Controlling the Traffic of Events** section.

Time to put all those event classes to use.

# Forwarding the Events to the Bloc

Open **quote_list_screen.dart**, which lives under the same directory you've been working on.

Find `// TODO: Forward subsequent page requests to the Bloc.` and replace it with:

```
_pagingController.addPageRequestListener((pageNumber) {
  final isSubsequentPage = pageNumber > 1;
  if (isSubsequentPage) {
    _bloc.add(
      QuoteListNextPageRequested(
        pageNumber: pageNumber,
      ),
    );
  }
});
```

The first thing to clear out here is that WonderWords uses the infinite_scroll_pagination (https://pub.dev/packages/infinite_scroll_pagination) package to handle the pagination of the quotes grid. The package takes care of several things: showing loading and error indicators, letting you know when the user is reaching the bottom of the page and you need more items to show, appending new items to the bottom, etc.

In the code above, you add a listener to `_pagingController`, which comes from that package. You need this listener so you know when the user's scroll is nearing the bottom of the page. When that happens, you forward that event to the Bloc so it can work on getting more items for the user.

> **Note**: If you want a deep dive into pagination and the `infinite_scroll_pagination` package, an excellent tutorial is Infinite Scrolling Pagination in Flutter (https://www.raywenderlich.com/14214369-infinite-scrolling-pagination-in-flutter).

Next, right below the place you inserted the previous code, replace `// TODO: Forward changes in the search bar to the Bloc.` with:

```
_searchBarController.addListener(() {
  _bloc.add(
    QuoteListSearchTermChanged(
      _searchBarController.text,
    ),
  );
});
```

This `_searchBarController` property holds a regular `TextEditingController` you attached to the screen's search bar. In the code above, you add a listener to it so you can notify your Bloc of any changes to the `TextField`'s value.

Now, scroll down a bit more and locate `// TODO: Forward pull-to-refresh gestures to the Bloc.`. Replace it with:

```
_bloc.add(
  const QuoteListRefreshed(),
);
```

This time, you're sending the `QuoteListRefreshed` event to the Bloc whenever the user pulls the list down from the top to force it to refresh. That gesture is known as pull-to-refresh (https://en.wikipedia.org/wiki/Pull-to-refresh).

That was all for this file. Now, for the last three events, go to **quote_paged_grid_view.dart**.

Replace `// TODO: Forward taps on the favorite button.` with:

```
bloc.add(
  isFavorite
    ? QuoteListItemUnfavorited(quote.id)
    : QuoteListItemFavorited(quote.id),
);
```

That one was pretty easy, right? When the user taps the favorite button for a quote, you send a `QuoteListItemUnfavorited` if that quote is already a favorite or `QuoteListItemFavorited` if it's not.

Now, for a more complex case, find `// TODO: Open the details screen and notify the Bloc if the user modified the quote in there.`. Replace it with:

```
// 1
final updatedQuote = await onQuoteSelected(quote.id);

if (updatedQuote != null &&
    // 2
    updatedQuote.isFavorite != quote.isFavorite) {
  // 3
  bloc.add(
    QuoteListItemUpdated(
      updatedQuote,
    ),
  );
}
```

This code executes whenever the user taps a quote. When that happens, your code will:

1. Call the `onQuoteSelected` callback this widget received on its constructor. If you trace back that callback's origin, you'll find its declaration in the **main** application package. What it does is simply open the quote details screen and then return the updated quote object to you when the user closes that screen.
2. Check if the user has favorited or unfavorited the quote while in the details screen.
3. If the user *did* change the quote's favorite status, send the updated quote object to the Bloc so it can replace the old one currently on screen.

To finish this file, you now have to send the taps on the main **Try Again** button to the Bloc. This button appears when you can't fetch the first page for any reason. Do this by replacing `// TODO: Request the first page again.` with:

```
bloc.add(
  const QuoteListFailedFetchRetried(),
);
```

Great job! Just one more section, and you'll be able to build and run your app.

This section was intentionally repetitive. Forwarding events is one of only two things that change in your codebase when using Blocs instead of Cubits. The second thing is the actual Bloc, which you'll dive into now.

## Scaffolding the Bloc

Still in the same directory you've been working on, open **quote_list_bloc.dart**.

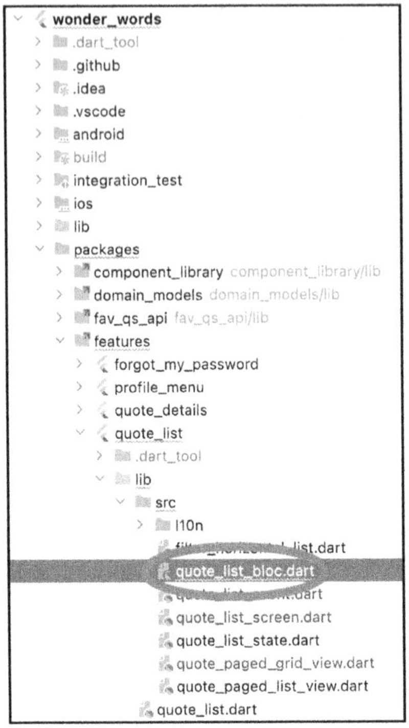


The Bloc's declaration is already there to save you some time. Take a look at it:

```
// 1
class QuoteListBloc extends Bloc<QuoteListEvent, QuoteListState>
{
  QuoteListBloc({
    required QuoteRepository quoteRepository,
    required UserRepository userRepository,
  })  :
        // 2
        _quoteRepository = quoteRepository,
        // 3
        super(
          const QuoteListState(),
        ) {
    // 4
    _registerEventHandler();

    // TODO: Watch the user's authentication status.
  }
```

```
  // 5
  late final StreamSubscription _authChangesSubscription;
  String? _authenticatedUsername;

  final QuoteRepository _quoteRepository;

  // Omitted code.
}
```

Nothing too fancy about it. Here's a walkthrough:

1. This `QuoteListBloc` class extends `Bloc` and specifies two generic types: the event class, `QuoteListEvent`, and the state class, `QuoteListState`.
2. `QuoteListBloc`'s constructor then receives two repositories and assigns one of them to the `_quoteRepository` property. You didn't have to assign `userRepository` to a property of the `QuoteListBloc` class — as you did for `quoteRepository` — because you'll only use it inside the constructor's code.
3. You then call the `super` constructor and pass it to your initial state, which is just a `QuoteListState` instantiated with all the default values.
4. Here, you're calling a function you'll implement later to handle all your events.
5. You'll learn all about these `_authChangesSubscription` and `_authenticatedUsername` properties in a moment.

Start *your* part of the work by replacing `// TODO: Watch the user's authentication status.` with:

```
_authChangesSubscription = userRepository
    // 1
    .getUser()
    // 2
    .listen(
  (user) {
    // 3
    _authenticatedUsername = user?.username;

    // 4
    add(
      const QuoteListUsernameObtained(),
    );
  },
);
```

Here's what's going on in there:

1. `UserRepository` has a `getUser()` function that returns a `Stream<User?>`. That `Stream` is useful for monitoring changes in the user's authentication status. When the user signs in, a new `User` object comes down that `Stream`. When they sign out, you get a `null` value instead.
2. You then subscribe to that `Stream` using the `listen()` function. The `listen()` function returns an object, called the **subscription**. You store the subscription object in the `_authChangesSubscription` property, so you can dispose of it later.
3. Every time you get a new value from that `Stream`, you store the new username inside the `_authenticatedUsername` property. This allows you to read that value from other parts of your Bloc's code.
4. This is a bit different from what you did before... Here, you're adding an event to the Bloc *from inside* the Bloc itself — so far, you've only used this `add()` function from the *widgets'* side.

Before you continue adding functionality to your Bloc's code, it's time to do some housekeeping. Dispose of the subscription you just created when your screen is closed. To do this, find `// TODO: Dispose the auth changes subscription.` and replace it with:

```
@override
Future<void> close() {
  _authChangesSubscription.cancel();
  return super.close();
}
```

Here, you're just overriding your Bloc's `close()` function to insert the code that cancels your subscription. This ensures your subscription won't remain active after the user closes the screen.

Now, before you write the code that actually handles incoming events, you'll create a utility function to support the logic you'll write there.

# Fetching Data

Replace `// TODO: Create a utility function that fetches a given page.` with:

```
Stream<QuoteListState> _fetchQuotePage(
  int page, {
  required QuoteListPageFetchPolicy fetchPolicy,
  bool isRefresh = false,
}) async* {
  // 1
  final currentlyAppliedFilter = state.filter;
  // 2
  final isFilteringByFavorites = currentlyAppliedFilter is
QuoteListFilterByFavorites;
  // 3
  final isUserSignedIn = _authenticatedUsername != null;
  if (isFilteringByFavorites && !isUserSignedIn) {
    // 4
    yield QuoteListState.noItemsFound(
      filter: currentlyAppliedFilter,
    );
  } else {
    // TODO: Fetch the page.
  }
}
```

This is the function you'll use to actually talk to the repository and get a new page from either the server or the cache. It returns a `Stream` instead of a `Future` because it can have up to two emissions if the `fetchPolicy` is `QuoteListPageFetchPolicy.cacheAndNetwork` – the page it got from the cache, followed by the fresh page it got from the server. In the code you just wrote, you:

1. Retrieve the currently applied filter, which can be either a search filter, favorites filter or tag filter.
2. Check if the user is currently filtering by favorites.
3. Check if the user is signed in.
4. Use the `yield` keyword to emit a new state to the new `Stream` you're generating within this function.

Notice this `_fetchQuotePage()` function you're working on doesn't emit anything to the UI. It just generates a `Stream` of `QuoteListStates`, which another part of your code can then subscribe to and finally send these emissions to the UI. You could only use the `yield` keyword because you added the `async*` to the function's declaration. You can check out this article (https://dart.dev/articles/libraries/creating-streams#creating-a-stream-from-scratch) if you want to learn more about this `Stream` generation mechanism of the Dart language.

Continue your work on this function by this time replacing `// TODO: Fetch the page.` with:

```
final pageStream = _quoteRepository.getQuoteListPage(
  page,
  tag: currentlyAppliedFilter is QuoteListFilterByTag
      ? currentlyAppliedFilter.tag
      : null,
  searchTerm: currentlyAppliedFilter is
QuoteListFilterBySearchTerm
      ? currentlyAppliedFilter.searchTerm
      : '',
  favoritedByUsername:
      currentlyAppliedFilter is QuoteListFilterByFavorites
          ? _authenticatedUsername
          : null,
  fetchPolicy: fetchPolicy,
);

try {
  // 1
  await for (final newPage in pageStream) {
    final newItemList = newPage.quoteList;
    final oldItemList = state.itemList ?? [];
    // 2
    final completeItemList = isRefresh || page == 1
        ? newItemList
        : (oldItemList + newItemList);

    final nextPage = newPage.isLastPage ? null : page + 1;

    // 3
    yield QuoteListState.success(
      nextPage: nextPage,
      itemList: completeItemList,
      filter: currentlyAppliedFilter,
      isRefresh: isRefresh,
    );
  }
} catch (error) {
  // TODO: Handle errors.
}
```

This is where the magic happens. Here, you:

1. Listen to the `Stream` you got from the repository by using this `await for` syntax. What it does is run the code inside the `for` block every time your `pageStream` emits a new item. The only time it actually emits more than one item, though, is when you build the `Stream` using the `QuoteListPageFetchPolicy.cacheAndNetwork` fetch policy, which you'll do when the user first opens the screen.
2. Then, for every new page you get, you append the new items to the old ones you already have on the screen. This is assuming the user isn't trying to refresh the data, in which case you'll instead *replace* the previous items.
3. `yield` a new `QuoteListState` containing all the new data you got from the repository.

You also have to be prepared for the case in which you *can't* get that new page for some reason. For example, the user might not have an internet connection. Do this by replacing `// TODO: Handle errors.` with:

```
if (error is EmptySearchResultException) {
  // 1
  yield QuoteListState.noItemsFound(
    filter: currentlyAppliedFilter,
  );
}

if (isRefresh) {
  // 2
  yield state.copyWithNewRefreshError(
    error,
  );
} else {
  // 3
  yield state.copyWithNewError(
    error,
  );
}
```

Here's what's happening in this code:

1. If the error is an `EmptySearchResultException`, you'll treat it differently. Instead of emitting an "error" state, which would cause the UI to show a **Try Again** button, you'll emit an empty state, which will show the user a more descriptive message saying you couldn't find any items for the current filters. It's the same state you use when a *signed out* user tries to filter by favorites.

2. You'll also emit a different state if this error occurred during a *refresh* request. When the user intentionally asks for a refresh, it means they already have some items on the screen, so there's no reason for you to hide those items and show a full-screen error widget. In that case, the best thing to do is notify them of the error with a snackbar (https://material.io/components/snackbars).

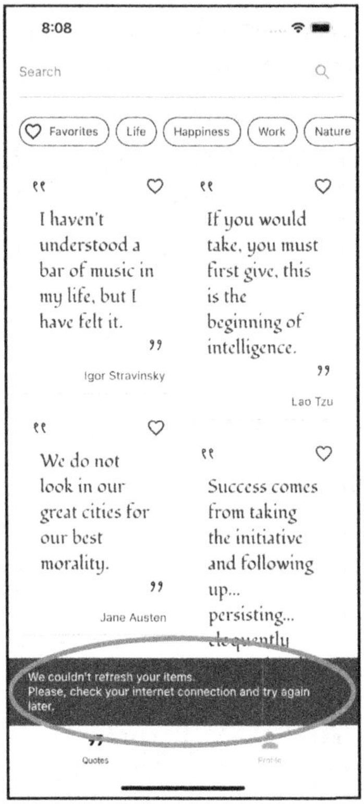

3. Finally, if this is an unexpected error, just re-emit the current state with an error added to it. The UI will take care of showing a full-screen error widget if the user is trying to fetch the first page. Otherwise, it will append an error item to the grid if this is a subsequent page request.

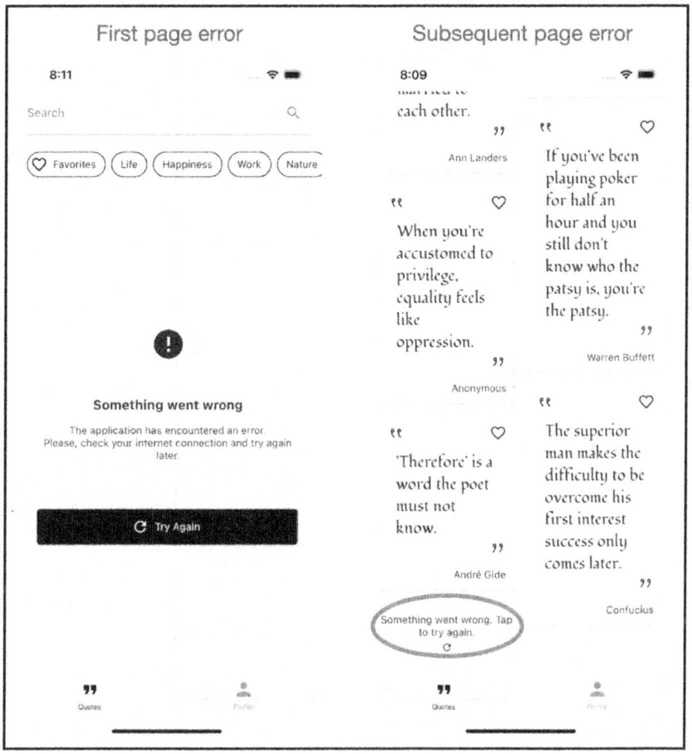


Wonderful! Your code should be free of errors now. Build and run to make sure you're on the right track. Since you haven't called the new `_fetchQuotePage()` function yet, you won't see anything but an infinite loading indicator on the screen.

Also, an error will print out to your console saying you haven't registered an event handler yet — you can just ignore it for now; you'll fix that next.

> **Note**: If you're having trouble running the app, it's because you forgot to propagate the configurations you did in the first chapter's starter project to the following chapters' materials. If that's the case, please revisit Chapter 1, "Setting up Your Environment".

# Receiving Events

Inside the `_registerEventHandler()` function, replace `// TODO: Take in the events.` with:

```
// 1
on<QuoteListEvent>(
  // 2
  (event, emitter) async {
    // 3
    if (event is QuoteListUsernameObtained) {
      await _handleQuoteListUsernameObtained(emitter);
    } else if (event is QuoteListFailedFetchRetried) {
      await _handleQuoteListFailedFetchRetried(emitter);
    } else if (event is QuoteListItemUpdated) {
      _handleQuoteListItemUpdated(emitter, event);
    } else if (event is QuoteListTagChanged) {
      await _handleQuoteListTagChanged(emitter, event);
    } else if (event is QuoteListSearchTermChanged) {
      await _handleQuoteListSearchTermChanged(emitter, event);
    } else if (event is QuoteListRefreshed) {
      await _handleQuoteListRefreshed(emitter, event);
    } else if (event is QuoteListNextPageRequested) {
      await _handleQuoteListNextPageRequested(emitter, event);
    } else if (event is QuoteListItemFavoriteToggled) {
      await _handleQuoteListItemFavoriteToggled(emitter, event);
    } else if (event is QuoteListFilterByFavoritesToggled) {
      await _handleQuoteListFilterByFavoritesToggled(emitter);
    }
  },
  // TODO: Customize how events are processed.
);
```

This is the heart of your Bloc. Here, you're finally listening to the incoming events and mapping them to functions you created to convert them to new states. In this code, you:

1. Call the `on()` function and use the angle brackets to specify the type of the events you want to register the handler for. In this case, it's `QuoteListEvent`, which encompasses all the event types you created at the beginning of this chapter.

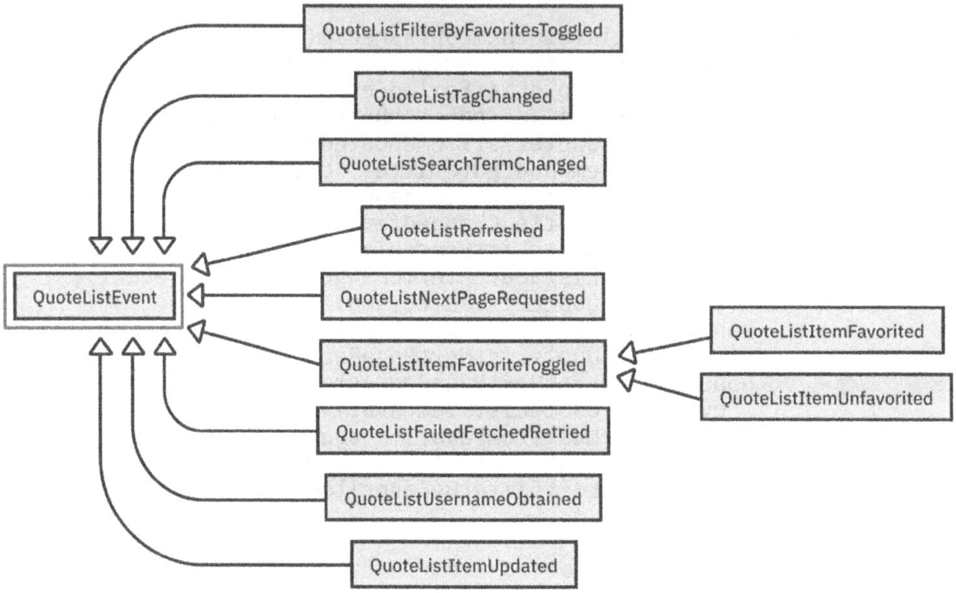


2. Pass in a callback to the `on()` function. That callback takes in the actual `event` object sent by the UI and an `emitter` object you have to use to send new states back to the UI.

3. Create `if` blocks for each type of event you can receive and then call the corresponding functions that handle each one of them.

Build and run one more time just to make sure you didn't break anything. This will be the last time you won't see anything different on the screen.

Now, you'll dive into some of these event-handling functions you're calling from your `if` blocks. Most of them are already complete, but a key one depends on your magical touch to start working.

# Handling Individual Events

Scroll down and find `// TODO: Handle QuoteListUsernameObtained.`. Replace it with:

```
// 1
emitter(
 QuoteListState(
    filter: state.filter,
  ),
);

// 2
final firstPageFetchStream = _fetchQuotePage(
  1,
  fetchPolicy: QuoteListPageFetchPolicy.cacheAndNetwork,
);

// 3
return emitter.onEach<QuoteListState>(
  firstPageFetchStream,
  onData: emitter,
);
```

Remember, you fire this `QuoteListUsernameObtained` event from your constructor on two occasions:

- When the user first opens the screen and you've retrieved their username – or `null` if the user is signed out.
- When the user signs in or out at any later time.

When any of these happen, the code you just wrote will:

1. Use the `emitter` to set the UI back to its initial state — with a full-screen loading indicator — while keeping any filters the users might have selected, like a tag, for example. Re-emitting the initial state makes no difference when the user first opens the app — since the screen will still be in the initial state — but is essential for when the user signs in or out at a later time.

> **Note**: Notice that even though the `emitter` is an *object* and not a *function*, you can still call it using the same syntax you use for functions: `emitter(something)`. You can do this because the `emitter` object implements the `call()` function internally.

2. Call the `_fetchQuotePage()` function you created in the previous section to get a new `Stream` you can subscribe to, to get the initial page.
3. Use the `onEach()` function from the `emitter` to handle subscribing to the `firstPageFetchStream` and sending out each new state it emits to the UI.

Take a moment to digest this.

You know the reason `_fetchQuotePage()` returns a `Stream` and not a `Future` is because it can emit up to two times when you specify the `cacheAndNetwork` fetch policy, which is *exactly* what you're doing here. So, what that `emitter.onEach()` call does is subscribe to `firstPageFetchStream` and use the `emitter` itself as a function to send the values from the `Stream` to the UI on each new emission.

To see this mechanism in play, build and run the app *twice* on your device. Twice? Yes! The first time, you should just wait until the app loads some quotes on the screen, and then you can close it — this ensures you have some quotes stored locally, or cached. Then, when you run the app for the second time, notice it *almost* instantly shows you the quotes you had the first time you opened the app — this is the first `firstPageFetchStream` emission. Then, after a few seconds, you can see the app replace those "old" quotes with fresh ones it got behind the scenes — your second emission. Cool, huh?

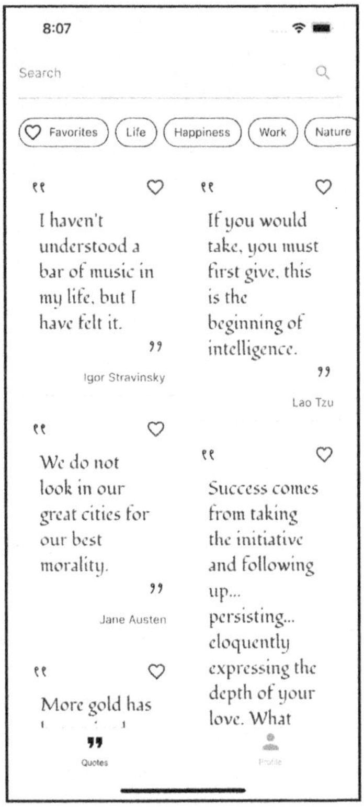


Before you proceed, take some time to look at the functions that handle the other events. They're basically variations of what you did for `_handleQuoteListOpened()`, and the code has lots of comments so you can understand everything that's going on.

# Controlling the Traffic of Events

Now, changing subjects, your home screen is in pretty good shape already, but have you tried using the search bar? You'd find two problems with it:

- As you type, the app triggers a *separate* HTTP request for *every* new character you enter. So, for example, a search for the word "life" would result in four sequential searches: "l", "li", "lif", and finally, "life".
- As you fire off these requests, there's no guarantee their results will arrive in the same order. For example, if the response for "lif" takes longer to process than the response for "life", the results you'd be showing the user wouldn't correspond to what's in the search bar.

You need finer-grained control over how your Bloc processes these events.

Instead of processing `QuoteListSearchTermChanged` events one by one, you want to process only the *last* one within a given timespan. For example, only send a request if one second has elapsed without the user typing anything new. This technique is known as **debouncing**.

Debouncing completely solves your first issue — of firing off too many requests. But it only *diminishes* the likelihood of the second one, where the results of an obsolete search might take over the results of a subsequent one. You're now guaranteeing that searches have at least one second separating them, but what if the server takes two seconds more to process your second-last search event?

To knock out this second issue, you'll need to stop processing an event if a newer one comes in. You'll call this the **canceling effect**.

You'll now see how to apply both the debouncing and the canceling effect on Blocs. In fact, the ability to apply these effects and change how your Bloc processes these events is exactly why you chose to use a Bloc for this screen. You couldn't do the same if you were using a Cubit — at least, not with the bloc library's support.

## Knowing the Transformer Function

Get back to the code, and, continuing on your Bloc's file, replace `// TODO: Customize how events are processed.` with:

```
transformer: (eventStream, eventHandler) {
  // TODO: Debounce search events.

  // TODO: Discard in-progress event if a new one comes in.
},
```

Here, you're specifying the `transformer` argument of the `on()` function. This `transformer` argument takes in a function where you have the ability to customize how you want to process events. You're receiving two values within that function:

- **eventStream**: The internal `Stream` from your Bloc where all the events come through.
- **eventHandler**: The function *you* wrote right above this one to process the events; the one that takes in an `event` and an `emitter` where you put all those `if` blocks.

In other words, within this `transformer` function, you have:

- The channel through which your events come in — the `eventStream`.
- The function you have to send your events to be taken care of — the `eventHandler`.

The only thing you have to do now is customize how you connect the two.

It's important to understand you don't necessarily *have to* specify a `transformer`. If you choose to go with the default implementation, your Bloc will perform just like a Cubit: processing events one by one as they arrive and not considering the order they came in when handling their results. The ability to *customize* the `transformer`, though, is the factor you should consider when deciding to pick Blocs over Cubits for a specific screen.

# Applying the Debouncing Effect

Pick up where you left off by replacing `// TODO: Debounce search events.` with:

```
// 1
final nonDebounceEventStream = eventStream.where(
  (event) => event is! QuoteListSearchTermChanged,
);

final debounceEventStream = eventStream
    // 2
    .whereType<QuoteListSearchTermChanged>()
    // 3
    .debounceTime(
      const Duration(seconds: 1),
    )
    // 4
    .where((event) {
  final previousFilter = state.filter;
  final previousSearchTerm =
      previousFilter is QuoteListFilterBySearchTerm
          ? previousFilter.searchTerm
          : '';

  final isSearchNotAlreadyDisplayed = event.searchTerm !=
previousSearchTerm;
  return isSearchNotAlreadyDisplayed;
});

// 5
final mergedEventStream = MergeStream([
  nonDebounceEventStream,
  debounceEventStream,
]);
```

Here's what's going on with the code above:

1. There are several functions you can call on `Streams` to generate a modified copy of them; we call these functions **operators**. Here, you use the `where` operator to generate a new `Stream` that *excludes* any `QuoteListSearchTermChanged` events.

2. Here, you're using the `whereType` operator to do the opposite of what you did in the previous step: generating a new `Stream` that excludes all *but* the `QuoteListSearchTermChanged` events. Both the `whereType` and the `debounceTime` operators you'll use next come from the RxDart (https://pub.dev/packages/rxdart) package, which adds several capabilities to Dart's `Streams`.

3. Now that you have a separate `Stream` for the `QuoteListSearchTermChanged` events, you applied the `debounceTime` operator to it so you can achieve that debouncing effect of one second without affecting all the other types of events.

4. Here, you're using the `where` operator to add another great feature to your searches: You're skipping searches where the term entered by the user is equal to the term of the search already on display. This can happen, for example, if the user adds a letter to the search bar, then regrets it and deletes it within the one-second timespan. If you didn't apply this `where` operator, this would trigger another request even though the search term hasn't changed.

5. In steps 1 and 2, you broke your `eventStream` into two other `Streams` just so that you could apply some operators exclusively to the search events. Now that you've finished that, you're merging the two `Streams` back together so you can continue implementing your `transformer`.

Great job! Now to the final touch...

# Applying the Canceling Effect

By default, Blocs process all incoming events in parallel. It works extremely well for the majority of situations — so much so that this is how all Cubits work — but it ends up being a problem for search bars:

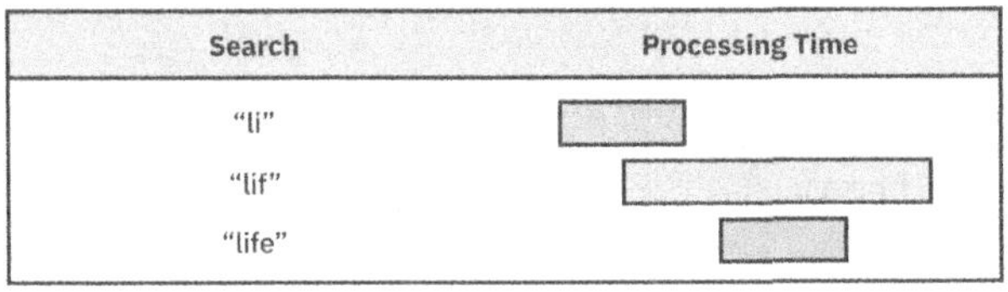


See the issue? Even though the search for "life" was last, you'll end up displaying the results for the "lif" query just because it took longer to process.

To solve this, you change this default behavior and cancel any previous event's processing when a new one comes in:

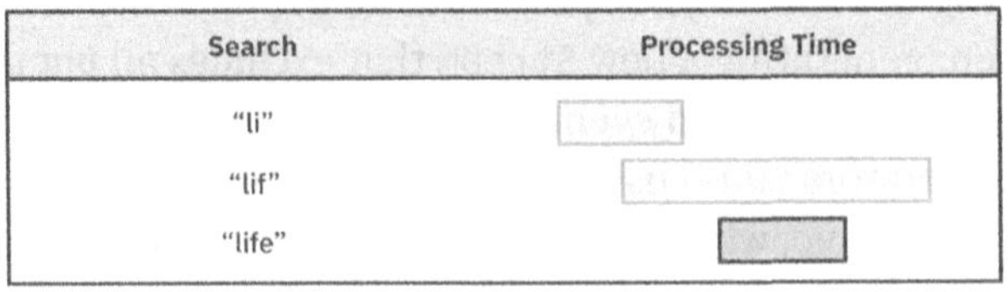

To do this, replace `// TODO: Discard in-progress event if a new one comes in.` with:

```
// 1
final restartableTransformer = restartable<QuoteListEvent>();

// 2
return restartableTransformer(mergedEventStream, eventHandler);
```

Here's what's happening:

1. This `restartable` function comes from the bloc_concurrency (https://github.com/felangel/bloc/tree/master/packages/bloc_concurrency) package, which is a dependency of this **quote_list** package's **pubspec.yaml**. This `restartable` function is the one that has the desired *canceling effect*, but the bloc_concurrency package provides a few different options as well:

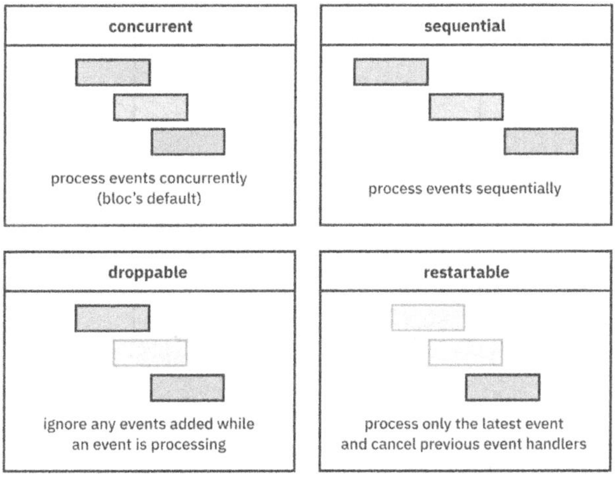


2. The `restartable` function actually returns another function. You then return the results from that function by passing them to your `mergedEventStream` and the `eventHandler`.

That's all for this chapter. Congratulations, you've made it! Build and run your app for the last time now and appreciate how smoothly your search bar works.

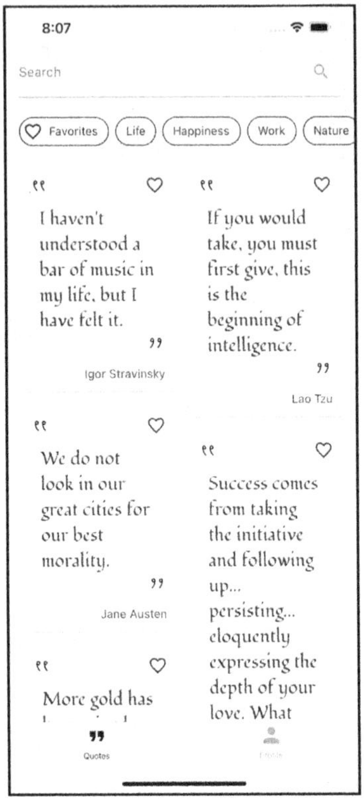

# Key Points

- You don't stop using **Cubits** once you know **Blocs**; one isn't better than the other.
- The only difference between Cubits and Blocs is how they *receive* events from the UI layer.
- While Cubits require you to create one function for each event, Blocs require you to create one class for each.
- As a rule of thumb, default to Cubits for their simplicity. Then, if you find you need to control the traffic of events coming in, upgrade to Blocs.
- If you don't customize the `transformer`, your Bloc will perform just like a Cubit: processing events one by one as they arrive and not considering their order when handing over the results.
- The ability to customize how events are processed is why you should pick a Bloc over a Cubit.

# Chapter 6: Authenticating Users

By Edson Bueno

In Chapter 4, "Validating Forms With Cubits", you used a `signIn()` function from a `UserRepository` class to ultimately send the server what the user entered in the email and password fields:

```
if (isFormValid) {
  try {
    await userRepository.signIn(
      email.value,
      password.value,
    );

    // ...
  } catch (error) {
    // ...
  }
}
```

Then, in Chapter 5, "Managing Complex State With Blocs", your path crossed that `UserRepository` class again, this time through a `getUser()` function:

```
_authChangesSubscription = userRepository.getUser().listen(
  (user) {
    _authenticatedUsername = user?.username;
    add(
      const QuoteListUsernameObtained(),
    );
  },
);
```

As you can see, `getUser()` returns a `Stream<User?>`, which you use to monitor changes to the user's authentication and refresh the home screen when the user signs in to or out of the app.

At this point, you might've noticed a strong connection between these two pieces of code above:

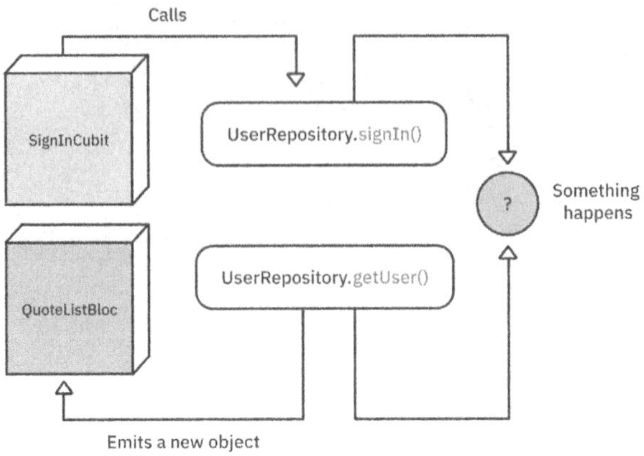


This chapter is where you'll fill in that gap and unravel the mysteries of user authentication. Along the way, you'll learn:

- What authentication is.
- The difference between app authentication and user authentication.
- How token-based authentication works.
- How to store sensitive information securely.
- How to use the **flutter_secure_storage** package.
- The difference between ephemeral state and app state.
- How to use the `BehaviorSubject` class from the RxDart package.

While going through this chapter, you'll work on the **starter** project from this chapter's **assets** folder.

# Understanding Authentication

**Authentication** is how you identify yourself and prove your identity to a server. That can be both at the **app level** and at the **user level**.

In Chapter 1, "Setting up Your Environment", you created an account at FavQs.com — the API server behind WonderWords — to generate something called the **API key**. You then learned how to configure compile-time variables in Dart to safely inject that key into your code, which you then set up to include that key in the headers of all HTTP requests. That was **app-level authentication**. You're passing the API key in your requests to prove to FavQs.com that you're not a random — or even malicious — app.

App-level authentication is sufficient for operations that aren't tied to a particular user, like getting a list of quotes. But how about *favoriting* a quote?

Favoriting, upvoting or downvoting a quote are examples of actions that need a user associated with them. When a user favorites a quote, it doesn't become a favorite for *all* users, only for the particular user who executed the action. Now, how does the server know which user it should favorite that quote for? Or, even further, how does the server know the client app is authorized to execute that action on behalf of the user? Here enters **user-level authentication**.

# Understanding Token-based User Authentication

To authenticate your *app*, all you had to do was generate a key on FavQs.com and include it in all your HTTP requests. But how do you authenticate *users*?

There are some different approaches, but the one used by FavQs.com — and most servers out there — is **token-based authentication**. It works like this:

1. The client app — WonderWords, in your case — prompts the user with a **Sign In screen**. Here, they can enter an email — to identify the user — and a password — to prove they own that user.
2. Once the user fills in that information and taps **submit**, the app sends a request to a "sign-in" endpoint on the server. The server then uses that email and password to generate a random-like `String`, the **user token**.
3. From then on, all the app has to do is include that user token — or access token — along with the app token — or API key — in the headers of the HTTP requests.

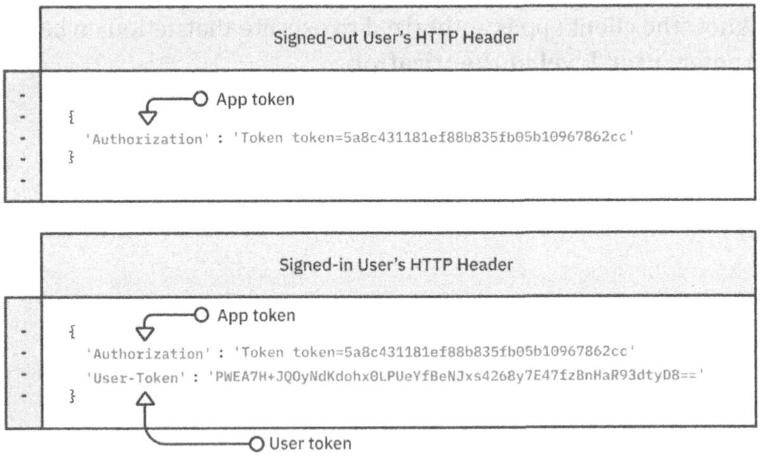

> **Note**: Some servers might generate user tokens that expire after a certain time, but FavQs.com doesn't. In those cases, the client application doesn't have to know what the token's duration is. When a token expires, and you send it to the server, the server lets you know by returning a specific error — often one with the 401 status code. Then, all you have to do is either prompt the user for their credentials again or start a background process known as token refresh (https://www.loginradius.com/blog/start-with-identity/refresh-tokens-jwt-interaction/). It depends on how sophisticated the API is.

## Storing Access Tokens Securely

Once you've called the "sign-in" endpoint and gotten the user's token, your next step is to store that token somewhere. But where? Compile-time variables aren't an option since you don't have the *user* token at *compile-time*, only at *runtime*.

Storing the token in a simple variable also wouldn't do because you need to keep the user signed in, even when they restart the app. Your next guess might be storing it in a local database, which wouldn't be entirely wrong... It just can't be *any* database.

User tokens, and any personally identifiable information (PII) such as emails and usernames, are extremely sensitive and shouldn't be stored in regular databases. The flutter_secure_storage (https://pub.dev/packages/flutter_secure_storage) package is your friend here.

**flutter_secure_storage** provides you with a simple key-value interface that, under the hood, leverages the most recommended secret storage on each platform: Apple's Keychain (https://developer.apple.com/documentation/security/keychain_services#//apple_ref/doc/uid/TP30000897-CH203-TP1) on iOS and Google's Keystore (https://developer.android.com/training/articles/keystore.html) on Android. Time to get your hands dirty.

## Creating a Secure Data Source

Use your IDE of choice to open the starter project. Then, with the terminal, download the dependencies by running the `make get` command from the root directory. Ignore all the errors in the project for now.

Wait for the command to finish executing, then look for the **user_repository** package and open the **user_secure_storage.dart** file inside **lib/src**.

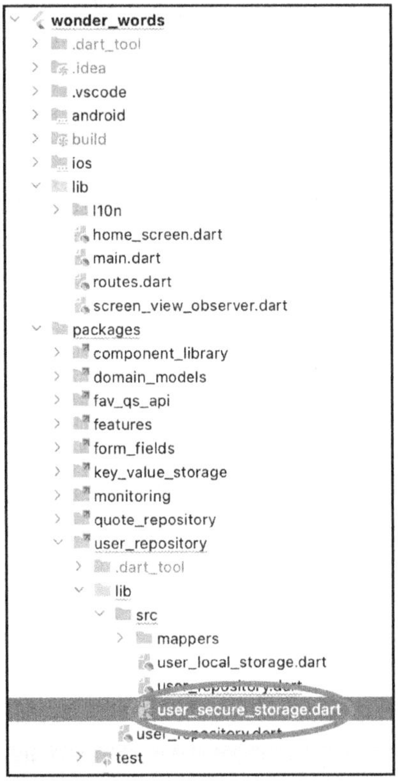

Kick things off by replacing `// TODO: Create a secure Data Source.` with:

```
// 1
class UserSecureStorage {
  static const _tokenKey = 'wonder-words-token';
  static const _usernameKey = 'wonder-words-username';
  static const _emailKey = 'wonder-words-email';

  const UserSecureStorage({
    // 2
    FlutterSecureStorage? secureStorage,
  }) : _secureStorage = secureStorage ?? const
```

```
FlutterSecureStorage();

  final FlutterSecureStorage _secureStorage;

  // 3
  Future<void> upsertUserInfo({
    required String username,
    required String email,
    String? token,
  }) =>
      // 4
      Future.wait([
        _secureStorage.write(
          key: _emailKey,
          value: email,
        ),
        _secureStorage.write(
          key: _usernameKey,
          value: username,
        ),
        if (token != null)
          _secureStorage.write(
            key: _tokenKey,
            value: token,
          )
      ]);

  Future<void> deleteUserInfo() => Future.wait([
        _secureStorage.delete(
          key: _tokenKey,
        ),
        _secureStorage.delete(
          key: _usernameKey,
        ),
        _secureStorage.delete(
          key: _emailKey,
        ),
      ]);

  Future<String?> getUserToken() => _secureStorage.read(
        key: _tokenKey,
      );

  Future<String?> getUserEmail() => _secureStorage.read(
        key: _emailKey,
      );

  Future<String?> getUsername() => _secureStorage.read(
        key: _usernameKey,
      );
}
```

Here's what's going on:

1. If you recall from Chapter 2, "Mastering the Repository Pattern", **data sources** are classes your repositories use to interact with external sources, like databases and the network. This `UserSecureStorage` class you're creating here will act as one of the data sources of your `UserRepository` class. Its role is to expose `UserRepository` to functions that help maintain the authenticated user's information.
2. The `FlutterSecureStorage` class comes from this **flutter_secure_storage** package you were reading about. Look at the functions' implementation in this file to see how easy it is to work with the package.
3. If you haven't seen this word before, **upsert** is a common neologism in software development that combines **up**date and in**sert**. In other words, it stands for: **Up**date the registry if one already exists or in**sert** if it doesn't.
4. This `Future.wait` function combines multiple `Futures` into one, allowing you to execute them simultaneously. This is useful when the `Future` calls aren't dependent on each other, that is, when you don't *have* to wait for one `Future` to complete to execute the next.

Done! That's all there is to "storing sensitive data" in Flutter and the **flutter_secure_storage** package. Easy, right?

You now have everything you need to jump to the `UserRepository` class and start connecting the dots.

# Signing in Users

Continuing in the same directory of the file you were working on before, open **user_repository.dart** this time.

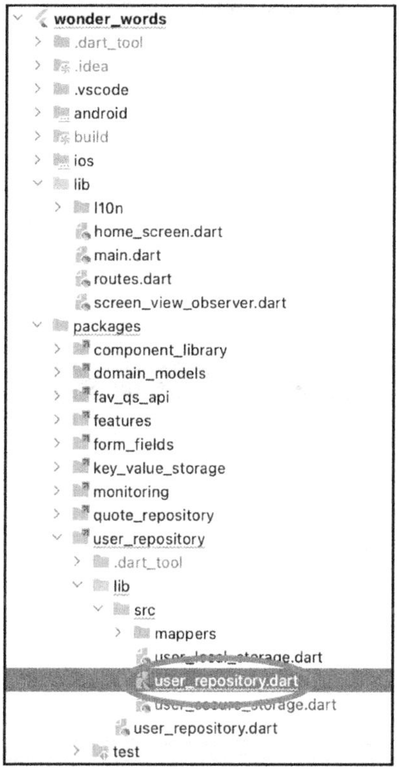


**Note**: Notice there are two **user_repository.dart** files, make sure you open the inner one within the **src** folder.

Scroll down until you find the `signIn()` function. This is the function that runs when the user taps the "Sign In" button on the Sign In screen.

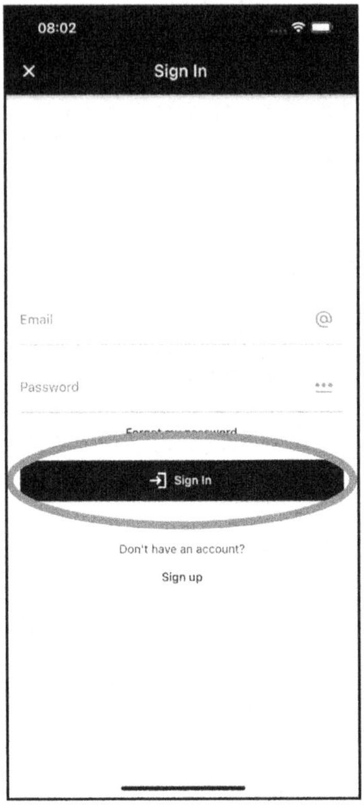


Replace `// TODO: Sign in the user by coordinating the Data Sources.` with:

```
try {
  // 1
  final apiUser = await remoteApi.signIn(
    email,
    password,
  );

  // 2
  await _secureStorage.upsertUserInfo(
    username: apiUser.username,
    email: apiUser.email,
    token: apiUser.token,
  );

  // TODO: Propagate changes to the signed in user.
} on InvalidCredentialsFavQsException catch (_) {
  // 3
```

```
    throw InvalidCredentialsException();
  }
```

This is an excellent refresher on Chapter 2, "Mastering the Repository Pattern". Here, you:

1. Called the "sign-in" endpoint on the server using the `remoteApi` property, which is of type `FavQsApi`. If the request succeeds, you get a `UserRM` object back from the server and assign it to the `apiUser` property. The `UserRM` class holds the recently signed-in user's token, email and username.
2. Used the `upsertUserInfo()` function you just created in the `UserSecureStorage` class.
3. Captured any `InvalidCredentialsFavQsExceptions` and converted them to `InvalidCredentialsExceptions`. Doing so is important because `InvalidCredentialsFavQsException` is only known by packages importing the **fav_qs_api** internal package, which won't be the case for users of this `UserRepository` class. `InvalidCredentialsException`, on the other hand, is part of the **domain_models** package and, therefore, is known to all features, making it possible for them to handle the exception properly.

The code you just wrote perfectly portrays the role of a repository: orchestrating different data sources. As you can see from this `signIn()` function, `UserRepository` is juggling between two data sources:

1. `remoteApi` of type `FavQsApi`, which talks to your remote API.
2. `_secureStorage` of type `UserSecureStorage`, which you created in the last section, uses the **flutter_secure_storage** package.

Before you continue knocking out more `TODOs` in the code, there's one important concept to clear up: the difference between **ephemeral state** and **app state**.

# Differentiating Between Ephemeral State and App State

You already know what **state** is: the conjunction of variables that describe what changed in your app since the user opened it.

If the app opens on the home screen, and now the user is on the sign-in screen, that's part of your state. If the fields on a sign-in screen were empty when you opened it, and now they contain input, that's also part of your state. Another way to think about it is: What information would you need to back up if you had to, from scratch, recreate your UI *exactly* as it is right now?

Now, some pieces of your state are related to a single widget, such as what's within an **email** field. That's **ephemeral state**. Others are broader and affect multiple parts of the app, such as "What user is currently signed in?". Here enters **app state**.

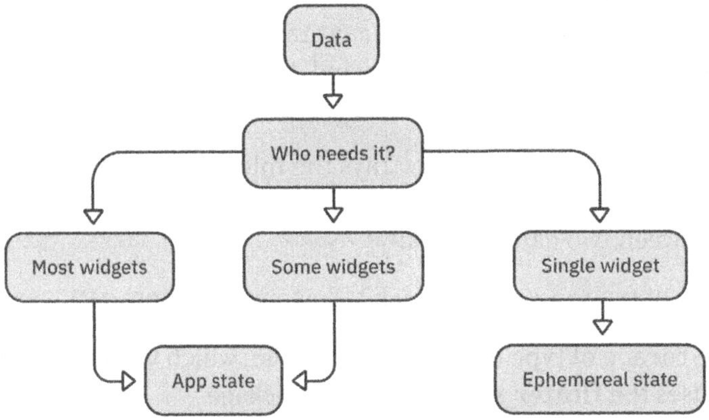


> Image recreated from Differentiate between ephemeral state and app state (https://docs.flutter.dev/development/data-and-backend/state-mgmt/ephemeral-vs-app#there-is-no-clear-cut-rule) and used under a Creative Commons Attribution 4.0 International License (https://creativecommons.org/licenses/by/4.0/#)

You won't find yourself managing app state as frequently as you do for ephemeral state — most of your app's state is taken care of by external packages or the Flutter framework itself, as it happens for the navigation stack.

In WonderWords, for example, there are only two situations where you're in charge of managing the app state:

1. The currently signed-in user's information.
2. The dark mode preference the user has selected for that device.

You know this book has a crush on the Bloc library (https://bloclibrary.dev) for managing ephemeral state. But how about app state? Well, here, things are grayer, and you need to take the specific situation into account more than ever. Cubits and Blocs can also do a great job here, but for the two situations from WonderWords outlined above, managing them inside the `UserRepository` itself makes the most sense. You'll now see how this looks in practice.

# Managing App State With BehaviorSubject

Still in **user_repository.dart**, find `// TODO: Create a listenable property.` and replace it with:

```
final BehaviorSubject<User?> _userSubject = BehaviorSubject();
```

`BehaviorSubject` is a class that:

1. Holds a value — from the type you specify within the angle brackets <>.
2. Provides a `stream` property that you can use to listen for any changes to that value. When a piece of code starts listening to a `BehaviorSubject`'s `stream`, it immediately gets the latest value on that property — assuming one has already been added — followed by all the subsequent changes to that value.

What else does one need to manage a piece of state? Think about it for a second: What's **state management** if not the art of watching a value and notifying interested parties of changes to that value?

You'll now see how to *use* that `BehaviorSubject`.

> **Note**: The `BehaviorSubject` class comes from the RxDart (https://pub.dev/packages/rxdart) package, which this **user_repository** package depends on.

## Notifying Changes in the User State

Scroll down back to the `signIn()` function and replace `// TODO: Propagate changes to the signed in user.` with:

```
// 1
final domainUser = apiUser.toDomainModel();

// 2
_userSubject.add(
  domainUser,
);
```

Here, you:

1. Used a mapper function, `toDomainModel()`, to convert the `apiUser` object from the `UserRM` type to the `User` type. `UserRM` is the type your network layer uses — **fav_qs_api** internal package — while `User` is the neutral model known by the rest of the codebase.
2. Replaced — or added, if this is the first sign-in — a new value to your `BehaviorSubject`.

All errors in your IDE should now be gone. Build and run your app to ensure you're on the right track, but don't expect the app to do much yet except for loading indefinitely.

**Note**: If you're having trouble running the app, it's because you forgot to propagate the configurations you did in the first chapter's starter project to the following chapters' materials. If that's the case, please revisit Chapter 1, "Setting up Your Environment".

## Providing a Way to Listen to Changes in the User State

You've seen how to *add* a value to a `BehaviorSubject`, and now's the time to see how to listen to changes in it.

Find `// TODO: Expose the BehaviorSubject.` and replace it with:

```
// 1
if (!_userSubject.hasValue) {
  final userInfo = await Future.wait([
    _secureStorage.getUserEmail(),
    _secureStorage.getUsername(),
  ]);

  final email = userInfo[0];
  final username = userInfo[1];

  if (email != null && username != null) {
    _userSubject.add(
      User(
        email: email,
        username: username,
      ),
    );
  } else {
    _userSubject.add(
      null,
    );
  }
}

// 2
yield* _userSubject.stream;
```

You're adding this code to the `getUser()` function, which exposes a `Stream` so users of `UserRepository` can monitor changes to the currently authenticated user. This is the same function you used in the previous chapter to refresh the home screen when the user signs in to or out of the app. In the code above, you:

1. Check if you've already added a value to `_userSubject`. If not, that means this is the first time the app has called this function. Therefore, you need to set the `_userSubject` with the values you have in the secure storage — which is what you do inside the `if` block.

2. Then, all you have to do is return the `stream` property of `_userSubject`. Well, you're not actually `returning` the `Stream`, but that's just because `getUser()` is an `async*` function, which makes it impossible to `return` anything. Instead, you use the `yield*` keyword, which generates a new `Stream` that just re-emits all the values from `_userSubject.stream`.

Amazing job! Build and run your app again, and this time you should have no problems loading your home screen:

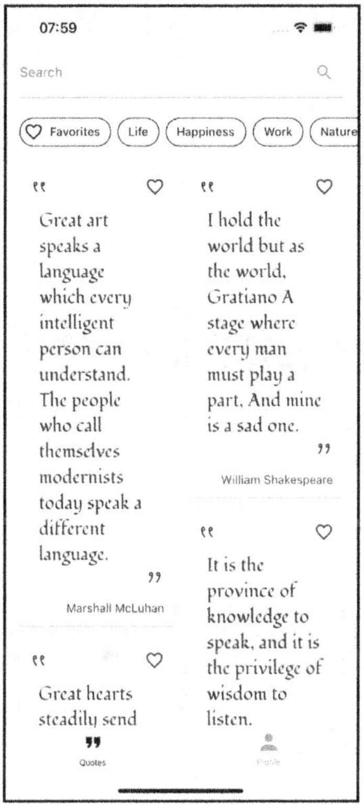

There's still one issue, though... When a user signs in, the **Profile** tab reflects that correctly, but the rest of the app doesn't. For example, the user's favorites aren't synced, and if you try to favorite a quote, you'll still see an error saying you're not signed in.

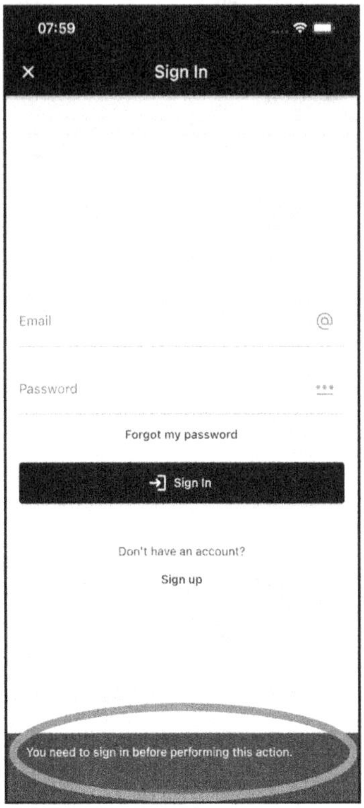


This is happening because you still have to implement the function that supplies the **user token** to the places that need it.

# Supplying the Access Token

Continuing on **user_repository.dart**, scroll up to `// TODO: Provide the user token.` and replace it with:

```
return _secureStorage.getUserToken();
```

And just like that, your code is complete. In the end, the **main** application package will take care of connecting the **fav_qs_api** package, which actually injects the token in the headers, to this `getUserToken()` function you added your code to. More on this in Chapter 7, "Routing & Navigating".

Build and run your app again, and you won't be disappointed this time. Play with the user's authentication for a bit... For example, open the **Profile** tab while signed out and notice it doesn't show the username at the top. Sign in, and see how the screen refreshes immediately — due to it listening to your `getUser()` function.

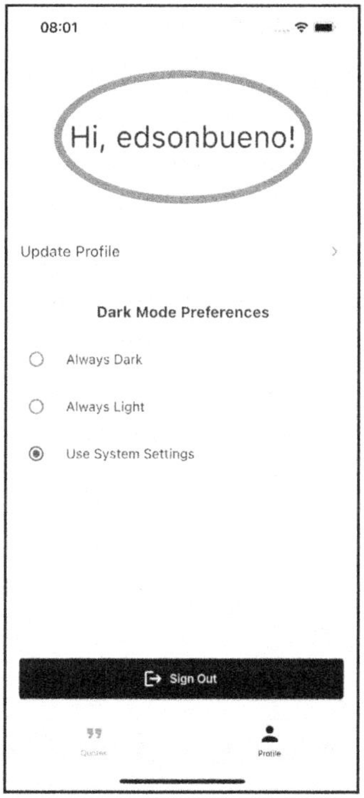


> **Note**: If you don't have an account, you can create one using the **Sign-up** feature within WonderWords itself or use the FavQs.com website.

# Key Points

- **App authentication** is how your app proves to the server there's a legit client app behind the requests.
- App authentication is usually accomplished by attaching a static long-formed `String` — the **app token** — to the headers of the requests. That token is the same across all installations of the app. You went over this process in Chapter 1, "Setting up Your Environment".
- On the other hand, **user authentication** is how your app proves to the server there's *a known user* behind the app. This is only required to *access and generate user-specific data within the server*, such as reading and marking favorites.
- User authentication is usually accomplished similarly to app authentication, where you attach a long-formed `String` — the *user token*, in contrast to the *app token* — to the header of your requests. The difference here is that *the server generates this token on the fly*, for every new sign-in request.
- **Token-based authentication** works like this: The client app makes a request to the server to exchange the user's email and password for a long-formed `String` — the **access token** or the **user token**. From then on, all the app has to do is attach that *user* token along with the *app* token to the headers of all HTTP requests.
- *Don't store your users' private data, such as JWTs and PII, in regular databases.* An alternative is using the **flutter_secure_storage** package, which gives you access to Apple's Keychain on iOS and Google's Keystore on Android.
- **Ephemeral state** is a piece of state associated with a *single* widget, as opposed to **app state**, which is related to *multiple* widgets.
- The `Future.wait` function generates a new `Future` that combines all the other `Futures` you pass. Use this to execute multiple `Futures` simultaneously.
- Using the `BehaviorSubject` class from the RxDart package is one of the most concise ways to manage app state.

# Chapter 7: Routing & Navigating

By Edson Bueno

Flutter has two routing mechanisms:

- **Navigator 1**: *Imperative* style
- **Navigator 2**: *Declarative* style

**Nav 1**, which you're probably most familiar with, is the oldest. It has a straightforward API and is very easy to understand. You can use Nav 1 in three different ways:

1. **Anonymous routes**

- When creating the app widget:

```
return MaterialApp(
  home: QuotesListScreen(),
);
```

- When pushing a new route:

```
Navigator.push(
  context,
  MaterialPageRoute(
    builder: (context) => QuoteDetailsScreen(
      id: id,
    ),
  ),
);
```

2. **Simple named routes**

- When creating the app widget:

```
return MaterialApp(
  initialRoute: '/quotes',
  routes: {
    '/quotes': (context) => QuotesListScreen(),
    '/quotes/details': (context) => QuoteDetailsScreen(
          id: ModalRoute.of(context)?.settings.arguments as
int,
        ),
  },
);
```

- When pushing a new route:

```
Navigator.pushNamed(
  context,
  '/quotes/details',
  arguments: 71, // The quote ID.
);
```

3. **Advanced named routes**

- When creating the app widget:

```
return MaterialApp(
  initialRoute: '/quotes',
  onGenerateRoute: (settings) {
    final routeName = settings.name;
    if (routeName == '/') {
      return MaterialPageRoute(
        builder: (context) => QuotesListScreen(),
      );
    }

    if (routeName != null) {
      final uri = Uri.parse(routeName);
      if (uri.pathSegments.length == 2 &&
          uri.pathSegments.first == 'quotes') {
        final id = uri.pathSegments[1] as int;
        return MaterialPageRoute(
          builder: (context) => QuoteDetailsScreen(
            id: id,
          ),
        );
      }
    }

    return MaterialPageRoute(
```

```
      builder: (context) => UnknownScreen(),
    );
  },
);
```

- When pushing a new route:

```
Navigator.pushNamed(
  context,
  '/quotes/71',
);
```

Each of these has its pros and cons:

- Anonymous routes are the easiest to learn but can give you a hard time when trying to reuse code — if two places in the app can open the same screen, for example.
- Simple named routes solve the code reuse issue but still have the flaw of not allowing you to parse arguments from the route name. For example, if the app runs on the web, you can't extract the quote ID from a link like `/quotes/73`.
- Lastly, advanced named routes let you parse arguments from the route name but aren't as easy to learn as their siblings.

As you can see, Navigator 1 has alternatives for all tastes. Why, then, did they have to come up with a Navigator 2?

Nav 1 — and all its variants — has a foundational flaw: It's very hard to push or pop multiple pages at once, which is terrible for **deep links** or Flutter Web in general.

**Deep linking** is the ability to send the user a link — the deep link — that, when opened on a smartphone, launches a specific screen within the app instead of opening a web page. Pay attention to the fact that the link doesn't simply launch *the app*; it launches *a specific screen within the app* — hence the "deep" in the name.

Deep links can be helpful to allow users to share links or enable your app's notifications to take the user to particular content when tapped. You'll leave the actual deep link implementation for the next chapter. The vital thing to have in mind now is: *A solid routing strategy must be good at deep linking*. Here enters Navigator 2.

Nav 2 completely nails any of the issues you can think of for Nav 1, but it comes with a cost: It's *dang hard* to learn and use. Fortunately for you, that's an easy problem to solve: The community has developed a plethora of packages that wrap over Nav 2 and make it easy to use. In this chapter, you'll learn how to use Routemaster (https://pub.dev/packages/routemaster), a package that makes Nav 2 as straightforward as simple named routes. Along the way, you'll also learn how to:

- Quickly identify what the routing strategy of a codebase is.
- Switch from Nav 1 to Nav 2.
- Support nested navigation for tabs.
- Manage and inject app-wide dependencies.
- Connect your feature packages without coupling them.

Throughout this chapter, you'll work on the **starter** project from this chapter's **assets** folder.

# Getting Started

Use your IDE of choice to open the starter project. Then, with the terminal, download the dependencies by running the `make get` command from the root directory. Wait for the command to finish executing, then build and run your app. For now, expect to see nothing but a giant X on the screen:

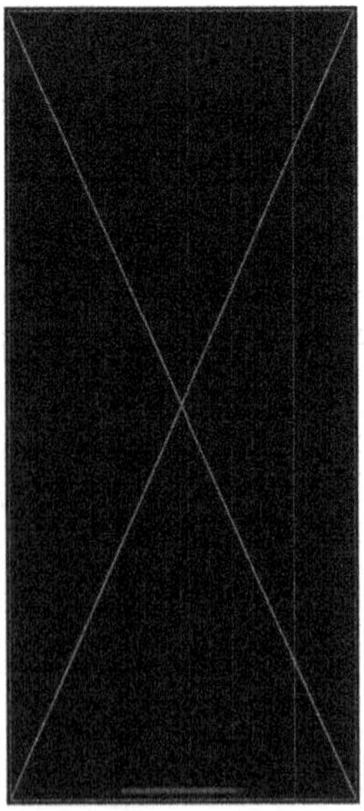

> **Note**: If you're having trouble running the app, it's because you forgot to propagate the configurations you did in the first chapter's starter project to the following chapters' materials. If that's the case, please revisit Chapter 1, "Setting up Your Environment".

You can tell what routing strategy an app uses just by looking at how it instantiates `MaterialApp`:

- **Anonymous routes**: Characterized by `MaterialApp(home:)`.
- **Simple named routes**: Characterized by `MaterialApp(routes:)`.
- **Advanced named routes**: Characterized by `MaterialApp(onGenerateRoute:)`.
- **Navigator 2**: Characterized by `MaterialApp.router(routerDelegate:, routeInformationParser:)`.

Open the starter project's **lib/main.dart** file. You'll see that the code is currently using the anonymous route form to set a `Placeholder` widget as the app's home screen — which explains the X you're seeing. Starting with the next section, you'll work on migrating your app to Navigator 2 and using it to display and connect all the screens you have in your feature packages.

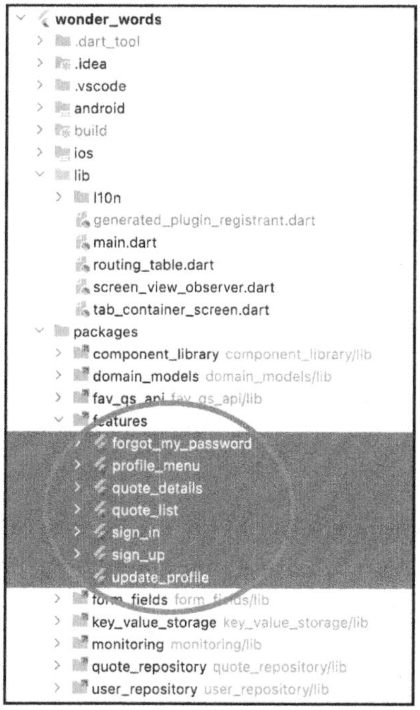

# Switching to Navigator 2

As you can see in the diagram below, Navigator 2 has quite a few moving parts:

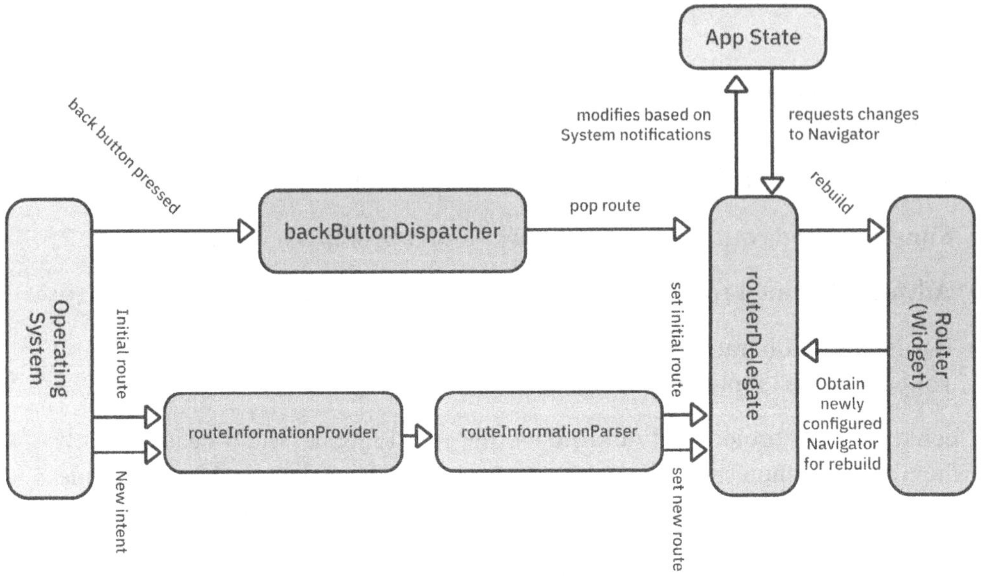


Image recreated from Learning Flutter's new navigation and routing system (https://medium.com/flutter/learning-flutters-new-navigation-and-routing-system-7c9068155ade) and used under a Creative Commons Attribution 4.0 International License (https://creativecommons.org/licenses/by/4.0/#)

Complicated, huh? But don't worry. You're only in charge of providing the two pieces in pink:

- **routerDelegate** (an object of the type `RouterDelegate`): Takes calls like `setInitialRoutePath(T configuration)` and `setNewRoutePath(T configuration)` and reacts to them by rebuilding an actual `Navigator` widget with all your screens piled up.
- **routeInformationParser** (an object of the type `RouteInformationParser`): Does the back-and-forth between URLs and that `configuration` object that the `RouterDelegate` takes in.

The Routemaster package eases your life by giving you a fully baked `RouteInformationParser` class and a half-baked `RouterDelegate` class — which you just need to supplement with your own routing table before being able to use it. In the end, the whole process will be pretty similar to using simple named routes, where you just need to provide a `Map` that defines all your routes.

Before you replace that X in your app with some actual screens, you'll first switch your navigation system to Nav 2 without changing anything else. To start the work, open **lib/main.dart** if you haven't done this yet.

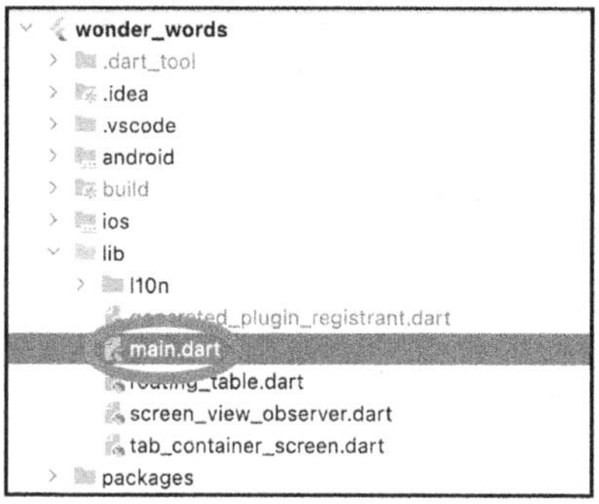


Find `// TODO: Instantiate the RouterDelegate.`, and replace it with:

```
// 1
late final _routerDelegate = RoutemasterDelegate(
  // 2
  routesBuilder: (context) {
    return RouteMap(
      routes: {
        // 3
        '/': (_) => const MaterialPage(
          child: Placeholder(),
        ),
      },
    );
  },
);
```

Here's what's happening:

1. You're creating a `late` property to hold a `RoutemasterDelegate` object — you'll understand why the `late` later on. `RoutemasterDelegate` is Routemaster's implementation of the Nav 2's `RouterDelegate` class you read about a few paragraphs ago. You're able to import this class because the Routemaster package is already listed as a dependency in your **pubspec.yaml**.

2. To instantiate a `RoutemasterDelegate`, you have to supply the `routesBuilder` parameter. `routesBuilder` takes in a function that receives a `BuildContext` and returns a `RouteMap` object.

3. To instantiate a `RouteMap`, you have to supply the `routes` parameter. Here's where Routemaster's approach gets close to simple named routes. The `routes` parameter receives a `Map<String, PageBuilder>`, which links every path you want to support in your app to a function that builds the corresponding `Page` object.

In Nav 2, you have to envelop your screen widgets around `Page` objects because that's what the `Navigator` class manages. It's similar to how, in Nav 1, you had to wrap your screens around `Route` objects. Besides holding the widget to be displayed, a `Page` also contains information about *how* you want to display that widget. The code above uses the `MaterialPage` class, which uses different transition animations for iOS and Android.

Now, to use the delegate you just created, continue on the same file and scroll down until you find the following line:

```
child: MaterialApp(
```

Then, replace the entire line with:

```
child: MaterialApp.router(
```

This is what characterizes the migration from Nav 1 to Nav 2, going from the `MaterialApp` default constructor to the `MaterialApp.router` one. Now, a little lower down, replace `home: const Placeholder()` with:

```
routeInformationParser: const RoutemasterParser(),
routerDelegate: _routerDelegate,
```

That's it! A few paragraphs ago, you read that Navigator 2 requires *you* to provide two pieces of the gear: a `RouterDelegate` and a `RouteInformationParser`. This is how you supply both. The first one — `RouterDelegate` — you built with the Routemaster package's help. The second one — `RouteInformationParser` — was a complete gift to you; you didn't have to worry about customizing anything.

Your app is now officially using Navigator 2 — too bad it doesn't show anything cool yet, but at least you're on the right path. Build and run the app to make sure the migration went smoothly. Expect to see the same thing as before — just a `Placeholder` on the screen.

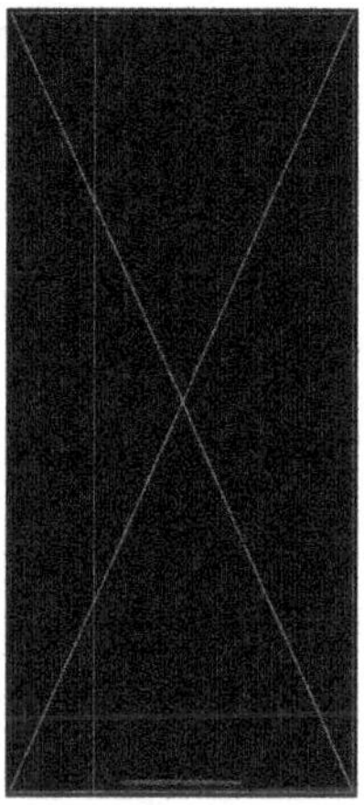

Next on your plate is replacing that `Map` you passed on to the `routes` property with another one containing some actual screens.

# Supporting Bottom Tabs With Nested Routes

Alongside deep linking, one of the most common challenges when approaching routing in mobile apps is the ability to have **nested routes**. But what are nested routes?

Notice that when you tap a quote in WonderWords, part of the screen stays in place: the bottom navigation bar.

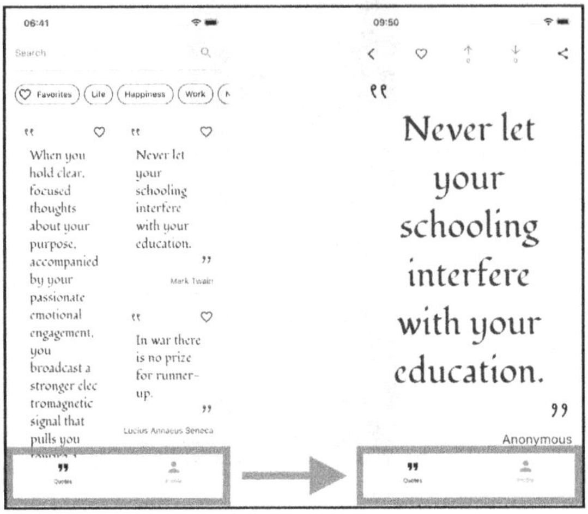


But that isn't always the case. For example, when you go from the profile to the sign-in screen, the new screen completely covers what was on the screen before.

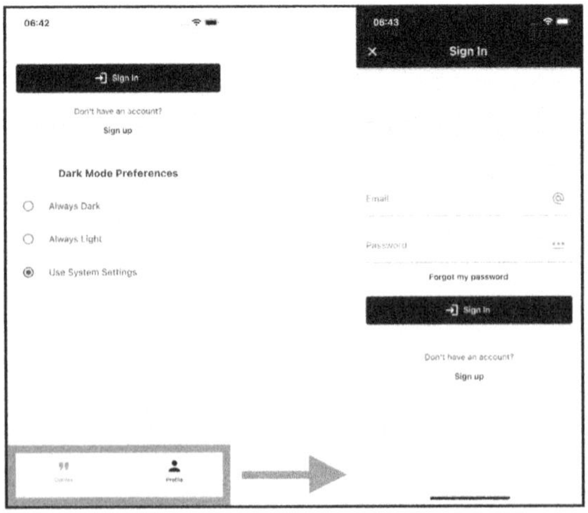

That means you have three navigation stacks:

1. An external one that controls the entire window.
2. A nested one that holds what's above the bottom navigation bar when the **Quotes** tab is selected.
3. A nested one that holds what's above the bottom navigation bar when the **Profile** tab is selected.

The good news is that, with the Routemaster package, achieving nested routes is easier than you might think. To see it with your own eyes, open **lib/tab_container_screen.dart**.

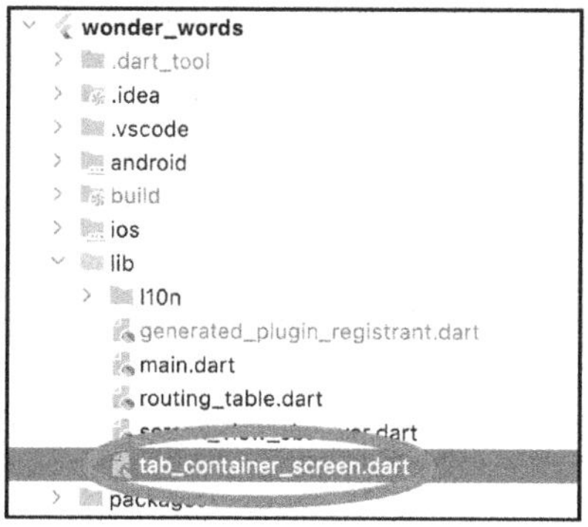


Now, replace `return Container();` with:

```
final l10n = AppLocalizations.of(context);
// 1
final tabState = CupertinoTabPage.of(context);

// 2
return CupertinoTabScaffold(
  controller: tabState.controller,
  tabBuilder: tabState.tabBuilder,
  tabBar: CupertinoTabBar(
    items: [
      BottomNavigationBarItem(
        // 3
        label: l10n.quotesBottomNavigationBarItemLabel,
        icon: const Icon(
          Icons.format_quote,
        ),
      ),
      BottomNavigationBarItem(
        label: l10n.profileBottomNavigationBarItemLabel,
        icon: const Icon(
          Icons.person,
```

```
            ),
          ),
        ],
      ),
    );
```

Here's what's going on with the code above:

1. `CupertinoTabPage` is a class that comes from the Routemaster package. As you can see a few lines below, `CupertinoTabPage` gives you the two pieces you need — a `controller` and a `tabBuilder` — to set up the tabbed layout structure using Flutter's `CupertinoTabScaffold`. `tabBuilder` is responsible for building the inner screens you want to display for each tab. Meanwhile, `controller` controls the state of the bottom bar — which index is selected and such.
2. The simplest way to implement bottom-tabbed screens is using this `CupertinoTabScaffold` from the **cupertino** library. Notice this is the first time you're using a widget from **cupertino** instead of **material**. A nice historical background to have in mind is that bottom-tabbed layouts were first popularized by iOS apps — the opposing standard on Android used to be navigation drawers (https://material.io/components/navigation-drawer). Bottom tabs quickly became as popular on Android as they were on iOS. Even Google apps started adopting them — YouTube is a great example.
3. This is how you retrieve a localized `String` in WonderWords. Don't worry about this for now; you'll learn all about it in Chapter 9, "Internationalizing & Localizing".

The code above won't work out of the gate. You first need to do some setup to connect this `TabContainerScreen` widget to the rest of the app and ensure there will be a `CupertinoTabPage` available when the `CupertinoTabPage.of(context)` call executes. To address this, open **routing_table.dart**.

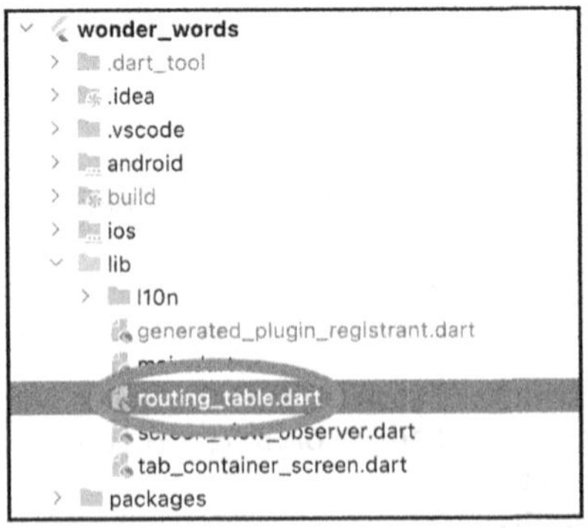

Now, replace `// TODO: Define the app's paths.` with:

```
class _PathConstants {
  const _PathConstants._();

  static String get tabContainerPath => '/';

  static String get quoteListPath => '${tabContainerPath}
quotes';

  static String get profileMenuPath => '${tabContainerPath}
user';

  static String get updateProfilePath => '$profileMenuPath/
update-profile';

  static String get signInPath => '${tabContainerPath}sign-in';

  static String get signUpPath => '${tabContainerPath}sign-up';

  static String get idPathParameter => 'id';

  static String quoteDetailsPath({
    int? quoteId,
  }) =>
      '$quoteListPath/${quoteId ?? ':$idPathParameter'}';
}
```

This is a class you're creating to centralize all your screens' paths. So, for example, the quotes list screen is `/quotes`, while the quote details screen is `/quotes/:id`, where `:id` is the placeholder for the actual quote ID. Notice the `quoteDetailsPath()` function can be used in two ways:

- If you pass `null` for the `quoteId` parameter, it'll return the path with the `:id` placeholder, which is useful for when you're declaring the route.
- If you pass a value for the `quoteId` parameter, the generated path will have an actual ID instead of the placeholder, which is useful for when you're using the `_PathConstants` class to navigate to the quote details screen.

You'll see these two use cases shortly. For now, you'll get back to the bottom-tabbed layout. Now that you have your path constants, you have everything you need to continue from where you left. Still in the same **routing_table.dart** file, replace `// TODO: Create the app's routing table.` with:

```
// 1
Map<String, PageBuilder> buildRoutingTable({
  // 2
  required RoutemasterDelegate routerDelegate,
```

```
    required UserRepository userRepository,
    required QuoteRepository quoteRepository,
    required RemoteValueService remoteValueService,
    required DynamicLinkService dynamicLinkService,
  }) {
    return {
      // 3
      _PathConstants.tabContainerPath: (_) =>
        // 4
        CupertinoTabPage(
            child: const TabContainerScreen(),
            paths: [
              _PathConstants.quoteListPath,
              _PathConstants.profileMenuPath,
            ],
          ),
      // TODO: Define the two nested routes homes.
    };
  }
```

Here, you're creating a function you'll call shortly from the **main.dart** file to replace the fake routes map you have in there right now. Here's what you have in the function so far:

1. The return type is a `Map<String, PageBuilder>`. As you've seen, this maps each path you want to support — the `String` — to the function that builds the corresponding page — the `PageBuilder`.
2. Most of the dependencies you'll need to instantiate your screens are already available on **lib/main.dart**, so you're asking them to be passed onto this function so you can reuse them.
3. The first path you declared is your app's entry point: the `/`. The screen you're assigning to this path is the `TabContainerScreen` you've created two code snippets above. This is the outermost screen that will hold the bottom tab along with the two nested navigation stacks.
4. To achieve the nested navigation layout, you wrapped your `TabContainerScreen` widget inside a `CupertinoTabPage` class. You then leveraged its `paths` parameter to define which two routes should be the entry point for each internal flow.

To ensure you understand what's going on, go back to that **tab_container_screen.dart** file you were working on. Observe how the code you wrote there links to what you've done now: You use a `CupertinoTabPage.of(context)` call to retrieve the current `state` of the tab. That call only works because you've now wrapped your `TabContainerScreen` inside a `CupertinoTabPage` class.

Now, to finish the nested routing setup, you have to link your inner paths — `quoteListPath` and `profileMenuPath` — to the actual widgets that represent them. To do this, replace `// TODO: Define the two nested routes homes.` with:

```
_PathConstants.quoteListPath: (route) {
  return MaterialPage(
    // 1
    name: 'quotes-list',
    child: QuoteListScreen(
      quoteRepository: quoteRepository,
      userRepository: userRepository,
      onAuthenticationError: (context) {
        // 2
        routerDelegate.push(_PathConstants.signInPath);
      },
      onQuoteSelected: (id) {
        // 3
        final navigation = routerDelegate.push<Quote?>(
          _PathConstants.quoteDetailsPath(
            quoteId: id,
          ),
        );
        return navigation.result;
      },
      remoteValueService: remoteValueService,
    ),
  );
},
_PathConstants.profileMenuPath: (_) {
  return MaterialPage(
    name: 'profile-menu',
    child: ProfileMenuScreen(
      quoteRepository: quoteRepository,
      userRepository: userRepository,
      onSignInTap: () {
        routerDelegate.push(
          _PathConstants.signInPath,
        );
      },
      onSignUpTap: () {
        routerDelegate.push(
          _PathConstants.signUpPath,
        );
      },
      onUpdateProfileTap: () {
        routerDelegate.push(
          _PathConstants.updateProfilePath,
        );
      },
    ),
  );
},
```

```
// TODO: Define the subsequent routes.
```

Observe how this code fills in the gaps. In the previous code snippet, you defined that the two pages you want to display for each tab are `_PathConstants.quoteListPath` and `_PathConstants.profileMenuPath`. Now, you're telling Routemaster how to actually build these two pages. This is what should be new to you with the code above:

1. Assigning a `name` to your page isn't mandatory but will be helpful when you're writing analytics code in Chapter 12, "Supporting the Development Lifecycle With Firebase".
2. Here, you're using the `RoutemasterDelegate` you created on **main.dart** to navigate to a new screen. You can use it in this file because you asked for it as a parameter of this `buildRoutingTable` function.
3. The navigation here is a bit more complicated. The `quoteDetailsPath` route may return a result: the updated `Quote` object if the user interacted with the quote while on that screen — by favoriting it, for example. You then return that `Quote` object to the `onQuoteSelected` callback just so your `QuoteListScreen` can update that quote's list item if something changed.

The snippet above is very representative of a vital piece of WonderWord's architecture: Feature packages don't execute navigation. Notice all integration between the screens happens here through the callbacks. The only package that imports Routemaster, and thus *can* navigate, is the **main** package, the one you're working on right now.

Now, before you can run your code, go back to the **lib/main.dart** file. Inside the declaration of the `_routerDelegate` property, replace:

```
return RouteMap(
  routes: {
    '/': (_) => const MaterialPage(
      child: Placeholder(),
    ),
  },
);
```

With:

```
return RouteMap(
  routes: buildRoutingTable(
    routerDelegate: _routerDelegate,
    userRepository: _userRepository,
```

```
      quoteRepository: _quoteRepository,
      remoteValueService: widget.remoteValueService,
      dynamicLinkService: _dynamicLinkService,
    ),
  );
```

Here, you're finally replacing the fake routes map with the real one you just created inside the **routing_table.dart** file.

Build and run your code, and watch the `Placeholder` disappear. You'll now see the bottom navigation bar along with the root **Quotes** and **Profile** screens working just fine.

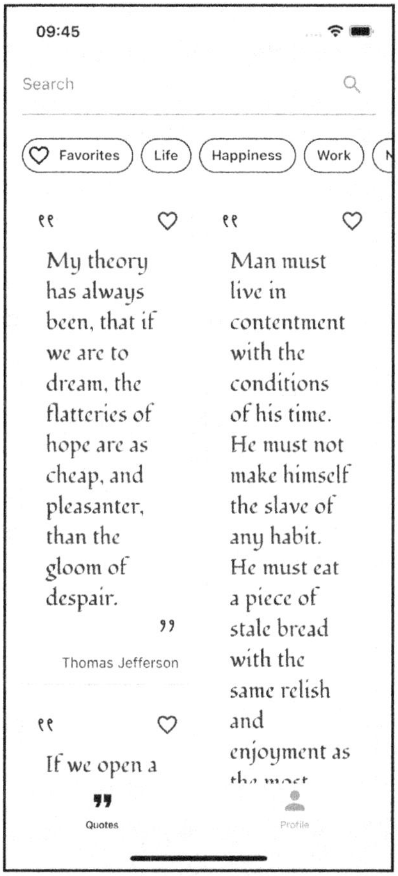


Finally, try tapping a quote so you can see an error on the screen. It should say that the route isn't defined yet. That's because you've only defined your root routes — the container screen and its two inner screens. You'll fix that now.

## Defining the Subsequent Routes

Go back to the **lib/routing_table.dart** file, find `// TODO: Define the subsequent routes.`, and replace it with:

```
_PathConstants.updateProfilePath: (_) => MaterialPage(
  name: 'update-profile',
  child: UpdateProfileScreen(
    userRepository: userRepository,
    onUpdateProfileSuccess: () {
      routerDelegate.pop();
    },
  ),
),
_PathConstants.quoteDetailsPath(): (info) => MaterialPage(
    name: 'quote-details',
    child: QuoteDetailsScreen(
      quoteRepository: quoteRepository,
      // 1
      quoteId: int.parse(
        info.pathParameters[_PathConstants.idPathParameter] ??
'',
      ),
      onAuthenticationError: () {
        routerDelegate.push(_PathConstants.signInPath);
      },
      // 2
      shareableLinkGenerator: (quote) =>
          dynamicLinkService.generateDynamicLinkUrl(
        path: _PathConstants.quoteDetailsPath(
          quoteId: quote.id,
        ),
        socialMetaTagParameters: SocialMetaTagParameters(
          title: quote.body,
          description: quote.author,
        ),
      ),
    ),
  ),
_PathConstants.signInPath: (_) => MaterialPage(
  name: 'sign-in',
  fullscreenDialog: true,
  child: Builder(
    builder: (context) {
      return SignInScreen(
        userRepository: userRepository,
        onSignInSuccess: () {
          routerDelegate.pop();
        },
        onSignUpTap: () {
          routerDelegate.push(_PathConstants.signUpPath);
```

```
          },
          onForgotMyPasswordTap: () {
            showDialog(
              context: context,
              builder: (context) {
                return ForgotMyPasswordDialog(
                  userRepository: userRepository,
                  onCancelTap: () {
                    routerDelegate.pop();
                  },
                  onEmailRequestSuccess: () {
                    routerDelegate.pop();
                  },
                );
              },
            );
          },
        );
      },
    ),
  ),
  _PathConstants.signUpPath: (_) => MaterialPage(
    name: 'sign-up',
    child: SignUpScreen(
      userRepository: userRepository,
      onSignUpSuccess: () {
        routerDelegate.pop();
      },
    ),
  ),
```

As big as this code snippet is, you should already understand most of it. The only two new things are:

1. This `info.pathParameters[_PathConstants.idPathParameter]` is how you extract a path parameter from a route. For example, when the user taps a quote on the quote list screen, you push a route with that quote's ID embedded within the path, such as `/quotes/13`. Here, you're extracting that 13 and passing it to the `QuoteDetailsScreen`. The reason you had to wrap it in an `int.parse()` call is because all path parameters come to you as `Strings`.

2. This is just using Firebase to generate a shareable link for a quote. You'll learn all about this in the next chapter, "Deep Linking".

That's all. Build and run your app for the last time, and now you should be able to navigate to inner screens just fine. For example, tap a quote and watch the details screen open just fine while still keeping the bottom navigation bar.

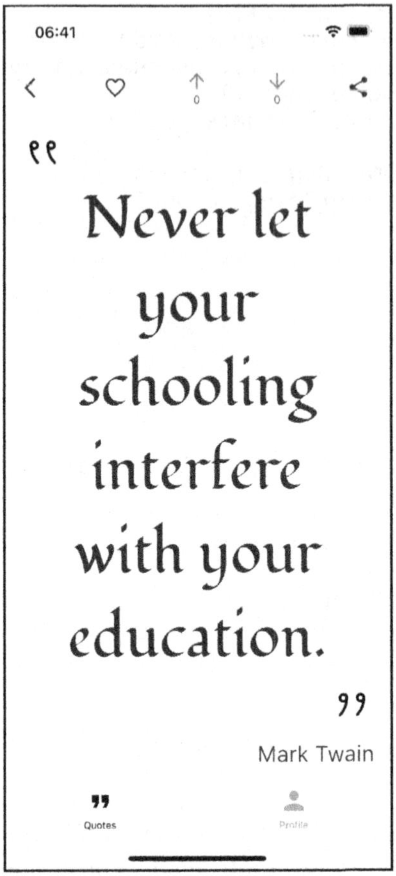

# Key Points

- **Navigator 1** is flexible and easy to use but not good at deep linking.
- A solid routing strategy must support **deep linking**.
- **Navigator 2** is very good at deep linking but comes with a cost: It's very hard to learn and use.
- The best way to cope with Navigator 2 is to use **wrapper packages**, such as Routemaster.
- With **Routemaster**, working with Nav 2 becomes almost as simple as using simple named routes from Nav 1.
- When architecting an app with **feature packages**, consider handling all integration between the features — i.e., the navigation — inside a package that's hierarchically above all of them.

# Chapter 8: Deep Linking

By Edson Bueno

You just went through an entire chapter on routing and navigation. Since this isn't a beginner's book, that surely wasn't a new topic for you at that point, but the reason it had to be covered was that the routing system you were probably familiar with, Navigator 1, doesn't have good deep link support.

You then learned how to use Flutter's Navigator 2, built from the ground up with deep links in mind. This chapter is where deep links finally come into play, and all the work from the previous chapter pays off. But what are deep links?

An app that supports deep links is an app that can launch in response to the user opening a link. Have you ever tapped a link, and that link opens an app instead of a web page? That's because that app supports deep links. Notice the link doesn't simply *launch* the app; it navigates to *specific content* within the app — hence the **deep** in the name.

Deep links are primarily used to allow users to share content — Spotify playlists, social media posts, etc. — the examples are countless. Another example of deep links in action is when you receive a notification, tap it, and that takes you to a related screen inside the app — you see that a lot in chat apps.

Adding deep link support to an app isn't as easy as one might imagine. It involves two different challenges:

- Making the system know it has to launch *your* app when the user opens certain links.
- Making your app take the user to the right screen once the system launches it.

The second part is pretty much complete, thanks to the robust routing strategy you already have in place. The first part, though, can be quite complicated, as it involves some web knowledge, like domains. Luckily, Firebase is your friend here. Firebase's specialty is saving client developers from having to know stuff they don't care about.

You'll implement deep links with the help of **Firebase Dynamic Links**. Firebase's solution works on top of an enhanced type of deep links, called **dynamic links**. Dynamic links are deep links that can:

- **Work across different platforms**: If a user opens the link on their phone, they can be taken directly to the linked content in your native app. If a user opens the same link in a desktop browser, they can be taken to the equivalent content on your website.
- **Work across app installs**: If a user opens the link on their phone and doesn't have your app installed, the user is sent to the Play Store or App Store to install it. Then, after installation, your app starts and opens the specific content.

Roll up your sleeves! In this chapter, you'll learn how to:

- Configure a Firebase project to support dynamic links.
- Generate dynamic links on the fly.
- Launch your app in response to a dynamic link.
- Respond to a dynamic link coming in when your app is already open.

Throughout this chapter, you'll work on the **starter** project from this chapter's **assets** folder.

# Getting Started

Use your IDE of choice to open the starter project. Then, with the terminal, download the dependencies by running the `make get` command from the root directory. Wait a while for the command to finish executing, then build and run your app *on an Android device* — either physical or virtual.

Why Android? You can't test dynamic links on iOS unless you have a paid Apple Developer Account; thus, very few readers of this book probably have one. Therefore, for brevity, this chapter will proceed using an Android emulator but will give you a link with the additional instructions you need for iOS.

After running your app, this is what you should see:

> **Note**: If you're having trouble running the app, it's because you forgot to propagate the configurations you did in the first chapter's starter project to the following chapters' materials. If that's the case, please revisit Chapter 1, "Setting up Your Environment".

Your app is pretty much complete, except it can't handle deep links yet. Tap a quote to go to the quote details screen, and you'll notice the **Share** button on the app bar doesn't respond when you tap it.

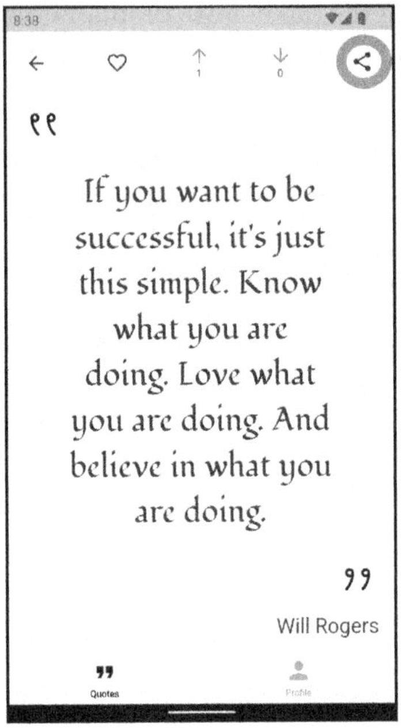


What that **Share** button *should* do is allow the user to share a deep link that, when opened, takes the recipient to that same exact quote inside the WonderWords app. From here on, your job is to make sure that:

- The button responds appropriately when users tap it.
- The app can open that same quote when the link is opened.

Your first step on that mission is to configure your Firebase's dashboard.

## Setting up Firebase

Go to Firebase's console (https://console.firebase.google.com/), and open the project you created in Chapter 1, "Setting up Your Environment".

On the left sidebar, expand the **Engage** section, then click **Dynamic Links**. Finally, click **Get Started**.

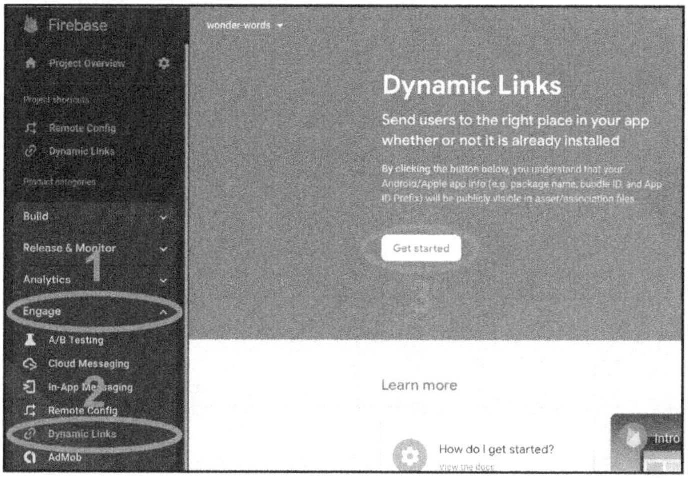


In the dialog that opens, you have to type what you want your links' prefix to be, that is, the domain. You have two options here:

- Use a custom domain that you might own, like **myproject.com**.
- Use a free domain provided by Firebase, like **myproject.page.link**.

The first option certainly looks more professional when you're doing this for a real project that you own, but it involves some additional steps — you can find the instructions here (https://www.raywenderlich.com/21376846-firebase-dynamic-links-getting-started#toc-anchor-008). Since you're only doing this for educational purposes now, the second option is more than enough.

Type in **wonderwordsSOMETHING_UNIQUE.page.link**, but don't forget to replace **SOMETHING_UNIQUE** with any unique value you know won't already be taken by other readers of this book. Finally, click **Continue**, and then **Finish**.

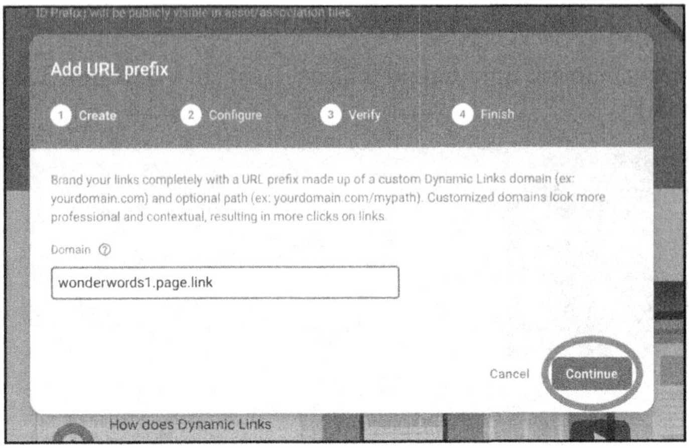


You'll see your domain listed in the Firebase console. Make sure to write it down because you'll need it later.

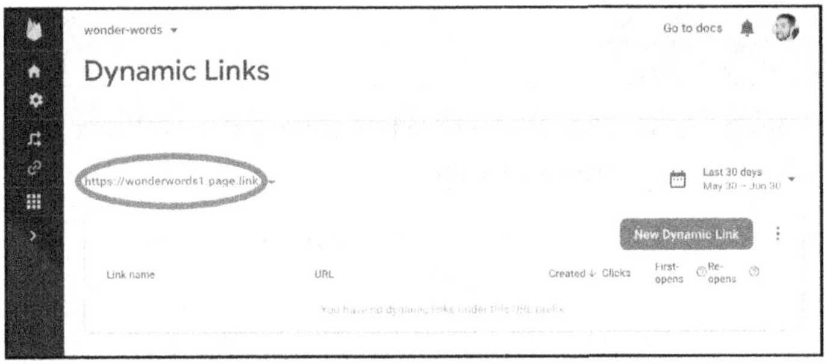


You'd need to perform a few more steps to make your links work on iOS. But again, as mentioned in the **Getting Started** section, that requires you to have both an Apple Developer Account and your app registered there. Since this is just an educational project and can't be published, it doesn't make sense to go through those steps right now. When configuring dynamic links for a project you own, just execute the additional steps outlined in the **Configuring Firebase Project Settings** section of the tutorial Firebase Dynamic Links: Getting Started (https://www.raywenderlich.com/21376846-firebase-dynamic-links-getting-started#toc-anchor-005).

Now, go back to your IDE. Your next task will be to create the logic to generate a dynamic link when users tap a quote's **Share** button.

## Building a Dynamic Link on Demand

You might think generating a dynamic link is just a matter of appending the path of the screen you want to open to the base URL you created on Firebase, something like: `https://wonderwords1.page.link/quotes/27231`. It's actually a bit more complicated than that.

A dynamic link is a complex link that contains several parameters. The actual link you want to open is encoded inside the last part of them, for example: `https://wonderwords1.page.link?sd=Abdul%20Kalam&st=You%20have%20to%20dream%20before%20your%20dreams%20can%20come%20true.&amv=0&apn=com.raywenderlich.wonder_words&ibi=com.raywenderlich.wonderWords&imv=0&link=https%3A%2F%2Fwonderwords1.page.link%2Fquotes%2F15140`.

It wouldn't be hard for you to create a function that builds a dynamic link by replacing the variable parts in the example above, but you'd still have one problem: That link is too ugly to share — shareable links should ideally be concise. There's an elegant solution for that: The package provided by Firebase Dynamic Links (https://pub.dev/packages/firebase_dynamic_links) has a function to help you build shortened versions of links like the one above. In the end, the result will be something like: `https://wonderwords1.page.link/jHcE`. Beautiful, right?

To see how this works in practice, open **lib/src/dynamic_link_service.dart** under the **monitoring** package.

> **Note**: WonderWords' architecture uses this **monitoring** package to encapsulate all the Firebase services you'll use throughout this book. The biggest advantage of doing this is that if one day you decide to replace Firebase with another tool, the only affected package will be this one.

This file holds a class named `DynamicLinkService`. The goal of this class is to wrap the Firebase Dynamic Links package and expose only the functionalities you'll need. Kick off your work on this class by replacing `// TODO: Create a constant to hold your dynamic link prefix.` with:

```
static const _domainUriPrefix =
'YOUR_FIREBASE_DYNAMIC_LINK_URL';
```

Don't forget to replace `YOUR_FIREBASE_DYNAMIC_LINK_URL` with the URL you got in the **Setting Up Firebase** section.

Next, find `// TODO: Create a function that generates dynamic links.`, and replace it with:

```
// 1
Future<String> generateDynamicLinkUrl({
  required String path,
  SocialMetaTagParameters? socialMetaTagParameters,
}) async {
  // 2
  final parameters = DynamicLinkParameters(
    link: Uri.parse(
      '$_domainUriPrefix$path',
    ),
    uriPrefix: _domainUriPrefix,
    androidParameters: const AndroidParameters(
      packageName: _androidPackageName,
    ),
    iosParameters: const IOSParameters(
      bundleId: _iOSBundleId,
    ),
    socialMetaTagParameters: socialMetaTagParameters,
  );

  // 3
  final shortLink = await
_dynamicLinks.buildShortLink(parameters);
  return shortLink.shortUrl.toString();
}
```

Here's what's going on with the code above:

1. You're creating a function that receives two parameters:* The path of the screen you want your link to open.* An optional `SocialMetaTagParameters` object that can contain information you want to appear when your link is shared in a social post, such as a short description and an image.
2. You then combine the parameters you received with some of the information you already had to build a `DynamicLinkParameters` object.
3. Finally, you delegate the link's construction to the `buildShortLink()` function from the `FirebaseDynamicLinks` class.

What you need to do now is connect this function to the quote details screen so that when the user taps the **Share** button in there, this code will run, giving the user a link to share.

Go back to the **main** package, and open the **routing_table.dart** file.

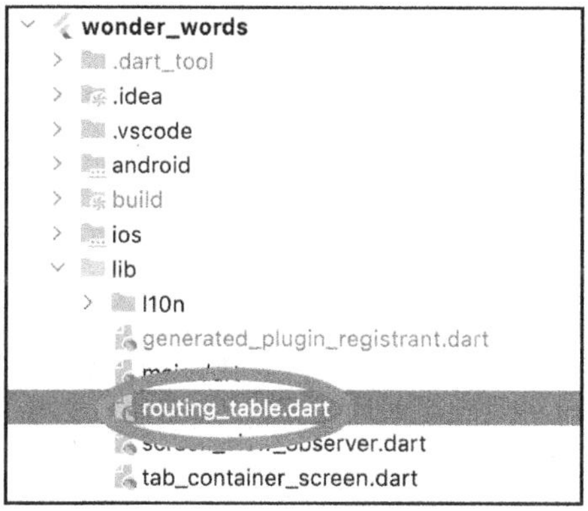


Scroll down to `// TODO: Specify the shareableLinkGenerator parameter.`, and replace it with:

```
// 1
shareableLinkGenerator: (quote) {
  // 2
  return dynamicLinkService.generateDynamicLinkUrl(
    path: _PathConstants.quoteDetailsPath(
      quoteId: quote.id,
    ),
    socialMetaTagParameters: SocialMetaTagParameters(
      title: quote.body,
      description: quote.author,
    ),
  );
},
```

First of all, observe *where* you're inserting this code. You dove into this **routing_table.dart** file in the last chapter. This is where you define all your routes and connect all your features. In the snippet above, you:

1. Specified the `shareableLinkGenerator` parameter of the `QuoteDetailsScreen` class. This parameter expects a function that the quote details screen can use to generate a dynamic link. That function receives a quote and must return a `Future<String>` containing the shareable link of that quote.
2. Then, to actually generate the link, you're calling the `generateDynamicLinkUrl()` function you created inside the `DynamicLinkService` class and provided it:

- The `path` of the quote details screen containing the ID for that specific quote the user wants to share.
- The `socialMetaTagParameters` containing some information about the quote, so the link looks good on social media.

Build and run your app to check on your progress. Tap any quote to open the quote details screen, and this time you'll be able to use the **Share** button in the upper-right corner. The only reason it wasn't working before is because you weren't specifying the `shareableLinkGenerator` parameter.

Tap the **Share** button and write down the link that appears in the bottom sheet. You'll use it later for testing.

> **Note**: The exact look of this bottom sheet might change depending on your Android version.

Great! Now that your app can properly generate dynamic links, your next job is to make sure you can open them as well.

When the user opens a dynamic link, your app can be in two states:

- Closed.
- Open — and minimized, since the user can only launch the link from another app.

You'll begin by handling the first scenario.

# Opening a Dynamic Link When Your App Is Closed

Go back to **lib/src/dynamic_link_service.dart** under the **monitoring** package.

Replace `// TODO: Create a function that returns the link that launched the app.` with:

```
Future<String?> getInitialDynamicLinkPath() async {
  final data = await _dynamicLinks.getInitialLink();
```

```
    final link = data?.link;
    return link?.path;
  }
```

That's it! The name of the function says it all. *If* the app was launched from a dynamic link, this function you just created is capable of returning that link to you so you can navigate to the corresponding screen.

You'll now put that function to use. Open the **main.dart** file under the **main** package.

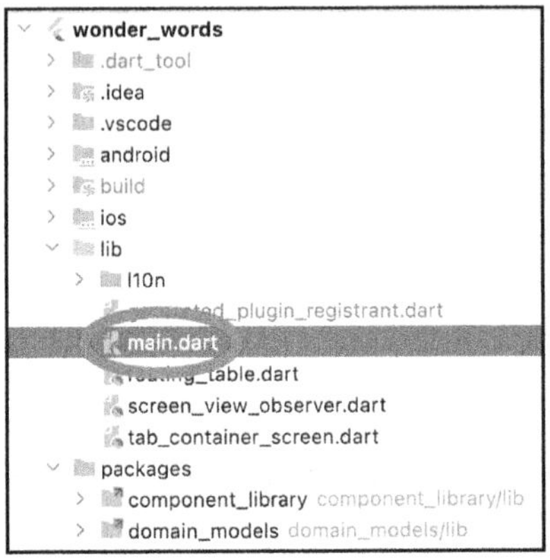


Replace `// TODO: Handle initial dynamic link if any.` with:

```
@override
void initState() {
  super.initState();

  _openInitialDynamicLinkIfAny();

  // TODO: Listen to new dynamic links.
}

Future<void> _openInitialDynamicLinkIfAny() async {
  // 1
  final path = await
_dynamicLinkService.getInitialDynamicLinkPath();
  if (path != null) {
    // 2
    _routerDelegate.push(path);
  }
}
```

Since you're adding this to the topmost widget in your app, this will run every time your app launches. The logic you wrote will then:

1. Check if a dynamic link launched the app.
2. If it did, then navigate to the appropriate path.

Time to test this. Build and run your app, so your new code gets deployed to your phone, but then hard close the app after that. Don't forget to make sure your app is really closed by swiping it out of the *recent apps* list.

Use a browser to open the link you generated using the **Share** button in the last section. Your app should open and navigate directly to a quote's details screen.

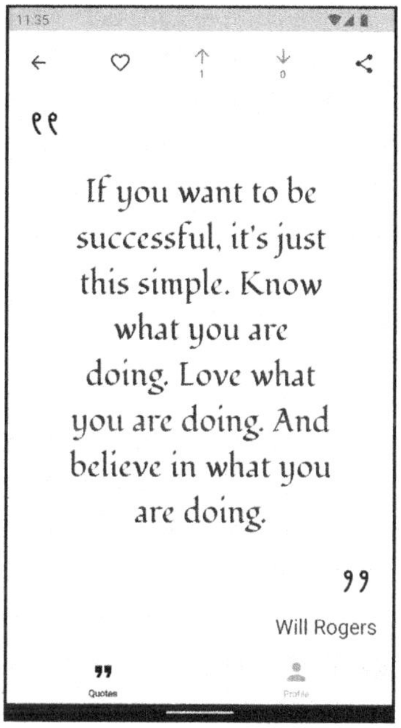


> **Note**: The quote you'll see will be different than the one above. It depends on which quote you generated your link for.

# Opening a Dynamic Link When Your App Is Already Open

You just covered the scenario in which a dynamic link *launches* your app. But what if your app was already open? To handle that, go back to the **monitoring** internal package and open **lib/src/dynamic_link_service.dart**.

Replace `// TODO: Expose a way to listen to new links.` with:

```
// 1
Stream<String> get onNewDynamicLinkPath {
  // 2
  return _dynamicLinks.onLink.map(
    (PendingDynamicLinkData data) {
      final link = data.link;
      final path = link.path;
      // 3
      return path;
    },
  );
}
```

Here's what's going on with this code:

1. You're creating a property that exposes a `Stream<String>` so that users of this function can listen to get notified about when a new link comes in.

2. The `FirebaseDynamicLinks` class contains an `onLink` property, which is pretty much what you need. You then just use the `map` function to change the data type of that `Stream` from `PendingDynamicLinkData` to a `String` containing just the path of the screen you need to open — which is the only thing you need to navigate.

Now, to finish your work for good, go back to the **main.dart** file.

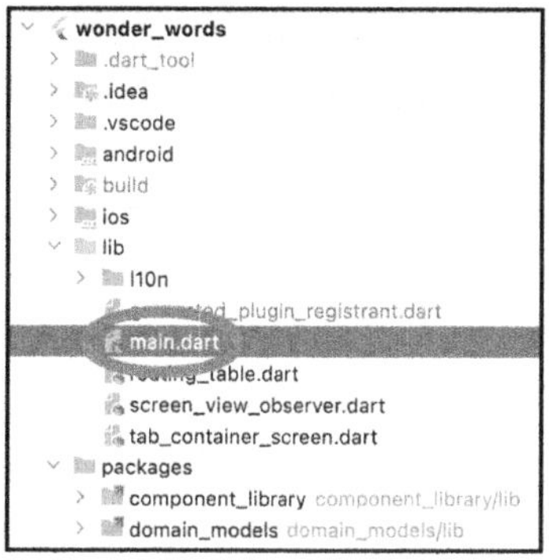


Replace `// TODO: Listen to new dynamic links.` with:

```
// 1
_incomingDynamicLinksSubscription =
    // 2
    _dynamicLinkService.onNewDynamicLinkPath.listen(
          // 3
          _routerDelegate.push,
        );
```

Here, you're:

1. Storing the result of the `listen()` call in the `_incomingDynamicLinksSubscription` property. This is necessary so you can `cancel()` the subscription when your widget gets disposed.
2. Using the `onNewDynamicLinkPath` property you just created inside the `DynamicLinkService` class.
3. Forwarding any new paths coming in from that `Stream` to the `push()` function of your `_routerDelegate` property. This is what makes the navigation happen.

Finally, build and run your app for the last time, but don't close it this time. Minimize the app just so you can open a browser, and try opening that same link from last time. If everything went fine, your app should be in that same quote details screen.

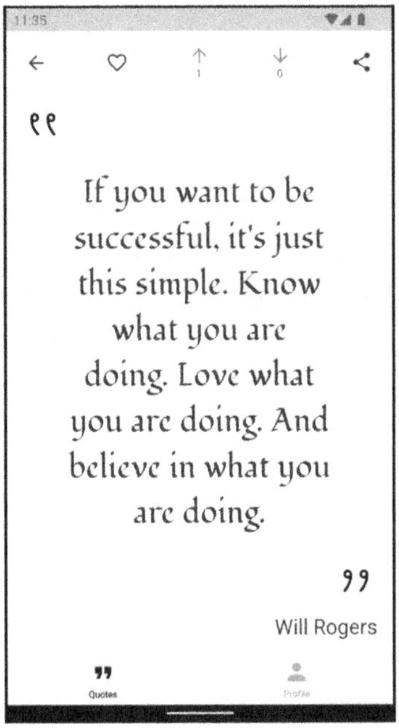


That's all for this chapter. Congratulations!

# Key Points

- An app that supports **deep links** can be launched in response to the user tapping a link.
- Using **Firebase Dynamic Links** is the easiest and most robust way to implement deep links in an app.
- When generating dynamic links, use the functions provided by the official package so you can build shortened links easily.
- When writing the code that handles an incoming dynamic link, you always need to consider that your app can be in two different states: closed or minimized.

# Chapter 9: Internationalizing & Localizing

By Edson Bueno

At its most basic form, **internationalization** is the process of removing **hard-coded** text from your codebase, like `Text('Hello')`, and replacing it with **dynamic properties**, like `Text(l10n.homeScreenGreetings)`. The first reason to do that is to have a more organized codebase, and the second is to lay the groundwork for **localizing** your app.

Localizing means adding support for another language. Spot the distinction between internationalization and localization:

- **Internationalization** is the engineering effort of making sure your app is *translatable*, even if you don't plan to support more than one language at the moment — or at *any* moment.
- **Localization** is taking advantage of an *already internationalized* codebase and feeding it the translations it needs to support another language.

But, of course, things can always be more complex. Internationalization and localization often go way beyond just text translation. Different regions write dates differently and can have different phone number formats, addresses, measurement units, currencies, etc. But that's not for today.

In this chapter, you'll learn how to:

- Internationalize your app.
- Best organize internationalized messages.
- Localize your app to add support for another language.
- Approach internationalization and localization in a multi-package codebase.

One quick explanation before you get your feet wet: Internationalization is also referred to as "**i18n**". Why? It encompasses the first and last letters of "internationalization" — "**i**" and "**n**" — and then substitutes the number "**18**" for the 18 letters in between — "**nternationalizatio**". It's the same reason people also call localization "**l10n**".

Throughout this chapter, you'll work on the **starter** project from this chapter's **assets** folder.

# Getting Started

Use your IDE of choice to open the starter project. Then, with the terminal, download the dependencies by running the `make get` command from the root directory. Wait for the command to finish executing, then build and run your app. This is what you'll see:

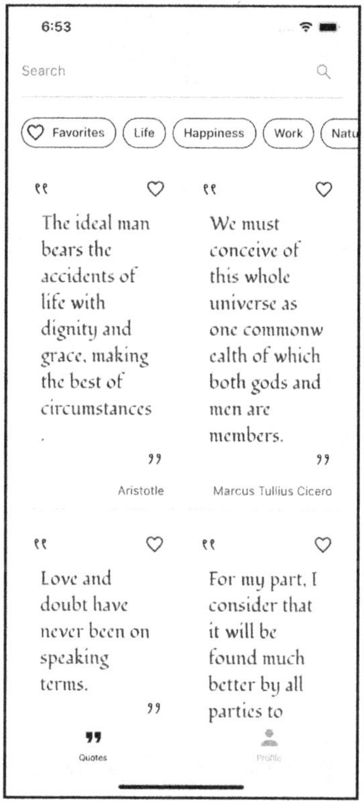


> **Note:** If you're having trouble running the app, it's because you forgot to propagate the configurations you did in the first chapter's starter project to the following chapters' materials. If that's the case, please revisit Chapter 1, "Setting up Your Environment".

Your app is pretty much complete, except that the only language it supports at the moment is English. Your goal from here on will be to add Portuguese support to it. Why Portuguese? The most populous country that speaks Portuguese is Brazil, which has the third-most app downloads worldwide, and a population where only 5% speaks English. That makes it an excellent target for localization.

> **Note**: You'll only localize text that's embedded in the codebase. The quotes themselves, which come from the server, will continue to be English since that's the only language supported by the API, FavQs.com.

## Generating Internationalization Files

The first thing to call out is that WonderWords is a multi-package project, where each screen in the app lives in an isolated package:

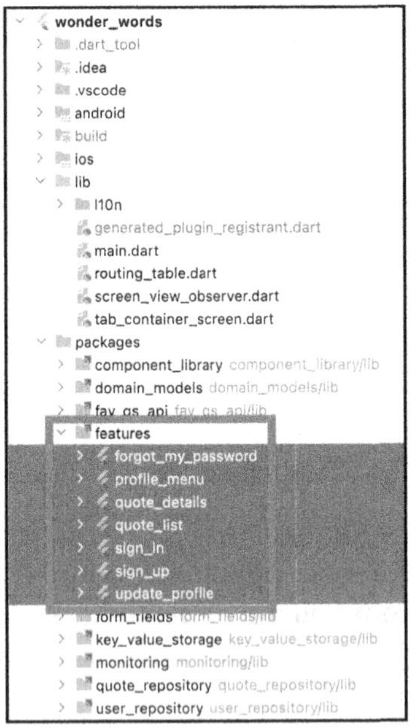

That means the internationalization process needs to happen individually for each one of these. To save you some time and repetitive work, most packages have already been taken care of for you. Your responsibility will be to handle **profile_menu**, which holds the code for the first screen on the Profile tab:

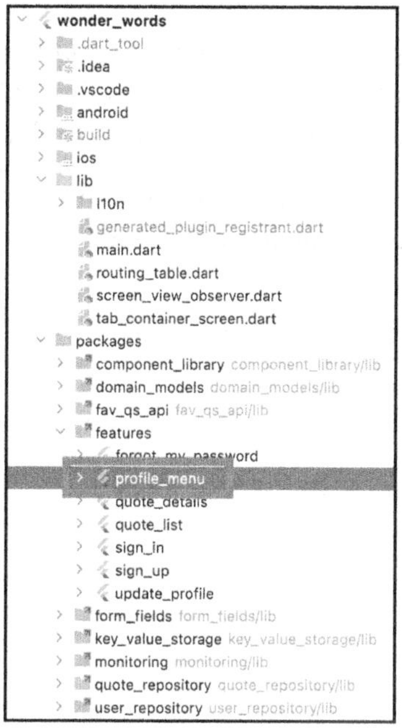


As of now, this screen's code contains only hard-coded text; your job will be to replace it with dynamic values. Kick off this work by opening the **profile_menu** package's **pubspec.yaml**:

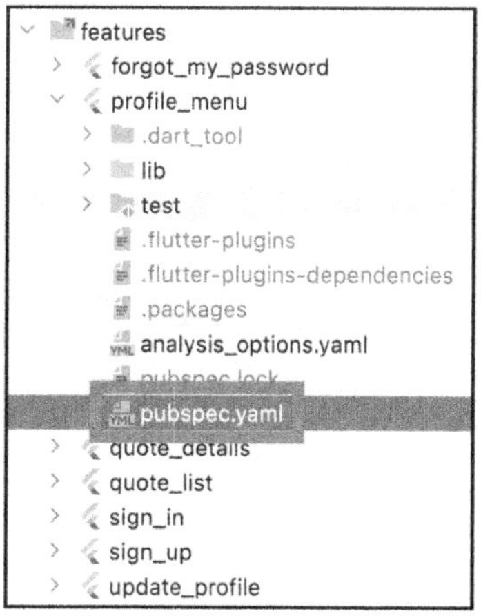

Now, replace `## TODO: Add l10n dependencies.` with:

```
flutter_localizations:
  sdk: flutter
intl: ^0.17.0
```

Done! Those are the two dependencies you need to add internationalization support to an app. Your IDE may warn you to re-fetch your dependencies since you've changed **pubspec.yaml**, but you don't *need* to do it in this case.

Next, still inside the **profile_menu** package, expand the **lib/src** directory and create a new folder there named **l10n** — please note that the first letter is a lowercase "L" and not a capital "I".

Then, create a new file under your new folder and name it **messages_en.arb**.

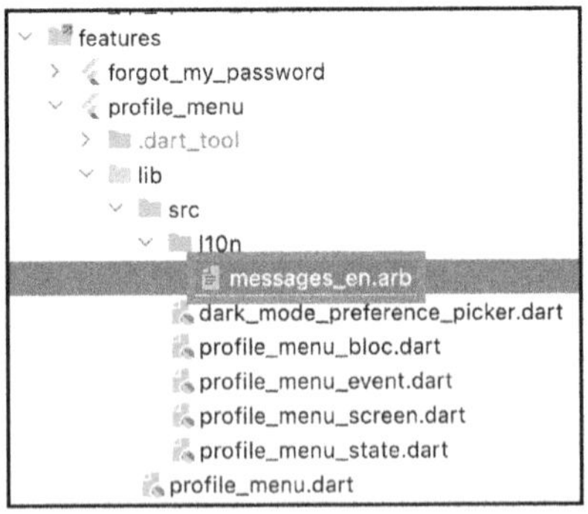

Add the following to the file you just created:

```
{
  "signInButtonLabel": "Sign In",
  "signedInUserGreeting": "Hi, {username}!",
  "@signedInUserGreeting": {
    "placeholders": {
      "username": {
        "type": "String"
      }
    }
  },
  "updateProfileTileLabel": "Update Profile",
  "darkModePreferencesHeaderTileLabel": "Dark Mode Preferences",
  "darkModePreferencesAlwaysDarkTileLabel": "Always Dark",
  "darkModePreferencesAlwaysLightTileLabel": "Always Light",
  "darkModePreferencesUseSystemSettingsTileLabel": "Use System
Settings",
  "signOutButtonLabel": "Sign Out",
  "signUpOpeningText": "Don't have an account?",
  "signUpButtonLabel": "Sign up"
}
```

This **messages_en.arb** file is what you'll use to maintain the English version of all the translatable text you have in this package. Notice the JSON format of the content you just inserted — **arb** files are simply JSONs with extra features.

Internationalization in Flutter works heavily based on code generation. Later, you'll run a command that will cause a Flutter tool to parse this **arb** file and generate a Dart class for you based on it. This generated class is then what you'll use to access these values from your Flutter code, like: `Text(l10n.signInButtonLabel)`.

There are two things worth noticing in the JSON snippet above:

1. Notice how you named your JSON properties. The keys describe *where* that message will be used and not the content of the message. For example, `signInButtonLabel` instead of just `signIn`. This is because you shouldn't reuse messages. If the same text appears in two different places of the app or screen, you should have two different entries in your **arb** file. The first reason for this is that the same text can have different translations depending on where you're using it. The second reason is you might want to change the value for one place without affecting the other.

2. Look at the `signedInUserGreeting` and `@signedInUserGreeting` entries. This is how you define a message with a dynamic parameter you want to inject from your Flutter code, like `Text(l10n.signedInUserGreeting(username))` — where `username` is a runtime value you got from the server, for example. For context, this `signedInUserGreeting` is the message that appears at the top of the screen for a signed-in user:

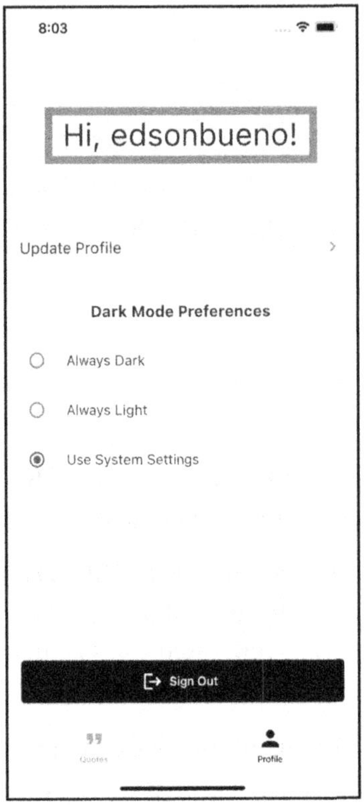


Awesome. Now that you have your messages' source in place — at least the English version — you need to put some configuration in place before being able to ask Flutter to generate the corresponding Dart code for you.

Create a new file named **l10n.yaml** under the **profile_menu** package's root folder.

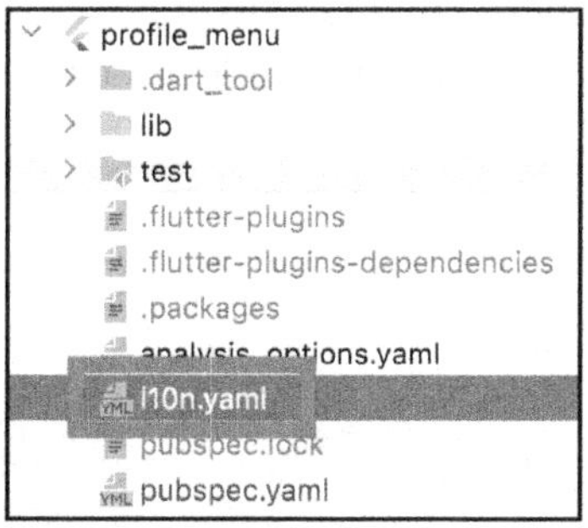


Add this content to your newly created file:

```
arb-dir: lib/src/l10n
template-arb-file: messages_en.arb
output-localization-file: profile_menu_localizations.dart
output-class: ProfileMenuLocalizations
nullable-getter: false
synthetic-package: false
```

This **l10n.yaml** configuration file is where you give Flutter the guidance it needs to generate the code you'll interact with. Here's a walkthrough of what each line in there is doing:

- **arb-dir**: Tells Flutter where it can find your **arb** files — you only have one at the moment, but you'll create another soon.
- **template-arb-file**: Tells Flutter what your *main* **arb** file is.
- **output-localization-file**: How you want it to name your generated Dart file. The default is **app_localizations.dart**, which is too generic for a project containing several packages.
- **output-class**: Same as the above, but now for the name of the actual Dart class instead of the file.
- **nullable-getter**: If this was set to `true`, you'd need to check for nullability whenever accessing a property from your Flutter code, like: `l10n?.signedInUserGreeting`.
- **synthetic-package**: By default, Flutter generates your localization files under a hidden/synthetic package that's only visible to the package you generated the files for. This doesn't work for WonderWords' multi-package structure; you need to be able to export your localization files so you can access them from your **main** package to plug them into your `MaterialApp`.

Finally, open the terminal, and using the `cd` command, navigate to the **profile_menu** package's root folder. From there, run the `flutter gen-l10n` command. Ensure the latest command generated two new files for you under the **l10n** folder you created a few steps ago.

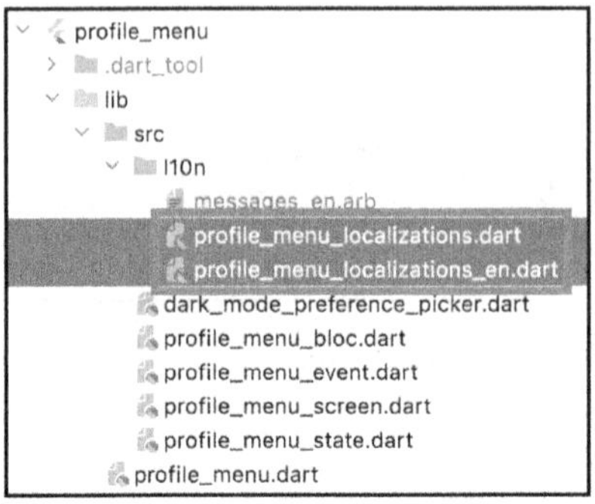


> **Note**: The command above will output a message to your console saying `Because l10n.yaml exists, [...]`. Just ignore it.

# Replacing Hard-Coded Text

You have everything you need to start internationalizing your app. Time for the main act.

Inside **lib/src**, open **profile_menu_screen.dart**.

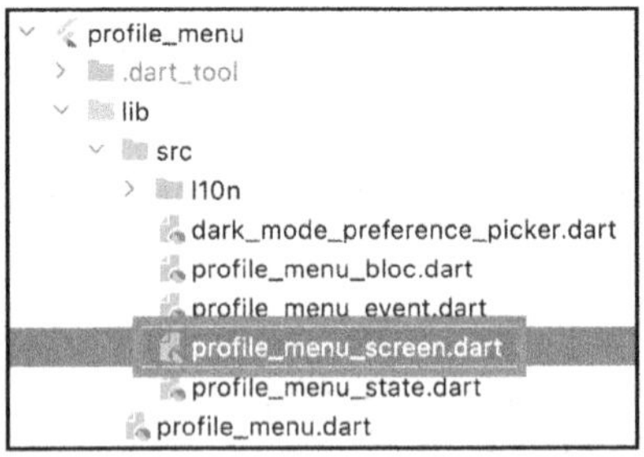


Add the following import line to the top of the file:

```
import 'package:profile_menu/src/l10n/
profile_menu_localizations.dart';
```

Now, replace *all three* instances of `// TODO: Get a ProfileMenuLocalizations instance.` in this file with:

```
final l10n = ProfileMenuLocalizations.of(context);
```

This `ProfileMenuLocalizations` is the class Flutter generated for you, mirroring the content you have in your **messages_en.arb** file. In fact, if you remember, the name `ProfileMenuLocalizations` was your choice inside **l10n.yaml**.

Notice you didn't instantiate `ProfileMenuLocalizations`. Instead, you used the `ProfileMenuLocalizations.of(context)` call, which will get you an instance based on the device's language. Since you only support English at the moment, this will always return an instance containing English messages.

Continuing on **profile_menu_screen.dart**, you'll now replace all the hard-coded text in this file with dynamic properties from these `l10n` variables you created. Do this by replacing:

1. `'Don\'t have an account?',` with `l10n.signUpOpeningText,`.
2. `'Sign up',` with `l10n.signUpButtonLabel,`.
3. `'Hi, $username!',` with `l10n.signedInUserGreeting(username),`.
4. `label: 'Update Profile',` with `label: l10n.updateProfileTileLabel,`.
5. `label: 'Sign In',` with `label: l10n.signInButtonLabel,`.
6. `label: 'Sign Out',` with `label: l10n.signOutButtonLabel,`. You'll find this one twice in this file; replace both.

That's all for this file! Now, you'll do the same for **dark_mode_preference_picker.dart**.

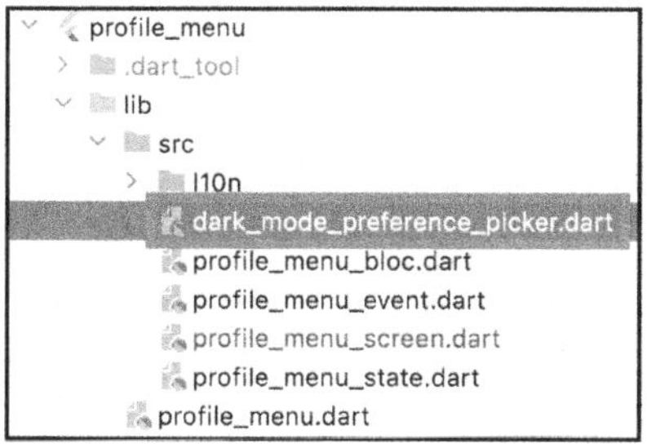

Start by replacing `// TODO: Get a ProfileMenuLocalizations instance.` with:

```
final l10n = ProfileMenuLocalizations.of(context);
```

Then, replace:

1. `'Dark Mode Preferences',` with `l10n.darkModePreferencesHeaderTileLabel,`.
2. `'Always Dark',` with `l10n.darkModePreferencesAlwaysDarkTileLabel,`.
3. `'Always Light',` with `l10n.darkModePreferencesAlwaysLightTileLabel,`.
4. `'Use System Settings',` with `l10n.darkModePreferencesUseSystemSettingsTileLabel,`.

Done! Your codebase is now completely free of hard-coded text.

# Pluging Localization Classes Into MaterialApp

Now, before running your project, you need to connect that `ProfileMenuLocalizations` class to the `MaterialApp` you have on **main.dart**. The problem is: As of now, `ProfileMenuLocalizations` is only visible within the **profile_menu** package, and your `MaterialApp` lives inside the **main** package.

To address that, open the **profile_menu.dart** file, which lives outside the **src** folder of the **profile_menu** package.

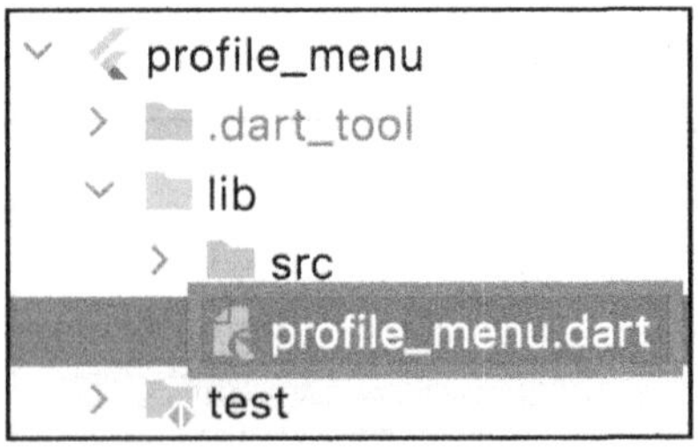

Delete `// TODO: Export ProfileMenuLocalizations.`, and add this instead:

```
export 'src/l10n/profile_menu_localizations.dart';
```

That's it! Now `ProfileMenuLocalizations` is visible to any packages depending on **profile_menu**.

Move on to the **main.dart** file in your root package.

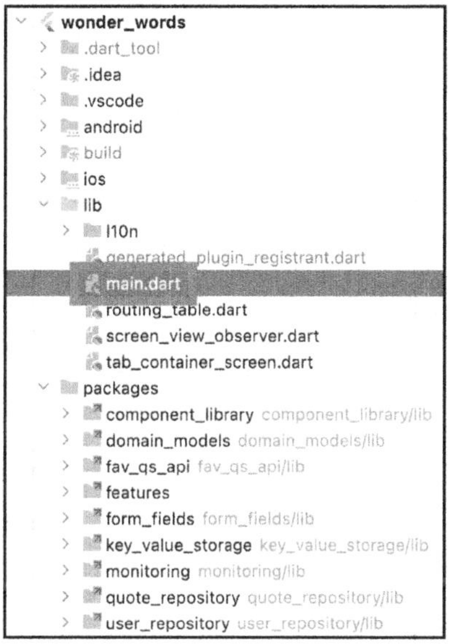


Scroll down until you find `// TODO: Add ProfileMenuLocalizations' delegate.`, and replace it with:

```
ProfileMenuLocalizations.delegate,
```

Here, you're plugging the `delegate` property of your `ProfileMenuLocalizations` class into your `MaterialApp`. This `delegate` property holds an object that knows how to create and recreate instances of `ProfileMenuLocalizations` based on the device's language. Notice that the other packages' delegates are already added for you in that same array.

Build and run your app. It will look exactly the same as before — still supporting English only — but it's now completely **internationalized** — meaning it doesn't contain hard-coded messages and is ready to support new languages.

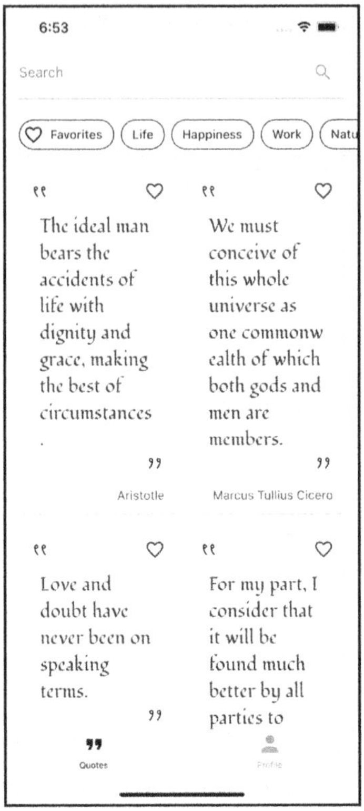


# Adding Portuguese Support

Head back to the **profile_menu** feature package and expand the **lib/src/l10n** folder. Create a new file in there named **messages_pt.arb**.

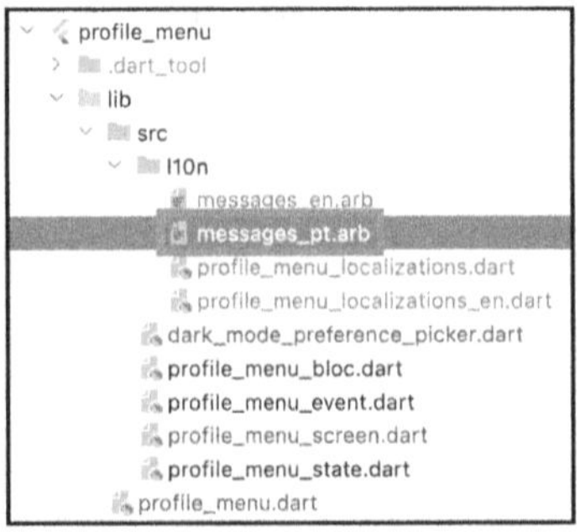

Insert the following code inside your new file:

```
{
  "signInButtonLabel": "Entrar",
  "signedInUserGreeting": "Olá, {username}!",
  "@signedInUserGreeting": {
    "placeholders": {
      "username": {
        "type": "String"
      }
    }
  },
  "updateProfileTileLabel": "Atualizar Perfil",
  "darkModePreferencesHeaderTileLabel": "Configurações de Modo
Noturno",
  "darkModePreferencesAlwaysDarkTileLabel": "Sempre Escuro",
  "darkModePreferencesAlwaysLightTileLabel": "Sempre Claro",
  "darkModePreferencesUseSystemSettingsTileLabel": "De Acordo
com o Sistema",
  "signOutButtonLabel": "Sair",
  "signUpOpeningText": "Não tem uma conta?",
  "signUpButtonLabel": "Cadastrar"
}
```

This mirrors what you have in **messages_en.arb**, but here the messages are all in Portuguese. Also, notice the pattern in the file names: **messages_LANGUAGE.arb**. Now, all you have to do is ask Flutter to regenerate the localization files for you.

Using a terminal, navigate to the **profile_menu** package's root folder and, from there, run the `flutter gen-l10n` command one more time. You'll see a **profile_menu_localizations_pt.dart** file pop up under the **l10n** folder.

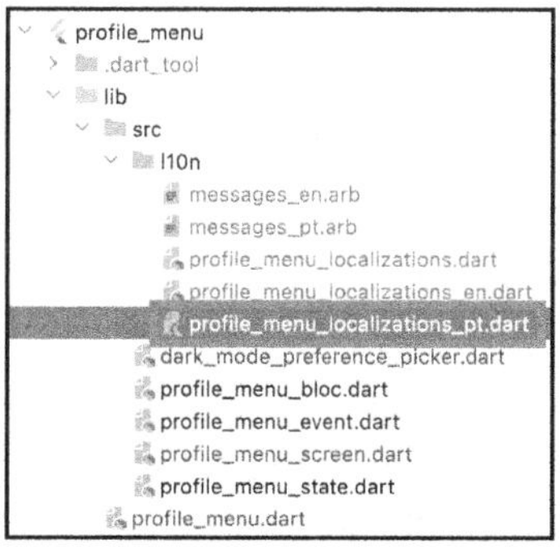


> **Note**: Notice you didn't have to change **l10n.yaml** to specify your new arb file. It already knows which folder to scan.

Now, you have to explicitly say to your `MaterialApp` that you want to support Portuguese. For that, go back to the **main.dart** file.

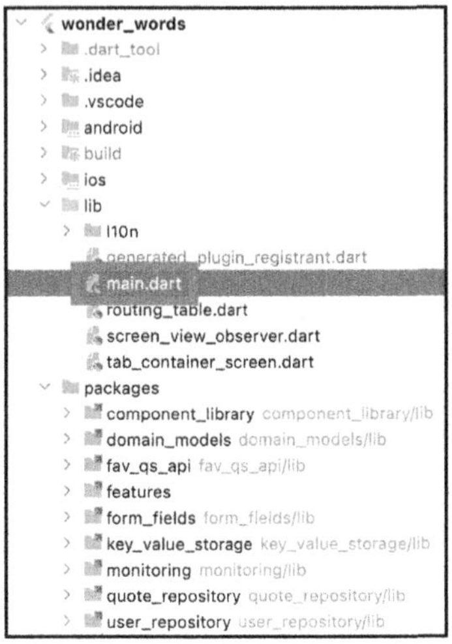


Replace `// TODO: Add supported locales.` with:

```
supportedLocales: const [
  Locale('en', ''),
  Locale('pt', ''),
],
```

Pretty straightforward, right? This is how you tell `MaterialApp` which languages you want to enable for your app.

Lastly, you need to add two more delegates to the `localizationsDelegates` list. Do this by replacing `// TODO: Add Flutter's delegates.` with:

```
GlobalCupertinoLocalizations.delegate,
GlobalMaterialLocalizations.delegate,
```

Here's what's going on: The other delegates that were already sitting on this `localizationsDelegates` list cover localizations for custom code created *by you*. Now that you officially listed Portuguese as one of your supported languages, you're also adding the delegates that handle localizations for Flutter's stock components — from both the Material and the Cupertino libraries.

Test all the work you did by first changing your device's language to Portuguese — from either Brazil or Portugal. Then, build and run your app for the last time. Your app's messages should all now be in Portuguese — don't forget the quotes will continue to be in English. Take a special look at the Profile tab's first screen, which is the one *you* internationalized. Congratulations!

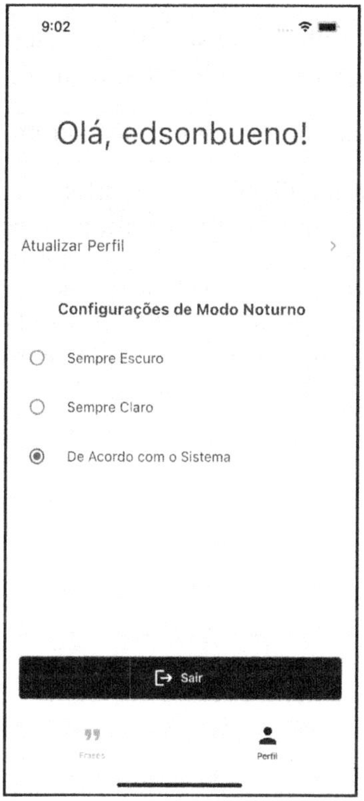

# Key Points

- **Internationalization** is the process of removing any hard-coded values in your codebase that would need to change if you were to support another language. That can include text images, units, date formats, etc.
- **Localization** is the process of adding another language's translations to the translatable resources you have in an internationalized codebase.
- Ideally, you should internationalize your projects from the start.
- Always name your internationalized `Strings` after the place they appear in your app. The same text can have different translations depending on where it appears.
- **Text internationalization** in Flutter is heavily based on **code generation**. All you have to do is maintain your text in JSON-like files and ask Flutter to parse those files and generate Dart versions of them for you to consume from your code.

# Chapter 10: Dynamic Theming & Dark Mode

By Vid Palčar

When thinking about mobile apps — or even apps in general — **dark mode** might instantly cross your mind. It's one of the most expected features for every new app developed. However, it's hard to imagine supporting either dark or light mode without using some type of **theming**. For a beginner who's just started the journey of developing mobile apps, it's usually most intuitive to specify colors and styles on the fly when they're needed. After gaining some experience developing apps, however, you'll quickly realize that this approach is unsustainable and hard to maintain. Imagine switching a specific color in the app for a darker shade — you'd have to go through all the appearances of the color previously used and switch it to the new one. This is where theming saves the day!

Theming in Flutter apps allows you to share colors and styles throughout whole or specific parts of the app. You can set up the theme in your Flutter app in a few ways. You'll look at different methods of setting up the theme in just a moment.

The way you'll choose to create a theme in most cases relies heavily on the `InheritedWidget` class. Therefore, check the key concepts and theory behind `InheritedWidget` in the previous chapter, Chapter 9, "Internationalizing & Localizing". In this chapter, you'll:

- Take a quick look at different approaches to setting up a theme in your Flutter app.
- Use your knowledge on `InheritedWidget` to add dynamic theming to your app.
- Learn about best practices and how to define colors and styles for the theme.
- Learn how to implement dynamic theming based on user preferences.

Throughout this chapter, you'll work on the **starter** project from this chapter's **assets** folder.

It's time to get started by looking at different ways to theme your app.

# Ways to Theme Your App

As already mentioned, you have numerous ways to set up the theme for your project. For this chapter, you'll only look at a few ways with a bit more focus on the one that's the most appropriate for the WonderWords app.

The purpose of this chapter is to provide you with options so that when you're facing different feature requirements and app architectures, you can choose the option that works the best for your case. Since there isn't much sense in using multiple theming solutions for your app, this chapter is more theoretical. You'll use only one theming solution for WonderWords and then look at examples of other options.

## Basic App Theming

Look at the following code snippet:

```
@override
Widget build(BuildContext context) {
  return MaterialApp(
    title: 'Flutter Demo',
    theme: ThemeData(
      primarySwatch: Colors.blue,
    ),
    home: const MyHomePage(title: 'Flutter Demo Home Page'),
  );
}
```

> **Note**: Notice that the code in this section isn't part of the WonderWords app. Therefore, you won't find it in the materials. It's here only for demonstrational purposes and doesn't require any action on your part.

The code above should look very familiar — it's the initial code generated when you run the `flutter create {app_name}` command. You can see it contains a very primitive theme.

From its initial releases, Flutter supported light and dark themes. It allows you to define the theme data for the app one time — like fonts, shapes and colors — then use that theme throughout the app.

In the following example, you see how to define those in the theme:

```
theme: ThemeData(
  // 1
  primaryColor: Colors.blueGrey,
  // 2
  fontFamily: 'Georgia',
  // 3
  textTheme: const TextTheme(
    headline1: TextStyle(
      color: Colors.black,
      fontSize: 36.0,
      fontWeight: FontWeight.bold,
    ),
  ),
),
```

In the example above, you can see how to define:

1. The color in the theme.
2. The font family for your project. Note that the usage of custom fonts might be a bit more complicated than just adding the font's name to the theme — Flutter has a limited number of fonts supported by default. Sometimes, you might have to add a specific font as an asset to the project or use a third-party package such as google_fonts (https://pub.dev/packages/google_fonts) to use a custom font. In the case of **Georgia**, no special steps are required.
3. A custom text theme. In this case, the theme for only one text style was defined by providing a color, font size and font weight.

> **Note**: When defining the theme in the way shown above, things can get messy very quickly. Therefore, a good practice is isolating the code in a separate file or even creating a custom class for it.

Now, as you know how to define the theme for your app, look at how you'll use the defined theme in your UI:

```
Text(
  'Title',
  style: Theme.of(context).textTheme.headline1,
),
```

In the example above, you use the style defined in your theme for a `Text` widget.

Similar to a light theme, you can also define a dark theme. Use the `ThemeData` widget on the `darkTheme` attribute of `MaterialApp` to define a dark theme:

```
theme: ThemeData(
  // definition of light theme
),
darkTheme: ThemeData(
 // definition of dark theme
),
```

Now, you might be wondering how the app will know which theme to use if you define both themes. The `themeMode` attribute of `MaterialApp` has you covered:

```
themeMode: ThemeMode.light,
```

The line of code above activates light mode for the app. By applying `ThemeMode.dark`, the app uses dark mode. If you don't define it, the app uses `ThemeMode.system`, which sets the mode based on the phone's settings.

This way of defining the theme might be enough in some cases, but it has a fairly noticeable downside. It limits you to only using the predefined parameters of the theme as well as not providing you with a good out-of-the-box solution to let your users change the theme mode when they'd like to.

## Using a Third-party Package

Thanks to the very strong developer community, quite a few excellent third-party solutions exist to handle theming for your Flutter app. The various packages might be more or less appropriate for your use case. One such package is adaptive_theme (https://pub.dev/packages/adaptive_theme), which is fairly popular in the developer community. It represents a holistic theming solution for your app by covering all the important features connected to theming. In the following section, you'll dive deeper into the usage of this package.

> **Note**: The following code examples are only for demonstration purposes. Therefore, you're not required to adjust any code in the starter project materials, and it won't be accessible in the final project.

Similar to all packages, the first thing you need to do is add it to your project. You can achieve that by running the `flutter pub add adaptive_theme` command or by adding the following line in the **pubspec.yaml** file under **dependencies**:

```
adaptive_theme: ^3.1.0
```

Because this book focuses on the package-based architecture of the app — to refresh your memory on that, review Chapter 1, "Setting up Your Environment" — you have to take into consideration choosing the right package to add this package. Best practice is to specify the theme of the app in the **component_library** package, as you'll need to access the theme in other packages.

Take a look at the basic usage of the package:

```
@override
Widget build(BuildContext context) {
  // 1
  return AdaptiveTheme(
    // 2
    light: ThemeData(
      // implementation of light theme
    ),
    dark: ThemeData(
      // implementation of light theme
    ),
    // 3
    initial: AdaptiveThemeMode.light,
    // 4
    builder: (theme, darkTheme) => MaterialApp(
```

```
      title: 'Flutter Demo',
      // 5
      theme: theme,
      darkTheme: darkTheme,
      home: const MyHomePage(title: 'Flutter Demo Home Page'),
    ),
  );
}
```

Look carefully, and you'll notice quite a few similarities with the implementation of the theme in the previous section. This is what's going on in the code above:

1. With the help of the `AdaptiveTheme` widget, handle app theming.
2. Use `ThemeData` to define both dark and light themes.
3. Define the theme initially used for the app. In the example above, the app will use a light theme.
4. Use `builder` to add `MaterialApp` to the widget tree.
5. Apply light and dark themes defined above in the `AdaptiveTheme` widget to `MaterialApp`.

The code above does basically the same as the final example of the previous section. Next, look at how to change the theme mode:

```
// 1
AdaptiveTheme.of(context).setDark();

// 2
AdaptiveTheme.of(context).setLight();
// 3
AdaptiveTheme.of(context).setSystem();
```

Using the code above:

1. Changes the theme to dark mode.
2. Sets the theme to the light mode.
3. Changes the theme according to the system settings of the users' devices.

This feature of the package can come in handy when implementing the app's settings. But it would be a bit impractical if the user changes the theme mode in the settings, then when opening the app next time, the theme reverts to light mode. Fortunately, this package also has you covered in this situation:

```
void main() async {
  WidgetsFlutterBinding.ensureInitialized();
  final themeMode = await AdaptiveTheme.getThemeMode();
  runApp(MyApp(themeMode: themeMode));
}
```

Calling `AdaptiveTheme.getThemeMode()` in `main()` lets you access the last theme set in the app. By providing it as a parameter to the `MyApp` widget, you can set this mode as the initial mode as follows:

```
initial: themeMode ?? AdaptiveThemeMode.light,
```

Notice that `AdaptiveTheme.getThemeMode()` can return a null value in cases where the theme mode has never been set. Therefore, you have to add a fallback mode, which in the case above, is light mode.

The **adaptive_theme** offers plenty of cool features — it's worthwhile to go through its official documentation. Before continuing with the next section, one more thing is worth mentioning.

In some situations, you might want to fetch the theme from a remote source. This could be a case when you want to change the app appearance without actually rolling out a new version. This is quite common when developing B2B (business to business) apps. The businesses, which in this case are your clients, will provide their clients with your app but still want to distinguish themselves from other clients. Therefore, the app's themes will be defined somewhere remotely. Each business will use its theme configuration, so the same app will look different for different businesses. With the help of the **adaptive_theme** package, you can achieve this by using the following code snippet:

```
AdaptiveTheme.of(context).setTheme(
  light: ThemeData(
    // new specification of light theme
  ),
  dark: ThemeData(
    // new specification of dark theme
  ),
);
```

This code replaces the light and dark themes defined before. Notice that this will replace the initially defined themes only while the app is running. By diving deeper into this issue, you can save the new theme to local storage and access it without fetching the theme from a remote source every time the app restarts.

Although this option gives you a good out-of-the-box solution for switching between light and dark themes, it still limits you to predefined parameters for your themes.

# Using Inherited Widget for Theming

Finally, it's time to implement dynamic theming for your WonderWords app. As mentioned in the introduction, it will depend on `InheritedWidget`. As theming is an essential part of the app's architecture, quite a few things are already prepared for you.

## WonderTheme as InheritedWidget

You'll start by opening **wonder_theme.dart** located in **packages/component_library/lib/src/theme**:

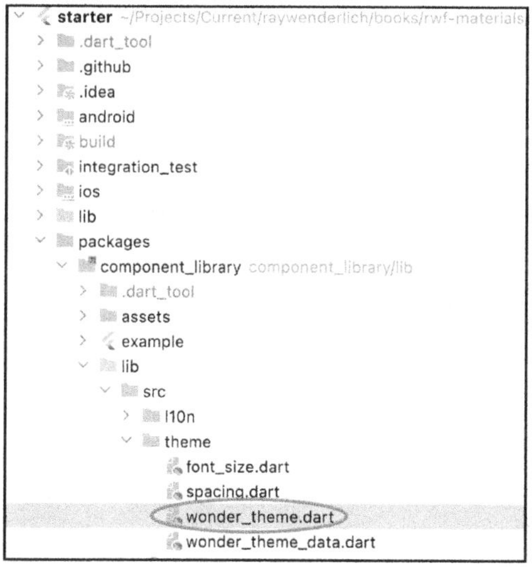


Look at the implementation of the `WonderTheme` class:

```
class WonderTheme extends InheritedWidget {
  const WonderTheme({
    required Widget child,
    required this.lightTheme,
    required this.darkTheme,
    Key? key,
```

```
  }) : super(
        key: key,
        child: child,
      );

  final WonderThemeData lightTheme;
  final WonderThemeData darkTheme;

  // TODO: replace with correct implementation of
updateShouldNotify
  @override
  bool updateShouldNotify(WonderTheme oldWidget) {
    return false;
  }

  // TODO: replace with correct implementation of service
locator function
  static WonderThemeData of(BuildContext context) {
    return LightWonderThemeData();
  }
}
```

There's nothing very special about the code above. `WonderTheme` takes light and dark themes of the `WonderThemeData` type as an attribute — which you'll learn about in a few moments — as well as a child, which allows you to properly position in the widget tree.

A definition of the `of()` method plays the role of a service locator, which lets you access theme data in your UI. As the `WonderTheme` class extends `InheritedWidget`, you have to implement one required override: `updateShouldNotify()`. You'll start by fixing the implementation of this override. Start by replacing the current implementation of the override of `updateShouldNotify()`, which is under `// TODO: replace with the correct implementation of updateShouldNotify`, with the following code:

```
@override
bool updateShouldNotify(WonderTheme oldWidget) =>
    oldWidget.lightTheme != lightTheme || oldWidget.darkTheme !=
darkTheme;
```

`updateShouldNotify()` notifies all the widgets that inherit `WonderTheme` so they can be rebuilt, and therefore, they'll reflect the change. It notifies them exclusively when the dark or light theme of an old widget is different from the current widget. This prevents unnecessary rebuilds.

Next, you'll add a correct implementation of the `of()` method. Replace the current implementation under `// TODO: replace with correct implementation of service locator function` with the following code:

```
static WonderThemeData of(BuildContext context) {
  // 1
  final WonderTheme? inheritedTheme =
      context.dependOnInheritedWidgetOfExactType<WonderTheme>();
  // 2
  assert(inheritedTheme != null, 'No WonderTheme found in
context');
  // 3
  final currentBrightness = Theme.of(context).brightness;
  // 4
  return currentBrightness == Brightness.dark
      ? inheritedTheme!.darkTheme
      : inheritedTheme!.lightTheme;
}
```

The code above:

1. Obtains the nearest widget in the widget tree of the `WonderTheme` type and stores it in the variable.
2. If no widget of the `WonderTheme` type is in the widget tree, it interrupts the normal execution of the code. This is important during the development process, so you don't forget to add your `InheritedWidget` in the widget tree. In just a moment, you'll see what happens if you forget to add `WonderTheme` at the top of your widget tree.
3. Stores the current brightness in the variable.
4. Based on current brightness, returns either a light or dark theme.

As already mentioned, you'll now see what happens if you forget to add `WonderTheme` to the widget tree. Open **main.dart** located in the **lib** folder at the root of the project. Locate `// TODO: replace build() method for demonstration purposes`, and replace the implementation of `build()` with the following:

```
// TODO: remove changes after testing
@override
Widget build(BuildContext context) {
  return MaterialApp.router(
    theme: ThemeData(),
    darkTheme: ThemeData(),
    themeMode: ThemeMode.light,
    supportedLocales: const [
      Locale('en', ''),
```

```
        Locale('pt', 'BR'),
      ],
      localizationsDelegates: const [
        GlobalCupertinoLocalizations.delegate,
        GlobalMaterialLocalizations.delegate,
        AppLocalizations.delegate,
        ComponentLibraryLocalizations.delegate,
        ProfileMenuLocalizations.delegate,
        QuoteListLocalizations.delegate,
        SignInLocalizations.delegate,
        ForgotMyPasswordLocalizations.delegate,
        SignUpLocalizations.delegate,
UpdateProfileLocalizations.delegate,
      ],
      routerDelegate: _routerDelegate,
      routeInformationParser: const RoutemasterParser(),
    );
  }
```

Compare your code with the implementation you had before. You'll see the only thing that's changed is that the widget tree doesn't contain the `WonderTheme` widget anymore. Run the app to see the changes:

> **Note**: If you're having trouble running the app, you might have forgotten to propagate the configurations you did in the first chapter's starter project to the following chapters' materials. If that's the case, please revisit Chapter 1, "Setting up Your Environment".

As explained before, the fact that you didn't add `WonderTheme` to the widget tree causes the issue. This is important because you're trying to access it with the help of the `of()` method in multiple places in the UI to reflect the theme specification you defined.

Remove the changes you just did in **main.dart**, and hot refresh the app. This is what you'll see:

## Defining Custom Theme Data

In **wonder_theme_data.dart**, under the **themes** folder, you'll see an `abstract` class and its two implementations: `LightWonderThemeData` and `DarkWonderThemeData`. Quite a few things are already prepared for you. `WonderThemeData` has declarations of the theming elements, such as colors and fonts, but there are two different implementations of this class with different values assigned to those declarations. You'll **override** these declarations in the implementation classes.

In the same file, you'll find the `ThemeData` type getter in the `WonderThemeData` class:

```
ThemeData get materialThemeData;
```

`materialThemeData` will assign themes to the `MaterialApp` widget. The data from `materialThemeData` differs for both light and dark themes, so you'll implement it in the implementation classes. Locate `// TODO: Add light theme implementation for materialThemeData` under the `LightWonderThemeData` class. Notice that an override for the `materialThemeData` getter already exists, which is implemented under the comment. This is because, without correct overrides, the `WonderThemeData` class will cause issues that prevent you from running the app. Proceed by replacing the current implementation with a new one:

```
@override
ThemeData get materialThemeData => ThemeData(
  // 1
  brightness: Brightness.light,
  // 2
  primarySwatch: Colors.black.toMaterialColor(),
  // 3
  dividerTheme: _dividerThemeData,
);
```

Before explaining the code, you'll do the same with the implementation of `materialThemeData` located in the `DarkWonderThemeData` class under `// TODO: Add dark theme implementation for materialThemeData`:

```
@override
ThemeData get materialThemeData => ThemeData(
  // 1
  brightness: Brightness.dark,
  // 2
  primarySwatch: Colors.white.toMaterialColor(),
  // 3
  dividerTheme: _dividerThemeData,
  // 4
  toggleableActiveColor: Colors.white,
);
```

Here's what these code snippets do:

1. `Brightness`'s `light` and `dark` values set the theme for all the elements in `ThemeData`. This assignment initializes the `ThemeData` elements with the default light or dark theme values. So, if you don't specify elements like `scaffoldBackgroundColor` in `ThemeData`, then the app uses the default ones from the Flutter framework.
2. The **light theme** and **dark theme** implementations of `materialThemeData` assign `black` and `white` colors as the primary swatches.
3. This is the theme for the divider, which is the same for both light and dark themes. Therefore, you use a global variable to define it.
4. An additional color for active toggle is defined for the dark theme, as it doesn't use color from `primarySwatch`.

> **Note**: `primarySwatch` is the driving factor for all the primary colors in the app. For example, all the text in the app gets the colors from this swatch. `toMaterialColor` is an extension method in **wonder_theme_data.dart** that generates the swatch from any color. Feel free to look at the implementation of this extension.

## Setting up Colors

Similar to `materialThemeData`, other `WonderThemeData` attributes are also defined. One, for example, is colors. Notice the multiple `Color` getters in the `WonderThemeData` abstract class. You use these to declare all the various sets of colors you use in the app. Look at the example that's already been prepared for you. The color is declared in the `WonderThemeData` abstract class as follows:

```
// 1
Color get roundedChoiceChipBackgroundColor;
```

The values for a light mode are assigned in the `LightWonderThemeData` class:

```
// 2
@override
Color get roundedChoiceChipBackgroundColor => Colors.white;
```

And values for dark mode are assigned in the `DarkWonderThemeData` class:

```
// 3
@override
Color get roundedChoiceChipBackgroundColor => Colors.black;
```

Here's what the code snippets above mean:

1. This is the declaration for a background color for the rounded choice chip.
2. Assigns the `white` color to rounded choice chip background for the light theme.
3. Assigns the `black` color to rounded choice chip background for the dark theme.

As you haven't implemented the systematic of switching themes, take a look at the following image of how the code above affects the app's appearance. You'll be able to test it on your own in just a moment:

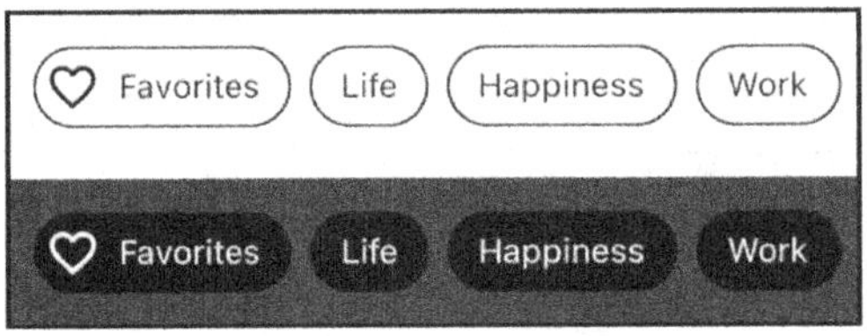


Now, you'll see how to use this data in an `InheritedWidget`.

## Switching Themes

You've already learned about switching themes in both of the previously mentioned theming approaches. When doing it with the help of an inherited widget, it's not much different.

Switching themes is as easy as providing a `ThemeMode` to `MaterialApp`. However, `MaterialApp` has to be aware of both the light and dark implementations of `materialThemeData` you defined in one of the previous sections.

Open the root **main.dart**, and replace the code under `// TODO: provide MaterialApp with correct theme data` with the following:

```
// TODO: wrap with stream builder
// 1
return WonderTheme(
  lightTheme: _lightTheme,
  darkTheme: _darkTheme,
  // 2
  child: MaterialApp.router(
    theme: _lightTheme.materialThemeData,
    darkTheme: _darkTheme.materialThemeData,
    // TODO: change to dark mode
    themeMode: ThemeMode.light,
    supportedLocales: const [
      Locale('en', ''),
      Locale('pt', 'BR'),
    ],
    localizationsDelegates: const [
      GlobalCupertinoLocalizations.delegate,
      GlobalMaterialLocalizations.delegate,
      AppLocalizations.delegate,
      ComponentLibraryLocalizations.delegate,
      ProfileMenuLocalizations.delegate,
      QuoteListLocalizations.delegate,
      SignInLocalizations.delegate,
      ForgotMyPasswordLocalizations.delegate,
      SignUpLocalizations.delegate,
      UpdateProfileLocalizations.delegate,
    ],
    routerDelegate: _routerDelegate,
    routeInformationParser: const RoutemasterParser(),
  ),
);
```

Here's what this code does:

1. Initializes `WonderTheme` with the data from the two themes.
2. `MaterialApp.router` uses both light and dark `materialThemeData` defined as an attribute of your implementations of `WonderThemeData`. With the help of `themeMode`, the UI reflects one theme or the other.

To see your progress so far, run the app. To test dark mode, replace `// TODO: change to dark mode` and the line of code after it with the following:

```
// TODO: change for dynamic theme changing
themeMode: ThemeMode.dark,
```

Hot restart the app, and this is how your app will look for light (left screen) and dark (right screen) modes:

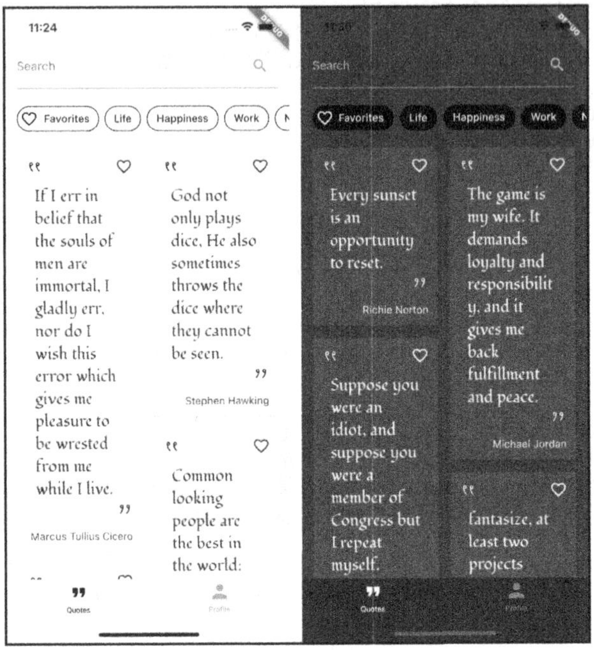


## Switching Themes With User Intervention

So far, you've manually switched themes by changing `themeMode` and rebuilding the app. That's not ideal, as your users won't rebuild the app once they install it. Instead, they want to select a light or dark theme according to their preference. Now, you'll add this capability to WonderWords.

## Different Theme Modes

Just as Flutter's theme provides three different modes for theming, your app will also support three theme modes. They're predefined for you as `DarkModePreference` enumeration in **dark_mode_preference.dart** located in the **lib/src** folder of the **domain_models** package:

1. **alwaysDark**: The app will always use dark mode.
2. **alwaysLight**: The app will always use light mode.
3. **useSystemSettings**: The app will use the current system theme, which could be either light or dark.

## Upserting and Retrieving Theme Mode

To set and use the currently set theme mode, you'll use `BehaviorSubject`, which you learned about in Chapter 6, "Authenticating Users". To refresh your memory on the topic, look back at that chapter.

Look at its declaration and initialization in **user_repository.dart** located in the **lib/src** folder of the **user_repository** package:

```
final BehaviorSubject<DarkModePreference>
_darkModePreferenceSubject =
      BehaviorSubject();
```

`_darkModePreferenceSubject` holds the value of the current theme mode and will provide you with `Stream`, which you'll listen to. This will let you update the UI appearance accordingly to the changes in theme mode.

To enable setting the theme mode, replace `// TODO: add logic for upserting theme mode` with the following method:

```
// 1
await _localStorage.upsertDarkModePreference(
  preference.toCacheModel(),
);
// 2
_darkModePreferenceSubject.add(preference);
```

This code:

1. Saves the selected theme mode of type `DarkModePreference` to the local storage. You won't go into details on how to save theme mode to the local storage using Hive. To refresh your memory on this, review Chapter 2, "Mastering the Repository Pattern".
2. Sets `_darkModePreferenceSubject` to the current theme mode.

Next, look at how to retrieve the currently saved theme from local storage. This function is already implemented for you, as it's crucial for the proper function of the starter project. Look at the following code:

```
Stream<DarkModePreference> getDarkModePreference() async* {
  // 1
  if (!_darkModePreferenceSubject.hasValue) {
    final storedPreference = await
_localStorage.getDarkModePreference();
    _darkModePreferenceSubject.add(
        storedPreference?.toDomainModel() ??
          DarkModePreference.useSystemSettings,
    );
  }
  // 2
  yield* _darkModePreferenceSubject.stream;
}
```

This is what the code above does:

1. Initially, when `_darkModePreferenceSubject` is empty, the code fetches the theme mode from local storage and adds it to the subject. If no theme mode is stored in the local storage, the default preference `DarkModePreference.useSystemSettings` is set, which indicates either light or dark mode based on the device's settings, and goes into the subject.
2. Provides you with the `BehaviorSubject`'s stream, which you'll listen to for the changes in the following steps.

## Changing Theme Through UI

At this point, you can access the theme preference selection UI in the **Profile Menu Screen** by switching to the **Profile** tab from the home screen. There, you'll notice a list of radio buttons specifying the three **Dark Mode Preferences**.

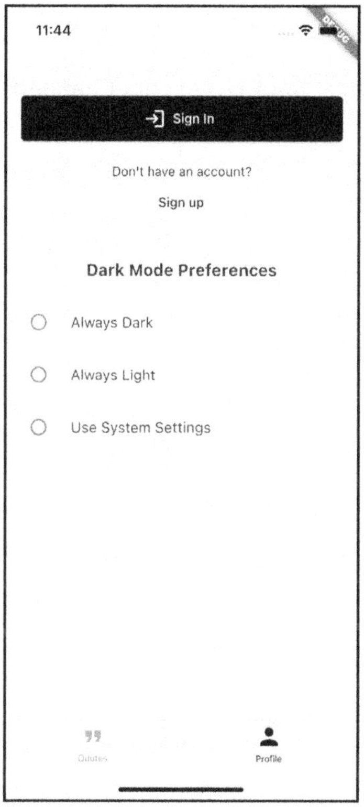


However, you may notice that none of them is selected, and tapping them doesn't change the starter project's theme yet. To fix this, you need to do the following two tasks:

1. Assign the new theme to the app when pressing the radio button on the profile menu screen.
2. Reflect the change of the theme mode preference in the UI.

You'll start by fixing the first issue.

Start by opening **dark_mode_preference_picker.dart** located in **packages/features/profile_menu/lib/src**. Locate `// TODO: add ProfileMenuDarkModePreferenceChanged triggering for dark mode`, and replace it with the following code:

```
bloc.add(
  const ProfileMenuDarkModePreferenceChanged(
    DarkModePreference.alwaysDark,
  ),
);
```

Before explaining the code above, you'll do the same two more times for light and system theme modes. Replace `// TODO: add ProfileMenuDarkModePreferenceChanged triggering for light mode` with the following code:

```
bloc.add(
  const ProfileMenuDarkModePreferenceChanged(
    DarkModePreference.alwaysLight,
  ),
);
```

And replace `// TODO: add ProfileMenuDarkModePreferenceChanged triggering for system mode` with the following code:

```
bloc.add(
  const ProfileMenuDarkModePreferenceChanged(
    DarkModePreference.useSystemSettings,
  ),
);
```

The code snippets above trigger `ProfileMenuDarkModePreferenceChanged` with the `DarkModePreference` the user selected. Notice the parameter change in these calls: `alwaysDark`, `alwaysLight` and `useSystemSettings`.

Build and run the app, and your profile screen will look the same as before you applied changes.

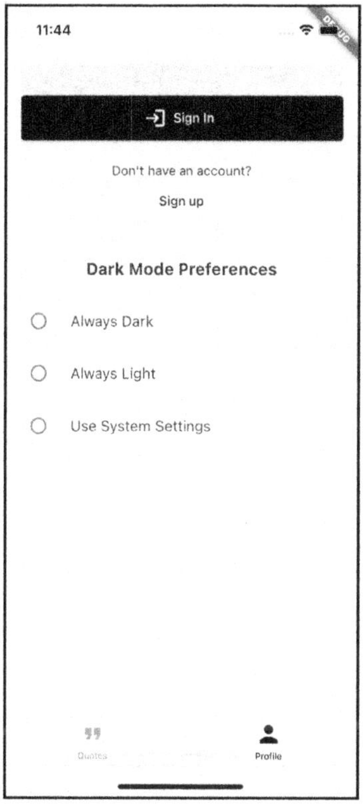


To fix the UI so it'll show the currently selected appearance, replace the line under `// TODO: set correct group value` for each theme mode preference with the following line of code. You have to do so three times — one time for each preference:

```
groupValue: currentValue,
```

`groupValue` is the attribute that assigns the currently selected value. If the `value` of any of these radio tiles matches the `groupValue`, that radio tile becomes active. If `value` isn't the same as `groupValue`, the button is inactive. `currentValue`, in this case, reflects the currently selected theme mode preference, which is part of the `ProfileMenuBloc` state — you won't go into details here, as you learned about that in Chapter 3, "Managing State With Cubits & the Bloc Library".

Hot restart the app, and you'll see the following change:

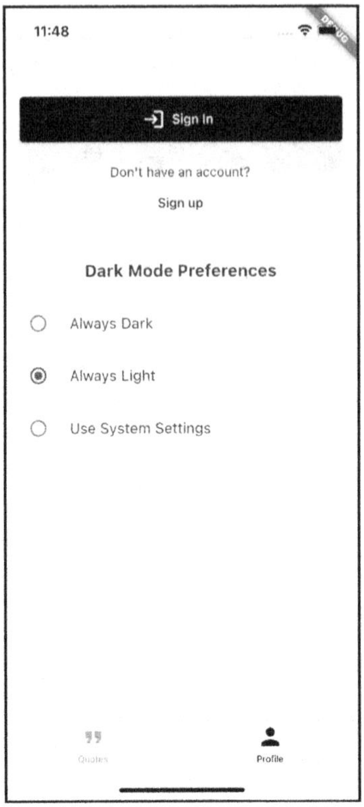


Now, you just need to take care of one more issue. If you change the theme mode preference to **Always Dark**, the app's theme still doesn't change to dark mode. To fix this, navigate to the root-level **lib** folder and open **main.dart**. Replace the entire content of `build()` under `// TODO: wrap with stream builder` with the following code:

```
// 1
return StreamBuilder<DarkModePreference>(
  stream: _userRepository.getDarkModePreference(),
  builder: (context, snapshot) {
    // 2
    final darkModePreference = snapshot.data;
    return WonderTheme(
      lightTheme: _lightTheme,
      darkTheme: _darkTheme,
      child: MaterialApp.router(
        theme: _lightTheme.materialThemeData,
        darkTheme: _darkTheme.materialThemeData,
        // 3
        themeMode: darkModePreference?.toThemeMode(),
```

```
          supportedLocales: const [
            Locale('en', ''),
            Locale('pt', 'BR'),
          ],
          localizationsDelegates: const [
            GlobalCupertinoLocalizations.delegate,
            GlobalMaterialLocalizations.delegate,
            AppLocalizations.delegate,
            ComponentLibraryLocalizations.delegate,
            ProfileMenuLocalizations.delegate,
            QuoteListLocalizations.delegate,
            SignInLocalizations.delegate,
            ForgotMyPasswordLocalizations.delegate,
            SignUpLocalizations.delegate,
            UpdateProfileLocalizations.delegate,
          ],
          routerDelegate: _routerDelegate,
          routeInformationParser: const RoutemasterParser(),
        ),
      );
    },
  );
```

Here's what the code above does:

1. Uses the `StreamBuilder` that reads the stream of `_darkModePreferenceSubject` from **user_repository.dart**.
2. The `builder` rebuilds the widget on the arrival of a new value. Here, you'll get the dark mode preference from the `snapshot` to use in the child widgets.
3. Sets the `themeMode` according to the user's dark mode preference. `toThemeMode()` is an extension method that converts `DarkModePreference` to `ThemeMode`. It's defined at the end of the **main.dart** file.

For one last time, build and run the app, and dynamic switching for the theme should work like a charm:

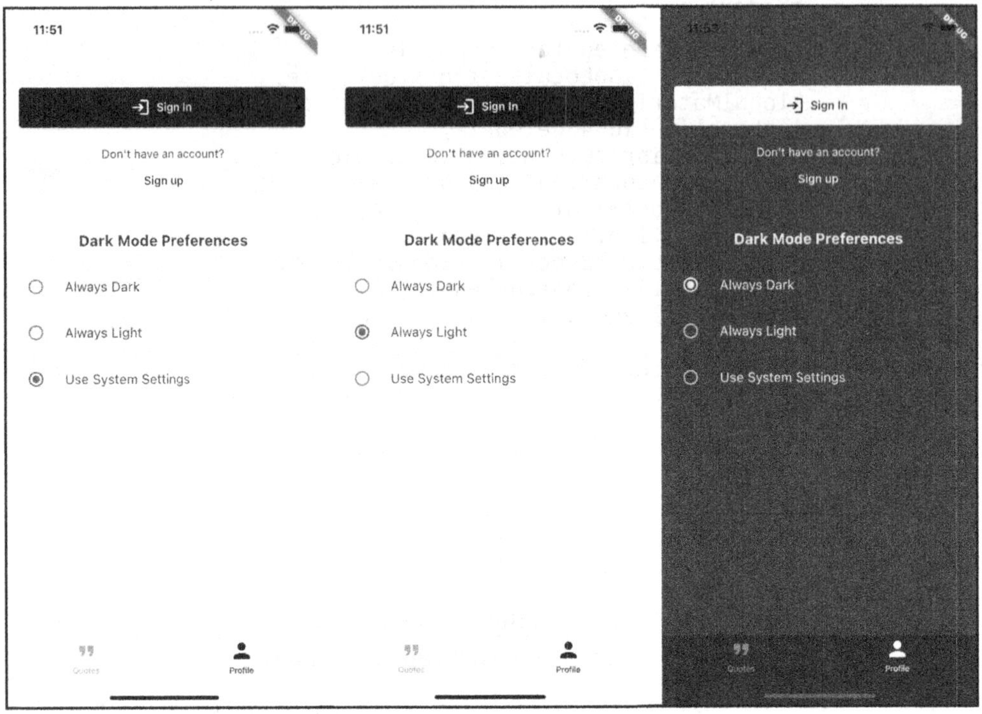

# Key Points

- Flutter offers a built-in solution for theming your app.
- Many other third-party theming solutions might work well for your project.
- You can implement a custom theme with the help of `InheritedWidget`.
- Usually, you want to support three different theme modes: **light**, **dark** and **system**.
- To hold the current theme mode preference, use `BehaviorSubject`. This provides you with a stream you can listen to for changes.
- To provide a great user experience, save the current theme mode preference in the local storage with the help of the **Hive** package.

# Where to Go From Here?

As already mentioned, it's important to be aware that you always have multiple options to achieve a specific goal or functionality. As you gain more and more knowledge, and therefore, become more and more experienced in Flutter development, it's important to consider this fact. Based on the requirements of your specific problem, you should use the solution that'll work best for you. Therefore, this chapter offers you a few different options for dealing with theming in your Flutter app. In the case of WonderWords, theming with the help of `InheritedWidget` works best, as it offers the most adjustability. In some other scenario, this might be too complicated of a solution, and therefore, it would just waste your time to implement it.

Flutter theming has quite a few other approaches that haven't been explained in this chapter, so feel free to dive deeper into the topic and explore other third-party solutions. You can also go through the WonderWords project and try to find instances of styles or colors that you can add to your theme.

# Chapter 11: Creating Your Own Widget Catalog

By Vid Palčar

By now, you're probably well aware that Flutter is all about the widgets. In the past few chapters, you've seen that a specific project can consist of hundreds — even thousands — of widgets, which can quickly get out of control. In this chapter, you'll learn about efficiently managing and maintaining all the widgets in real-world projects.

Duplicating your code *seems* to save you time... until you need to make a change. Now, you need to find *all* the places you used that code and make the changes over and over again. And if you miss any, it could cause serious and hard-to-diagnose problems. Flutter, on the other hand, lets you write a widget once, reuse it throughout your code, and have just one place to make any necessary changes. Easy!

Reusing already-created widgets can save you a lot of time and effort when creating and maintaining your projects. Many teams reuse widgets not only within a project, but even across numerous apps. That practice allows you to keep maintenance efforts low and makes the process of unifying the brand identity over multiple projects easier than ever. Having a **component library** with a **storybook** can be an invaluable tool for reusability of UI components. Although the two terms are often used interchangeably, you'll learn about the differences between them.

A component library is a package that consists of fairly small components: widgets. You use these widgets as building blocks when creating custom UIs across one or multiple apps. A storybook, on the other hand, allows you to present the components you've built to your fellow team members, product managers and designers. It allows them to better understand how a specific component/widget will render across multiple devices and orientations.

Since a component library is a separate package, you can easily use it in multiple products or share it with the world by publishing it to pub.dev. You can even add an example app to it. In your case, this storybook will run across multiple devices as a standalone app.

In this chapter, you'll learn:

- Reasons you need a component library and storybook.
- How to create a reusable component and add it to the component library.
- How to add a standalone example app to a package.
- The basic structure of a storybook.
- How to customize a storybook.

Throughout this chapter, you'll work on the **starter** project from this chapter's **assets** folder.

## Why Do You Need a Component Library?

You might be familiar with object-oriented programming (OOP), and widgets are one of the ways to implement it in Flutter. Taking it one step further, component libraries are a real-world approach to taking OOP across modules, apps, organizations and the external world.

Each component/widget in the component library acts like a small building block that you can use to create a more complex custom UI implementation. Breaking code into smaller components allows you to apply quick modifications to the UI with minimal effort. Remember the pain of reimplementing a component — or even a screen — for the fifth time because the design team came up with a brilliant new idea *again*?

Rather than going through all the appearances of the design feature in your app, you only have to modify a specific attribute of the widget or simply replace it with a new one. In no time, you're back on track — working on things that really matter.

Furthermore, a single widget for a specific purpose in the app gives the feeling of consistency in the design language. That increases the overall UI quality, which reflects higher user satisfaction.

## Customizing a Specific Component

Now that you have a better understanding of what a component library is, it's time to look at how you implement reusable components in the WonderWords app. Open the starter project and run the app. In the app, navigate to the login screen and look at the design of the **Sign In** button:

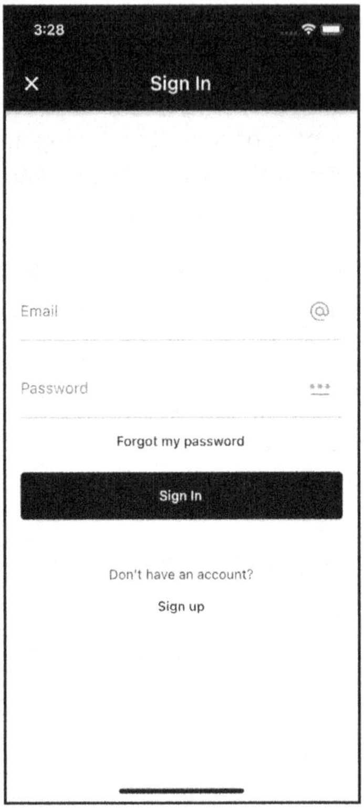


> **Note**: If you're having trouble running the app, you might have forgotten to propagate the configurations you did in the first chapter's starter project to the following chapters' materials. If that's the case, please revisit Chapter 1, "Setting up Your Environment".

You've probably noticed that this button looks quite boring. To spice up the UI, you'll add a simple icon to the button to further inform the user about this button's function.

All the reusable components for WonderWords are part of the internal package called **components_library**. This package is the component library for your app. Open the starter project from the **projects** folder of this chapter's downloaded assets. Navigate to the **expanded_elevated_button.dart** located in the **src** folder, which is a subfolder of **lib** in the **component_library** package.

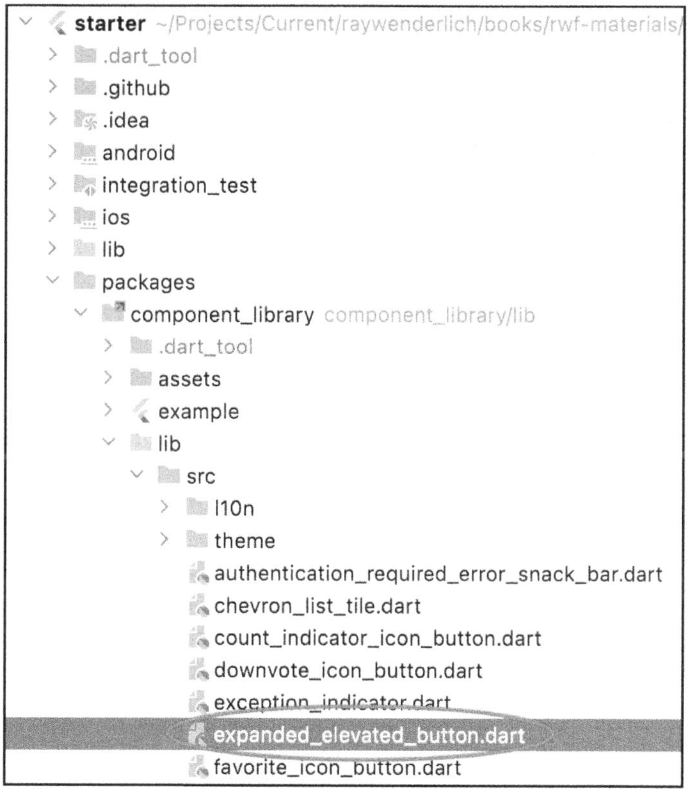

Locate `// TODO: replace child with button with icon` in the file, and replace `Widget`'s child — the current implementation of `ElevatedButton` with the following code:

```
// 1
child: icon != null
    // 2
    ? ElevatedButton.icon(
        onPressed: onTap,
        label: Text(
          label,
        ),
        icon: icon,
      )
    // 3
    : ElevatedButton(
        onPressed: onTap,
        child: Text(
          label,
        ),
      ),
```

Here's what the code above does:

1. Checks that `icon` is not null.
2. Returns `ElevatedButton.icon` if that icon isn't null, which takes `icon` as an attribute.
3. If `icon` wasn't provided to the widget as an attribute, it returns `ElevatedButton` without `icon`.

Now that you've changed the button, hot reload the app:

Go through the app and try to find other appearances of the same button component. You'll find one in the **Profile** tab, and you can see it's been updated accordingly. Now, you have a better idea of the power of using reusable components with a component library.

## Adding Components to the Component Library

Go to **quote_details_screen.dart** located in **features/quote_details/lib/src**, and look at the following code snippet for a moment:

```
// TODO: replace with centered circular progress indicator
const Center(
    child: CircularProgressIndicator(),
  ),
```

Now, go to **update_profile_screen.dart** located in **features/update_profile/lib/src** or go to **profile_menu_screen.dart** in **features/profile_menu/lib/src**, and you'll find almost the same code as above:

```
// TODO: replace with centered circular progress indicator
return const Center(
  child: CircularProgressIndicator(),
),
```

You know from the theory you've already learned that repeating the same snippet of code in multiple places isn't a good approach to writing reusable code. This is why you'll try to isolate the code snippet above into a reusable component in the component library.

Go to the **src** folder in the **component_library** package. Create a new file, name it **centered_circular_progress_indicator.dart**, and paste the following code snippet into the file:

```
import 'package:flutter/material.dart';

class CenteredCircularProgressIndicator extends StatelessWidget
{
  const CenteredCircularProgressIndicator({Key? key}) :
super(key: key);

  @override
  Widget build(BuildContext context) {
    return const Center(
      child: CircularProgressIndicator(),
    );
  }
}
```

With that code, you created a new component that positions the `CircularProgressIndicator` in the center of the screen. Next, replace `// TODO: export central circular progress indicator` with the following code snippet in **component_library.dart** located in the root of the **component_library** package:

```
export 'src/centered_circular_progress_indicator.dart';
```

Now that you've exported your new component, you'll be able to use it by importing the **component_library** package in other packages and the app itself. Lastly, you have to replace the repetitive code in the files listed above. Locate `// TODO: replace with centered circular progress indicator` in **quote_details_screen.dart**, and replace the code below the comment with:

```
const CenteredCircularProgressIndicator(),
```

Also, open **update_profile_screen.dart** and **profile_menu_screen.dart** files and replace the code below the `// TODO: replace with centered circular progress indicator` comment with:

```
return const CenteredCircularProgressIndicator();
```

It doesn't seem like a huge change. There's no visible difference in the app's UI or performance, but if the UI changes in the future, fixing the `CircularProgressIndicator` position might save you a lot of time.

# Why Do You Need a Storybook?

In learning about the component library, you've learned a good practice of writing maintainable, reusable code. But now, imagine the following situation: Suppose you have to build a new feature. To avoid duplicating the code, you have to check whether you or your fellow team members have already implemented a specific design feature. That can get very time-consuming as the project grows. By using a storybook, you can check if the specific component already exists as part of the **components_library** package, as well as modify some of its attributes to make sure it fulfills all the design requirements. You can also see widgets in different form factors as well as dark and light mode appearances in the cases when you've defined it for your widgets.

> **Note**: To get the most out of a storybook, you need to be aware of these good practices:
>
> 1.) Before creating a widget, always refer to the storybook.
>
> 2.) When you update a widget, update the storybook as well.

## Adding a Storybook to a Flutter App

A few open-source solutions (https://pub.dev/packages?q=storybook+flutter) allow you to add a customizable storybook to your component library. In this chapter, you'll use storybook_flutter (https://pub.dev/packages/storybook_flutter), as it stands out with the support of multiple features, such as **localization**, **dark mode**, **device previews** and others. It also has a **knob panel**, which allows you to adjust predefined attributes of a specific widget when testing it in real time.

> **Note**: In the starter project, the **component_library** package already has an **example** folder that contains **pubspec.yaml** and **analysis_options.yaml** files. To better understand the purpose of the example folder in an individual package, look at the "Creating an Example Project" section in Creating and Publishing a Flutter Package (https://www.raywenderlich.com/19421827-creating-and-publishing-a-flutter-package#toc-anchor-014).

Navigate to **pubspec.yaml** under the **component_library**'s **example** folder, and you'll see that storybook has already been added into the example project for you:

```
storybook_flutter: ^0.8.0
```

> **Note**: From now on, you'll only work on **component_library**'s **example** folder, so every file or folder mentioned in this chapter is contained in that folder.

## Basic Structure of Storybook UI

To give you a sneak preview and better understanding of the topic, here's what the WonderWords storybook will look like at the end of this chapter after running it in the browser:

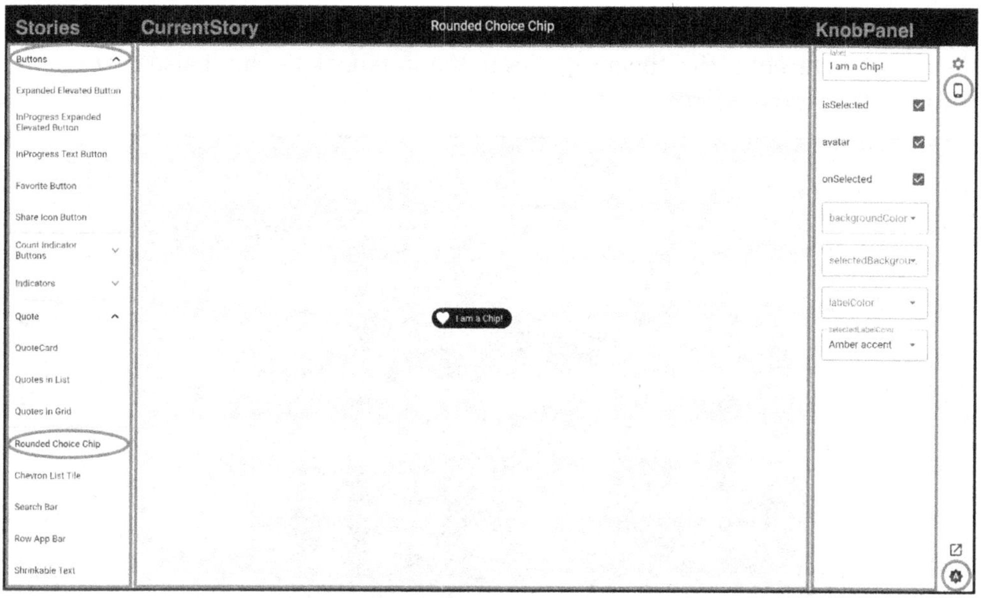


At first glance, the UI can look a bit confusing. It has a flood of tiles and strange controls, but when you take a proper look at it, everything starts to make sense.

Here's the explanation of the UI above. On the left side is a **Stories** panel, which consists of stories — or components — and story sections. For example, **Buttons** is the name of a section that can expand to a list of all buttons that exist in your **component_library** package. On the other hand, **Rounded Choice Chip** isn't part of any component group. In other words, it's not part of an expandable list.

In the middle is the **CurrentStory** panel, which shows the currently selected story.

To the right of the **CurrentStory** panel is the **KnobPanel**, which allows you to adjust the parameters and appearance of the currently displayed story.

Lastly, on the far right side is a sidebar for **device preview** selection and **theming** appearance toggling.

## Device Preview and Theming

In the image above, the top circled icon on the right enables you to show the current story in a device preview. You can select a device from a predefined set of devices and change its orientation.

The bottom-most circled icon is to toggle between light, dark or system default themes. The current active theme applies to the storybook UI, but it also changes the theme of the current story:

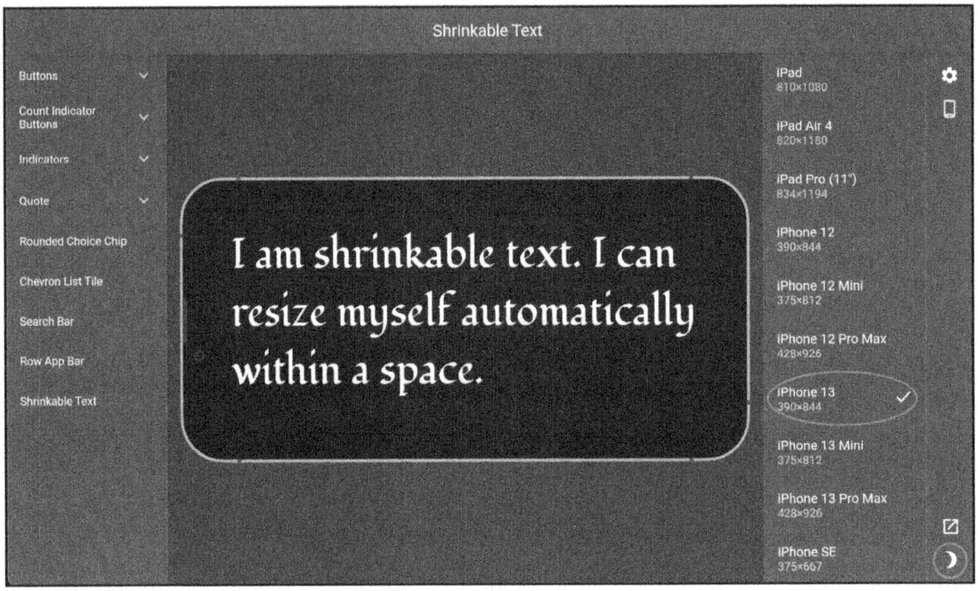


The image above is an example where dark mode is active, and the preview device is an **iPhone 13**. Isn't it fascinating having a preview device inside a browser?

You should now have a better understanding of the importance of being able to see and test different configurations of a specific widget across various devices, orientations, theme modes and even localization before even referencing them in an actual project.

## Storybook UI on a Mobile App

You already know that you can run the storybook on all three main platforms supported by Flutter: iOS, Android and web. All the storybook panels are also present on its mobile version, with the layout adjusting to the smaller screen size. Check it out:

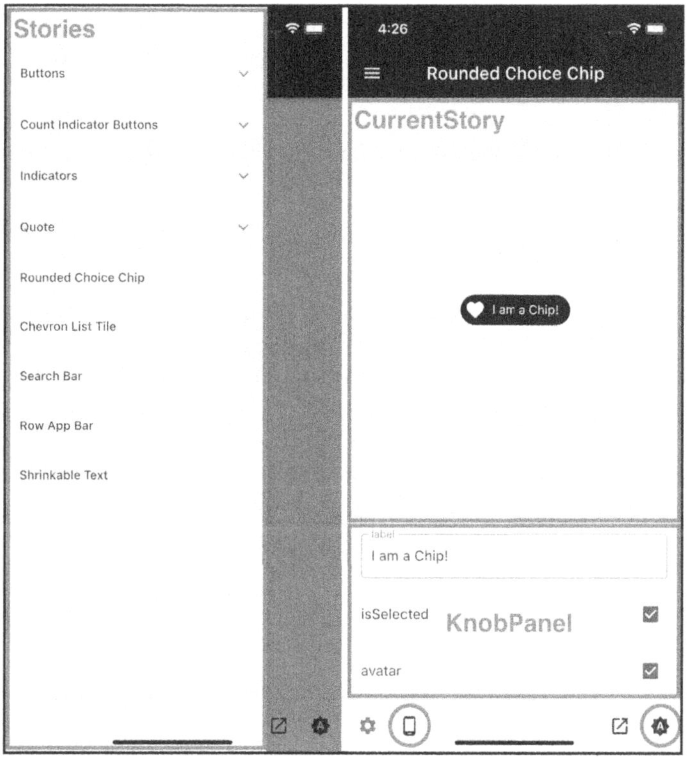


You only need to do one step before you can run the storybook on your own — and also eventually publish it to the Google Play Store, Apple Store or host it on the web. You have to add platform-specific files to your **components_library**'s **example** folder so it can run as a standalone app.

## Making the Storybook App Runnable

In the terminal, navigate to the **example** folder of **component_library** with the following command:

```
$ cd packages/component_library/example
```

Try to run the app by pasting the following command into the terminal:

```
$ flutter run
```

Did you notice anything strange about it? You probably weren't successful, and it returned the following stack:

```
Target file "lib/main.dart" not found.
```

If you think about that for a moment, it makes total sense. The **example** folder isn't a Flutter app yet, as it doesn't include the **main.dart** file. By running the `flutter run` command, Flutter tries to find the **main.dart** file and run the `main()` method located in that file. So, to run the app, you have to create one.

Navigate to the **lib** folder, create a new file named **main.dart**, and add the following content:

```
import 'package:flutter/material.dart';
// TODO: add missing import

void main() {
  runApp(
    // TODO: replace the MaterialApp placeholder later
    MaterialApp(
      home: Container(color: Colors.grey),
    ),
  );
}
```

The code above uses `Container` as a placeholder and will be replaced later with the `StoryApp` widget.

Try to execute `flutter run` again, and make sure Chrome, iOS Simulator or Android Emulator is running. See if you're more successful this time.

By trying to run the app again, you'll receive the following stack:

```
No supported devices connected.
The following devices were found, but are not supported by this
project:
sdk gphone64 arm64 (mobile) • emulator-5554 • android-arm64   •
Android 13 (API 33) (emulator)
macOS (desktop)             • macos         • darwin-arm64    •
macOS 12.6 21G115 darwin-arm
Chrome (web)                • chrome        • web-javascript •
Google Chrome 105.0.5195.125
If you would like your app to run on android or macos or web,
consider running `flutter create .` to generate projects
for these platforms.
```

**Note**: The actual terminal output is much longer than the output above. This output is trimmed to make it more readable and understandable.

From the output, you can see that even though all three devices are connected, the app doesn't run because the package doesn't contain **android**, **ios** or **web** folders. To fix this, run `flutter create .` in the terminal. You'll get the following output:

```
Recreating project ...
...
...
Wrote 122 files.

All done!

In order to run your application, type:

  $ cd .
  $ flutter run

Your application code is in ./lib/main.dart.
```

**Note**: Again, for better readability, the previously created files were replaced with `....`

As a result, you'll be able to find the **android**, **ios** and **web** folders located in the **example** folder:

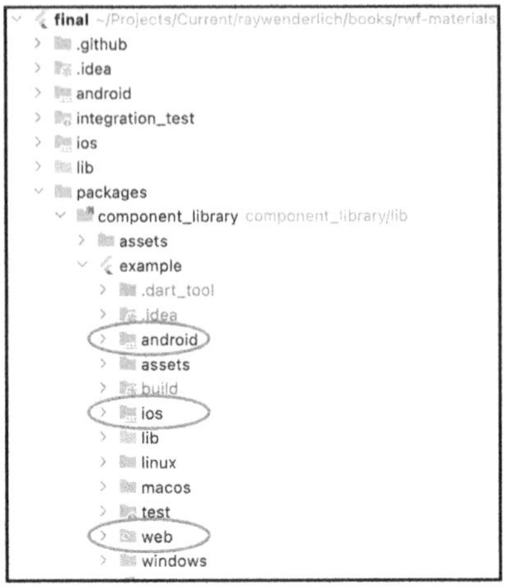


> **Note**: Additionally, there were also **macos**, **windows** and **linux** folders generated, but you won't use them in this example.

Now, for the last time, execute `flutter run`, and you'll see the app successfully run on any of the supported devices:

# Understanding Component Storybook

Now that you can successfully run the storybook app, you'll inspect what the source code from the **lib** folder does. First, open **component_storybook.dart** and look at the `build()` method of a `ComponentStorybook` widget. In the next few subsections, you'll learn how to configure a storybook for your needs.

## Specifying Stories and an Initial Story

As mentioned, a storybook is a collection of stories — or components — put together in an organized order. Take a closer look at its only required attribute, `children`, and the `initialRoute` attribute:

```
// 1
children: [
  ...getStories(theme),
],
// 2
initialRoute: 'rounded-choice-chip',
```

Here's what this code does:

1. The `children` attribute gets a `List<Story>`. You'll learn about the `Story` widget in detail in the next section. The `getStories()` method is present in the **stories.dart** file in the **lib** folder. It's better to keep the stories in a separate file to avoid duplicating them when you decide to add a `CustomStorybook` in addition to the default storybook.

> **Note**: The following section will further explain the `theme` argument.

2. The **flutter_storybook** library converts the `Story`'s name to hyphen-separated lowercase words. For example, if you specify the `Story`'s name as `Rounded Choice Chip`, its route becomes `rounded-choice-chip`. By giving `initialRoute`, you ensure a *specific* story is the current story. If you don't set `initialRoute`, you see a **Select story** message.

## Specifying Themes

The first two attributes of the storybook widget are `theme` and `darkTheme`:

```
@override
Widget build(BuildContext context) {
  // 1
  final theme = WonderTheme.of(context);
  return Storybook(
    // 2
    theme: lightThemeData,
    // 3
    darkTheme: darkThemeData,
    // TODO: add localization delegates
    children: [
      ...getStories(theme),
    ],
  );
}
```

Here's what the code above does:

1. Fetches the `WonderTheme` instance from ancestors. You'll provide `WonderTheme` from **main.dart** later.
2. Provides light and dark themes to the storybook. The storybook's widget also allows you to specify `themeMode`, which is set to `ThemeMode.system` by default.
3. Provides the stories with `theme`. Using the `WonderTheme` instance from ancestors in the storybook ensures that `theme` is unified across your main app and the storybook app.

## Specifying Localization

Next, you have to locate the `localizationDelegates` attribute in the storybook widget by replacing `// TODO: add localization delegates` with the following code snippet:

```
localizationDelegates: const [
  GlobalMaterialLocalizations.delegate,
  GlobalWidgetsLocalizations.delegate,
  GlobalCupertinoLocalizations.delegate,
  ComponentLibraryLocalizations.delegate,
],
```

Recall what you learned in Chapter 9, "Internationalizing & Localizing". Since this is a component storybook, you only need `ComponentLibraryLocalizations.delegate` along with the default ones.

# Applying StoryApp to runApp() Methods

Lastly, replace `// TODO: replace the MaterialApp placeholder later` in **main.dart**'s `StoryApp` with:

```
StoryApp()
```

Here, `StoryApp`, available in **story_app.dart**, is another widget that builds `WonderTheme`, much like the root-level **main.dart** file. Don't forget to import a missing import at the top of the file by replacing `// TODO: add missing import` with the following code:

```
import 'package:component_library_storybook/story_app.dart';
```

This is how your **main.dart** file should look like when you've applied those changes:

```
import 'package:component_library_storybook/story_app.dart';
import 'package:flutter/material.dart';

void main() {
  runApp(StoryApp());
}
```

Take a look at how `StoryApp` builds `WonderTheme` in the **story_app.dart** file:

```
@override
  Widget build(BuildContext context) {
    return WonderTheme(
      lightTheme: _lightTheme,
      darkTheme: _darkTheme,
      child: ComponentStorybook(
        lightThemeData: _lightTheme.materialThemeData,
        darkThemeData: _darkTheme.materialThemeData,
      ),
    );
  }
```

The `build()` method of the `StoryApp` widget returns the `WonderTheme` widget, which takes `lightTheme`, `darkTheme` and `child` as an argument. By wrapping `ComponentStorybook` with the `WonderTheme` widget, you ensure that you can get the current theme's instance using `WonderTheme.of(context)`. This enables dynamic changing of the theme per the currently active theme.

Build and run the storybook app on mobile to get the following screen:

Now that you've learned about storybook customizations, it's time to learn how to configure the most important element of a storybook — a story.

# Understanding a Story

You can create a `Story` a couple different ways — a **simple story** and a **complex story**. Choosing the right way varies from case to case, and it's important from the perspective of how informative your `Story` will be for the end user. In the case of `Storybook`, the end user might be a fellow developer, your lead UI designer or even a client. So, it has to be as configurable as possible.

# Defining a Simple Story

A `simple Story` is used in cases when the widget/component has no configuration options. You can figure out whether a specific widget should have configuration options by looking at its attributes. For example, among all the widgets present in **component_library**, `ShareIconButton`, `LoadingIndicator`, `SearchBar` and `RowAppBar` are simple widgets. Such widgets don't have any attributes that would define the way they should render.

Now, it's time to create a `simple Story`. Open **stories.dart** in the **lib** folder, copy the following code snippet, and replace `// TODO: Add Simple Expanded Elevated Button Story here` with:

```
// 1
Story.simple(
  name: 'Simple Expanded Elevated Button',
  section: 'Buttons',
  // 2
  child: ExpandedElevatedButton(
    label: 'Press me',
    onTap: () {},
  ),
  // TODO: add additional attributes to the story later
),
```

The code above:

1. Uses `simple` named constructor and provides a name and `section` to the `Story`. This name becomes the `title` of `ListTile` in the stories list, and `section` becomes the `title` of the `ExpansionTile`.
2. As `child`, you provide the widget you want to show in the storybook. In this specific example, this widget is `ExpandedElevatedButton`, which has two required attributes.

`name` and `child` are the only required attributes of a `simple Story` widget, but you can also provide some other customization attributes, such as `padding` and `background`. Replace `// TODO: add additional attributes to the story later` in the file above with the following code:

```
padding: const EdgeInsets.all(64.0),
background: Colors.cyanAccent,
```

Apply those two additional attributes and hot reload the app. Navigate to **Simple Expanded Elevated Button** located in the **Buttons** section by expending the side drawer hidden in the menu. You'll see the difference, as shown below. The first screen shows the implementation of `simple Story` without additional attributes, and the second screen shows the implementation of `simple Story` with additional attributes from above:

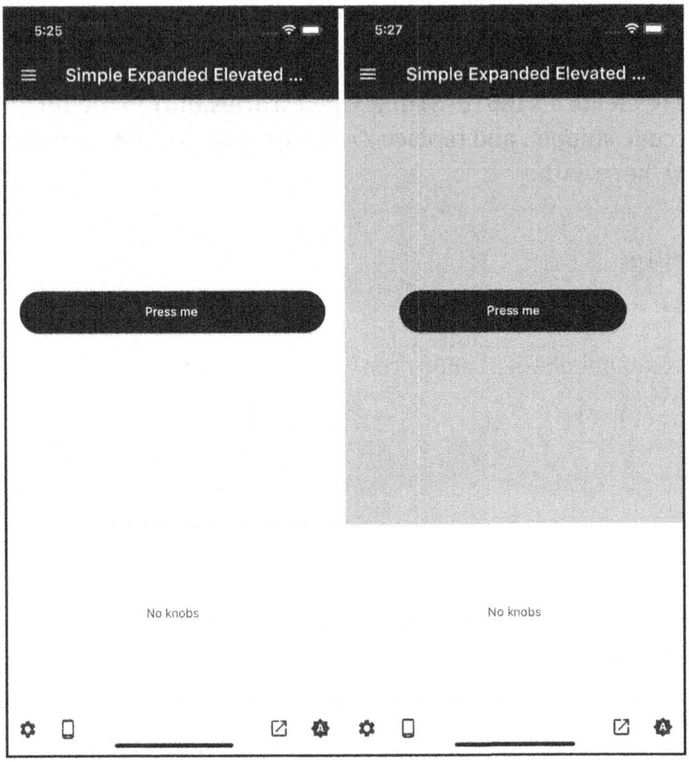


# Defining a Complex Story

`complex Story` isn't much different from `simple Story`. The only difference between the two is that `complex Story` uses `builder` instead of `child`. Using `builder` enables you to configure the knob panel for a widget. For example, look at the `ExpandedElevatedButton` widget that has the following fields:

```
final String label;
final VoidCallback? onTap;
final Widget? icon;
```

From the code above, you can see that `ExpandedElevatedButton` is much more configurable than the widgets listed above. It allows you to specify `label`, `onTap` and `icon`.

Getting back to your implementation of `simple Story`, you can see that it doesn't allow you to configure it. Here are two main disadvantages that you face by not configuring the story when this is possible:

1. When, as a developer, you're looking for a widget that you can provide with a custom label, `RoundedChoiceChip` looks useless, although it has a configurable `label`.
2. You don't get a good overview of what you can configure in a specific widget, which makes you visit the codebase. This completely devalues having a storybook in the first place.

To better understand how you offer the configuration options for the components, paste the following code snippet below your implementation of the `simple Story` for `ExpandedElevatedButton` and replace `// TODO: Add Complex Expanded Elevated Button Story here` with:

```
Story(
  name: 'Expanded Elevated Button',
  section: 'Buttons',
  builder: (_, k) => ExpandedElevatedButton(
    label: k.text(
      label: 'label',
      initial: 'Press me',
    ),
    onTap: k.boolean(
      label: 'onTap',
      initial: true,
    )
        ? () {}
        : null,
    icon: Icon(
      k.options(
      label: 'icon',
        initial: Icons.home,
        options: const [
          Option(
            'Login',
            Icons.login,
          ),
          Option(
            'Refresh',
            Icons.refresh,
          ),
          Option(
```

```
                'Logout',
                Icons.logout,
              ),
            ],
          ),
        ),
      ),
    ),
```

In the code above, you use `builder` instead of `child`, which will add the knob options to this specific widget/story. `builder` is a type of `StoryBuilder`, which is used by `BuildContext` and `KnobsBuilder` to build the story. `KnobsBuilder` allows you to configure simple data types such as `bool`, `string`, `int` and `double`, as well as any other custom data type. The code above will be explained in the following paragraphs.

### Adding a Knob for Text

Now, you'll take the `RoundedChoiceChip` story in the **stories.dart** file as a reference. You might notice it has a `k.text` method:

```
label: k.text(
  // 1
  label: 'label',
  // 2
  initial: 'I am a Chip!',
),
```

This method:

1. Provides a `label` to the text field for the knobs panel.
2. Gives an `initial` value to the text field.

As a result, notice the presence of a `TextField` in the knobs panel:

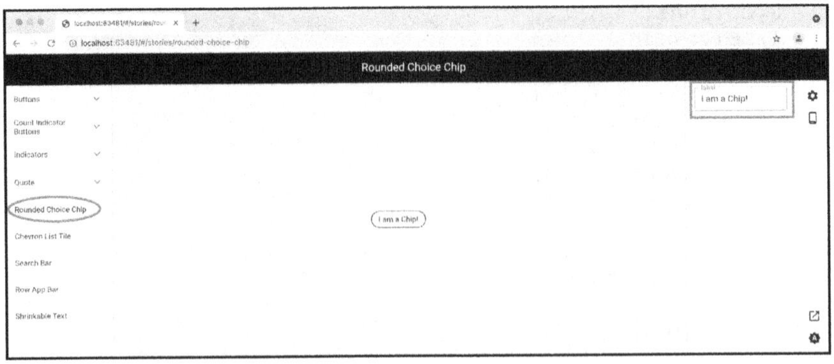

## Adding a Knob for a Boolean

In the same `RoundedChoiceChip` story, also notice a `k.boolean` method:

```
isSelected: k.boolean(label: 'isSelected', initial: false),
```

Since `RoundedChoiceChip` also has the `isSelected` attribute, which requires a Boolean value, you can use the `k.boolean` method. In the code sample above, this value is initially set to `false`. As a result, the knob panel has a field in the form of `CheckBox`, which enables you to change a value:

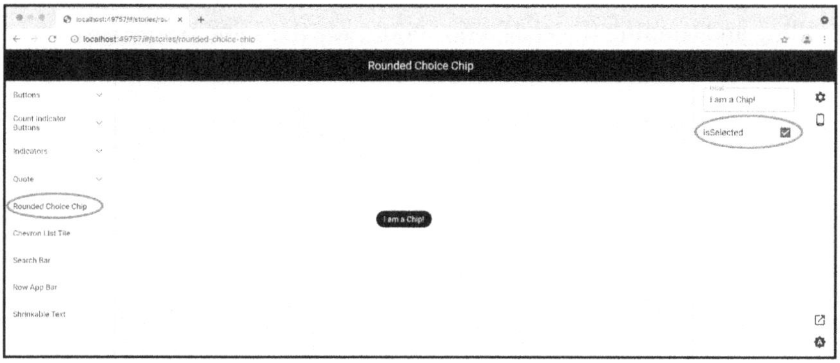


## Adding a Knob for int or double

Look at storybook on your mobile simulator or in your browser, and locate the **Upvote Icon Button** story under the **Counter Indicator Buttons** tile in the app. Go to the knob panel, and you'll see a slider to change the vote count. That's the knob for the `int` or `double` type field:

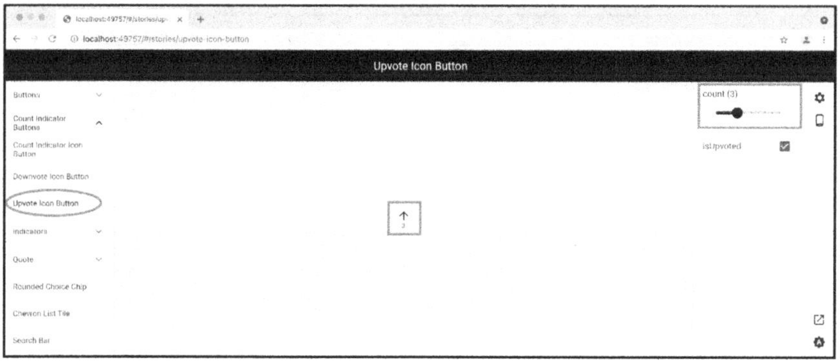

You can achieve this by adding the following implementation of `k.sliderInt` to the `UpvoteIconButton` story by replacing `// TODO: replace with implementation of int knob` located in **stories.dart** with the following code snippet:

```
count: k.sliderInt(
  label: 'count',
  max: 10,
  min: 0,
  initial: 0,
  divisions: 9,
),
```

After building and running the code, you should see the same result as shown in the image above.

Of all the offered parameters, `label` is the only one required. The rest are optional, whereas `max` defaults to 100 with as many divisions.

Take a look at how you can very similarly use `k.slider` for `double` values as follows:

```
k.slider(
  label: 'count',
  max: 10,
  min: 0,
  initial: 0,
),
```

For `double` values, you can't specify `divisions` because it's restricted in this library. But, if you're curious to add it, feel free to create an issue and raise a pull request for the package. The output of `slider` with and without divisions is shown in the images below:

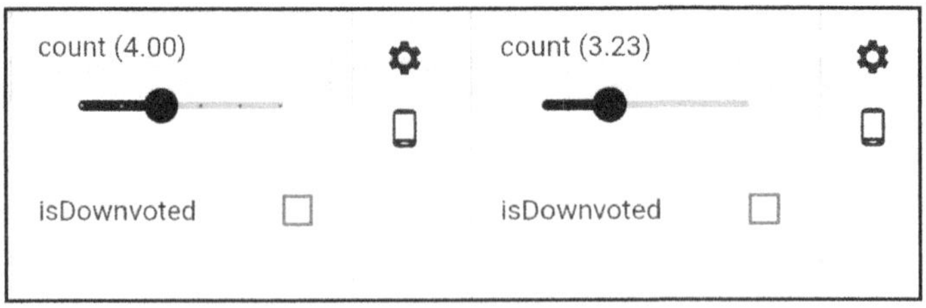

## Adding a Knob for Custom Types

So far, you've seen how to add knobs for primitive data types. Now, it's time to learn about the wildcard knob, which you can use for any custom type. Look back at the example of `RoundedChoiceChip`, which has customizable colors. The `color` type isn't a primitive Dart data type. In such scenarios, you should use `k.options`, as shown below:

```
backgroundColor: k.options(
  label: 'backgroundColor',
  initial: null,
  options: const [
    Option('Light blue', Colors.lightBlue),
    Option('Red accent', Colors.redAccent),
  ],
),
```

In the code above, using the `option` parameter, you can specify an infinite number of colors to select for the background color of the chip. As a result, a drop-down in the knob panel has the specified colors you can choose from. A `null` initial value ensures that there's no default value from options for background color:

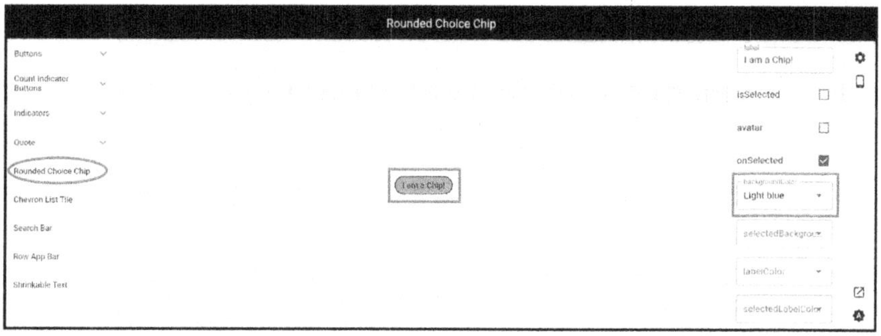


That's a deal-breaker, isn't it? However, the `k.options` method enables the storybook to be more configurable.

## Custom Wrapper for a Story

The storybook has one more customization option worth mentioning. You can add a custom wrapper to every single `Story` widget using `wrapperBuilder` for `Story`. So, suppose you want to see how the `QuoteCard` widget renders itself in `ListView`. You can easily achieve this by using `wrapperBuilder` here. Add the following code snippet to a complex `Story` with `Quotes in List` in **stories.dart**. To locate it easier, search for `// TODO: add wrapper builder for quotes list`:

```
// 1
wrapperBuilder: (context, story, child) => Padding(
  padding: const EdgeInsets.all(8.0),
  child: ListView.separated(
    itemCount: 15,
    // 2
    itemBuilder: (_, __) => child,
    separatorBuilder: (_, __) => const Divider(height: 16.0),
  ),
),
```

Here's what the code above does:

1. Wraps the `QuoteCard` in `ListView` with 15 items.
2. The widget returned by `builder` is the initial `child`.

When you run the app on a mobile device and select **Quotes in List** or **Quotes in Grid** in a side drawer, you'll see the output shown below:

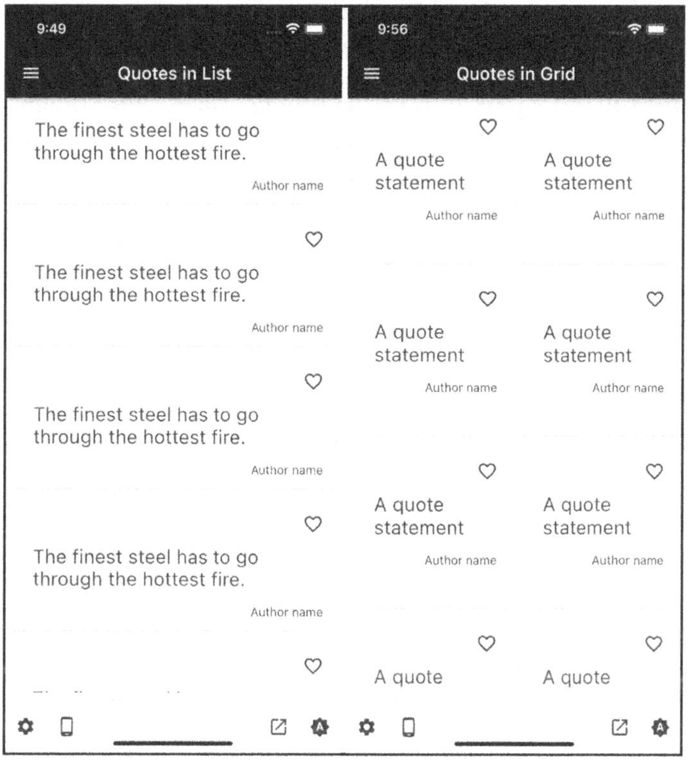

# Challenge

You accomplished a lot in getting through this chapter, and this is an excellent opportunity for you to test your knowledge.

Go to **stories.dart** in the starter project and find `// TODO: Challenge`. Add a new story for the `Downvote Icon Button` component and make all its attributes configurable in the knob panel. You can check your solution with the one in the challenge project.

# Key Points

- A **storybook** is a visual representation of the **component library**.
- A storybook can be a separate app or an integral part of your main app.
- Use the `flutter create .` command to add platform-specific folders.
- Configure the **knob panel** for fields you feel the user would like to change and test.

# Chapter 12: Supporting the Development Lifecycle With Firebase

By Vid Palčar

You've gotten through the first 11 chapters, and you've finished your app — well done! You've set up the data layer, written the app's business logic, spiced up the UI, and created custom components and packages. Just distribute it among the people, and your WonderWords app will be a hit.

But not so fast!

App development is an ongoing process that never stops. Once you finish the first version of your app, you must monitor its performance. Besides adding new features, you'll have to release new versions of the app to improve users' experience. This might be some UI and UX changes, adding a new feature or removing confusing ones, or just resolutions of the bugs that your QA team missed when testing the app.

Here, you might ask yourself how you can know what changes are required to make your app even better. Well, you have to monitor users' engagement with the specific features of the app as well as analyze their interaction with the app. You might want to track the app's crashes when users discover some side case you hadn't thought about. Or, maybe you'll have to run a few tests in your user group without necessarily releasing a new version of the app.

When dealing with these types of issues, **Firebase** can come in very handy. You've probably already heard a lot about Firebase. In this chapter, you'll look at a few tools you might not be very familiar with, but are essential in almost any real-world app. Those tools are Firebase **Analytics** and **Crashlytics**.

Firebase Analytics lets you understand information about your app's users, including:

- Which features of your app they use the most or least.
- How much time they spend on your app.
- Where they come from.
- Which devices they use.

By adding Firebase Crashlytics to your project, you may discover hidden issues in the app that you need to resolve immediately. Crashlytics does this by providing you with the record and stacktrace of an error or crash.

In this chapter, you'll learn how to:

- Add analytics on-screen view events.
- Record crashes and non-fatal errors.

Throughout this chapter, you'll work on the starter project from this chapter's **assets** folder.

# Firebase Analytics

Getting back to Chapter 1, "Setting up Your Environment", you might remember adding Firebase to the WonderWords app. When you finally added all the necessary files to the project, you might've taken a sneak peek into the Firebase Analytics console. If so, you'll remember that it offers a bunch of cool information about your audience. But in this section, you'll focus primarily on capturing a **screen_view** event when users visit a specific screen in the app.

**screen_view** is one of the predefined events in Firebase Analytics, although it enables you to define custom events as well. A **screen_view** event occurs when the user visits a screen in your app.

But before continuing, you'll look at some useful information that Firebase Analytics tracks for you automatically when you add it to your project. To check your behavior in the app, run WonderWords.

> **Note**: If you're having trouble running the app, you might have forgotten to propagate the configurations you did in the first chapter's starter project to the following chapters' materials. If that's the case, please revisit Chapter 1, "Setting up Your Environment".

Go to Firebase console (https://console.firebase.google.com/) and navigate to **Analytics ▸ Dashboard** from the left-side menu. The Dashboard shows various eye-catching graphs and analyses recorded automatically by Firebase Analytics when users run your app. Here are a few that will be the most relevant for you:

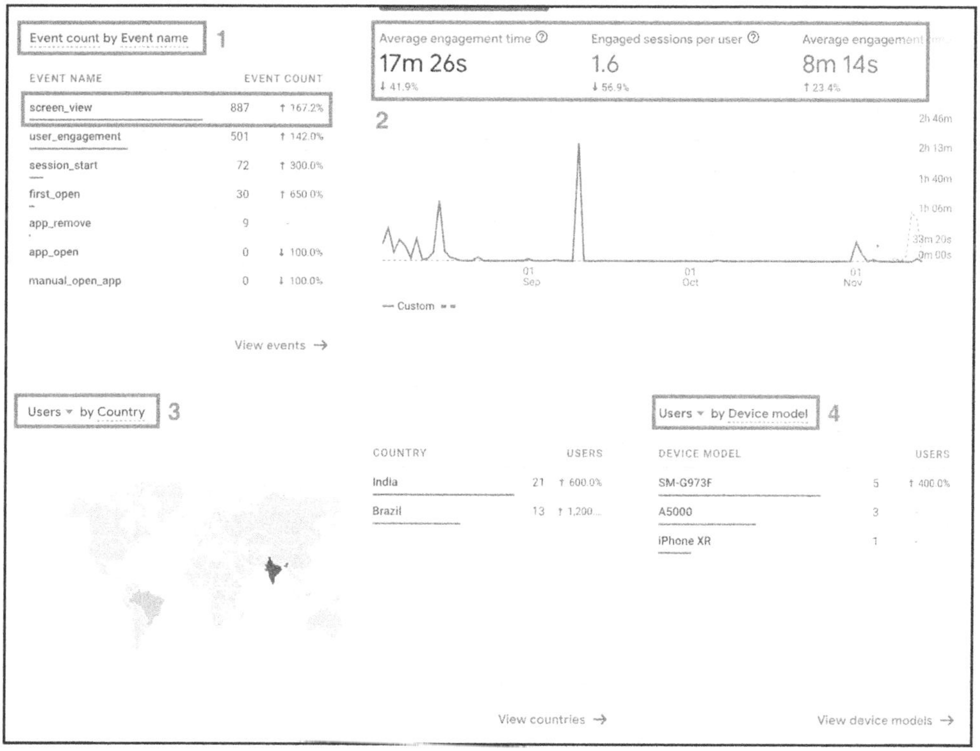

Going through the selected information panels in the previous image, you can see:

1. The first information panel, at the top-left, shows event counts for all users in descending order of their occurrence. The most interesting information for you in this section will be the **screen_view** event. By drilling down further into it, you can see which screens are most used by your users — but more about that later.
2. The second graph represents the recent average engagement time.
3. The third representation is a demographical view of user base distribution across countries.
4. The fourth shows a count of users who've installed the app on a specific device model.

Besides the useful information highlighted here, the Dashboard also has a lot more, such as user activity over time, users by app versions, user retention, revenue statistics, etc.

> **Note**: As soon as you add Firebase Analytics dependency in the project, it starts recording all this data automatically. This won't be the case for a few types of information, such as the **screen_view** event, which you have to implement separately. Note that the data in your console will be different from what you may see in the image above.

Next, click **screen_view** on the Firebase Analytics page to see the user engagement per screen in the app. Scroll farther down and locate the **User engagement** card.

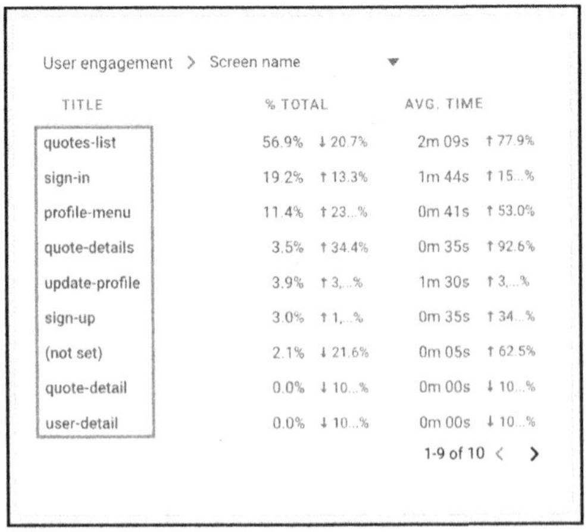

Compare the names listed in the **TITLE** column with the ones defined in the **lib/routing_table.dart** file. You can see that they match. All the titles are the names of `MaterialPages` in the `Routes` class. From the **% TOTAL** column, you can see that users use the **quotes-list** screen as much as they use all the other screens combined. You can also see the average time they spend on every single one of the pages. This small but meaningful information can help you determine which feature or screen your users spend the most time on. Using this analysis to enhance highly used features can be a great business strategy, especially when thinking about monetizing the app.

As you have a better overview of what Firebase Analytics offers, it's time to jump into its implementation in the app.

# Adding Firebase Analytics

Open **lib/routing_table.dart** at the root of the project:

Refer to the screen names in the `buildRoutingTable` function:

```
MaterialPage(
  name: 'quotes-list'
  ...
)

MaterialPage(
  name: 'profile-menu'
  ...
)
```

Once again, notice the name attribute for MaterialPage. In the buildRoutingTable function, you'll notice definitions for all MaterialPages, which, in other words, are all screens in the app. You'll use these names as unique identifiers for screens when capturing the **screen_view** event.

# Modifying ScreenViewObserver

WonderWords uses the Routemaster (https://pub.dev/packages/routemaster) package as a navigation solution. The package offersRoutemasterDelegate with the observer's attribute, which takes the list of RoutemasterObservers.

The RoutemasterObserver observes all screen in and out events, like when a new screen enters or when a screen exits.

Look at the implementation of the RoutemasterObserver class in the **screen_view_observer.dart** file located in the root-level **lib** folder. Locate // TODO: add _sendScreenView() helper method, and replace it with the following code snippet:

```
void _sendScreenView(PageRoute<dynamic> route) {
  // 1
  final String? screenName = route.settings.name;
  // 2
  if (screenName != null) {
    analyticsService.setCurrentScreen(screenName);
  }
}
```

The code above:

1. Extracts the name of the screen from route settings.
2. Once verified that the screen name is non-null, you record the screen view event by invoking the predefined setCurrentScreen method.

Notice that here you're invoking the setCurrentScreen method on the FirebaseAnalytics instance. Since this is in use in multiple places, you declared its instance at the file level in **analytics_services.dart** under **packages/monitoring/lib/src**.

When you open this file, you'll see an instance of Firebase Analytics declared as well as two methods — setCurrentScreen() and logEvent(). The first one takes screenName for a parameter and logs it to the Firebase Analytics service. You use it in the code snippet above to log screen views. The second one takes a custom event and logs it to the Firebase Analytics service.

Next, replace `// TODO: override didPush and didPop method` with the following code snippet:

```
@override
void didPush(Route route, Route? previousRoute) {
  super.didPush(route, previousRoute);
  if (route is PageRoute) {
    _sendScreenView(route);
  }
}

@override
void didPop(Route route, Route? previousRoute) {
  super.didPop(route, previousRoute);
  if (previousRoute is PageRoute && route is PageRoute) {
    _sendScreenView(previousRoute);
  }
}
```

When navigating to a new screen, the `didPush` method passes its route to your `_sendScreenView` method. When navigating back to the previous screen, the current screen disappears, and the previous screen reappears. That's when the `didPop` method passes the previous route to the `_sendScreenView` method instead of the current route. This will be important later to understand on which screen a specific error happened when Firebase Crashlytics reports it.

Lastly, assign `ScreenViewObserver` to `RoutemasterDelegate`. Open the root **main.dart** file and replace `// TODO: add observers to RoutemasterDelegate` with the following:

```
ScreenViewObserver(
    analyticsService: _analyticsService,
  ),
```

With that, you've added an observer to `RoutemasterDelegate`, which tracks navigation from one screen to another. You can see that the `observers` attribute is a type of `List`, which means that you could add multiple observers to observe users navigating from screen to screen.

To make sure that the analytics will record the screen views, you have to reinstall the app. After reinstalling the app, you can test what you've done so far. There's no difference in the appearance of your app, but you may see the result of your efforts in the Firebase Analytics console. The recorded events might take up to one day to reflect in the Firebase Analytics console's Dashboard. Instead, visit the **Analytics ▸ Realtime** screen to see events in real time.

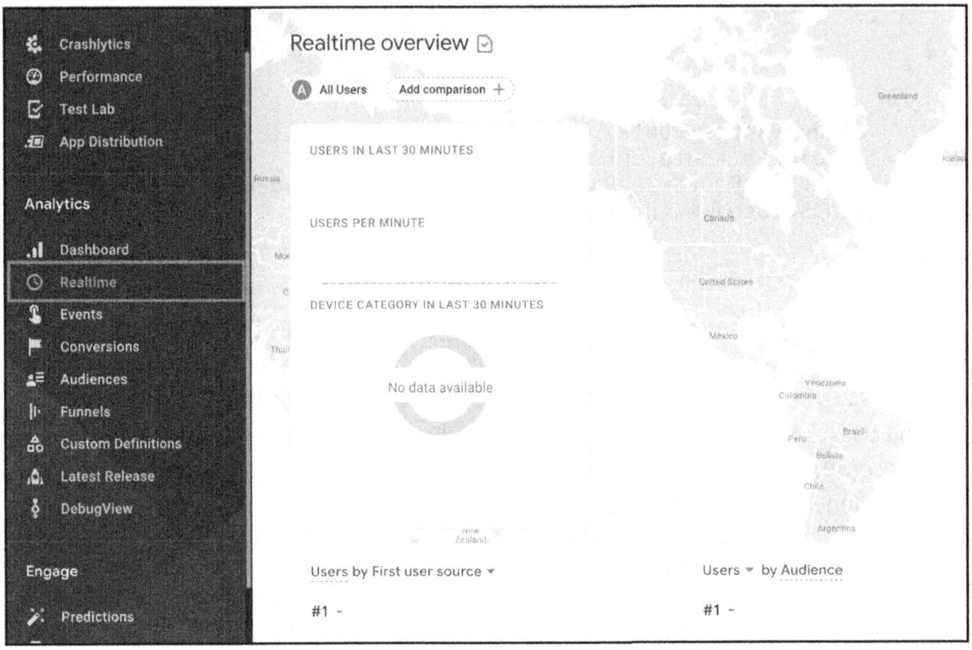


So far, you've learned that Firebase Analytics helps you record events that may occur in a known user journey, such as visiting a quotes list screen or a quote detail screen. But what if your app crashes while loading the quotes list or navigating to details, or it misbehaves for any reason? Then, your role as an app developer would be to find the root cause of that crash. It's very difficult to get this information directly from the user. Don't worry — Firebase Crashlytics can help you with that!

# Firebase Crashlytics

So far, you probably have a good understanding of why, in addition to users' engagement, you also have to track your app's crashes. So, you'll start by getting straight to the point.

There are two major groups of app crashes that you need to be able to distinguish between:

- **Fatal**: The app stops processing and terminates as soon as an error occurs.
- **Non-Fatal**: The app still runs after the error or warning was thrown.

You'll dig deeper into tracking both of these in just a moment. For now, it's worth noting that Firebase Crashlytics supports both of them, although, by default, Flutter tracks only non-fatal crashes. You can override that by changing the `fatal` parameter to `true` when calling the `recordFlutter()` method. But you'll get back to that later.

First, you'll look at how to add Firebase Crashlytics to your project.

# Enabling Firebase Crashlytics

Look at the Crashlytics tab in your Firebase console. Navigate to **Release & Monitor ▸ Crashlytics** in the menu on the left:

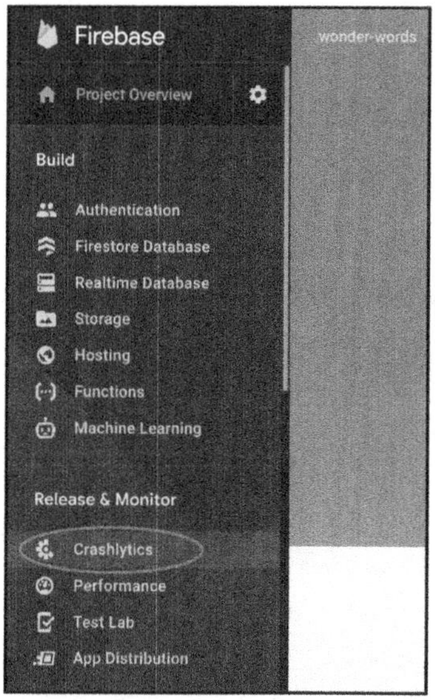

When you navigate to the Crashlytics screen, you'll see the following screen:

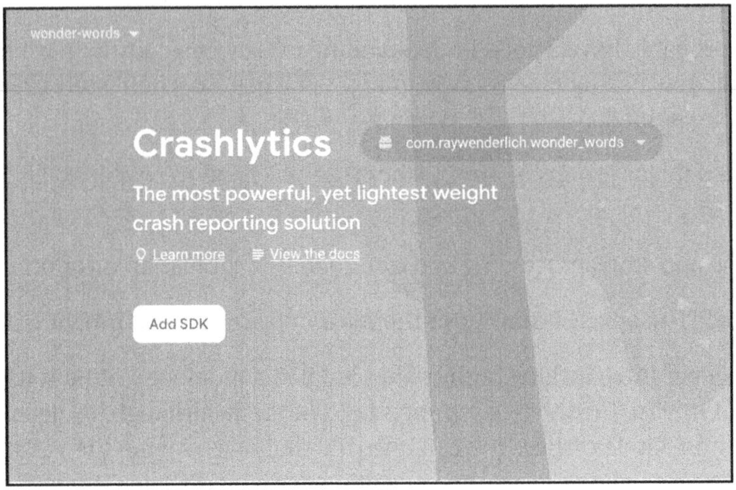


Before proceeding to the Crashlytics console, you have to add a few things to your WonderWords project.

## Setting up Firebase Crashlytics

Just like Firebase Analytics, Firebase Crashlytics is also a one-time setup. Add the required package in the monitoring package **pubspec.yaml** file located in **packages/monitoring** by replacing `# TODO: Add crashlytics packages` with the following code snippet:

```
firebase_crashlytics: ^2.8.4
```

With that, you've added both required packages.

> **Note**: When editing **pubspec.yaml** — or **yaml** files in general — be sure to use the correct indentation.

Before continuing with the next steps, run the `make get` command in the terminal at the root of the app.

With that, you enabled Dart-only Firebase error reporting. This means you can only track Dart exceptions. As you'll also want to report native Android and iOS exceptions, a few additional steps are required.

## Android-Specific Crashlytics Integration

Open **android/build.gradle** and add the following classpath under the `dependencies` group by replacing `// TODO: add Firebase Crashlytics classpath` with the following code:

```
classpath 'com.google.firebase:firebase-crashlytics-
gradle:2.7.1'
```

Next, open **android/app/build.gradle** and replace `// TODO: apply Firebase Crashlytics plugin` with the following line:

```
apply plugin: 'com.google.firebase.crashlytics'
```

You've successfully added all the necessary things for using Firebase Crashlytics for reporting native Android exceptions. Now, look at how you can achieve the same for iOS exceptions.

## iOS-Specific Crashlytics Integration

Use **Xcode** to open **Runner.xcworkspace** located in the root-level **ios** folder. Select **Runner** in the **TARGETS** section. Go to the **Build Phases** tab and add **New Run Script Phase**, as shown in the image below:

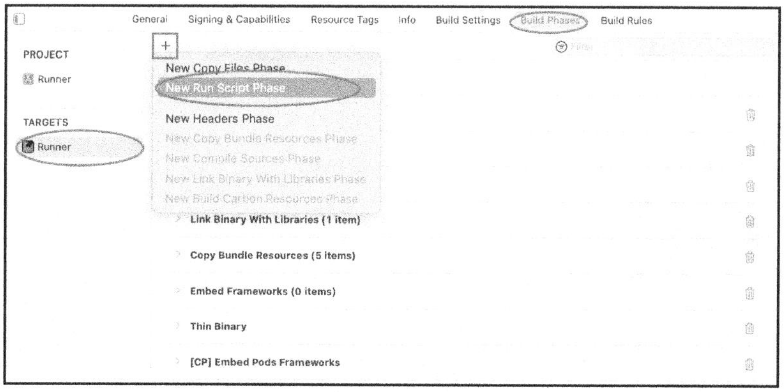

When you add a **New Run Script Phase**, it should appear at the end of the list with all scripts. Expand its list tile and focus on the text box underneath the **Shell** property:

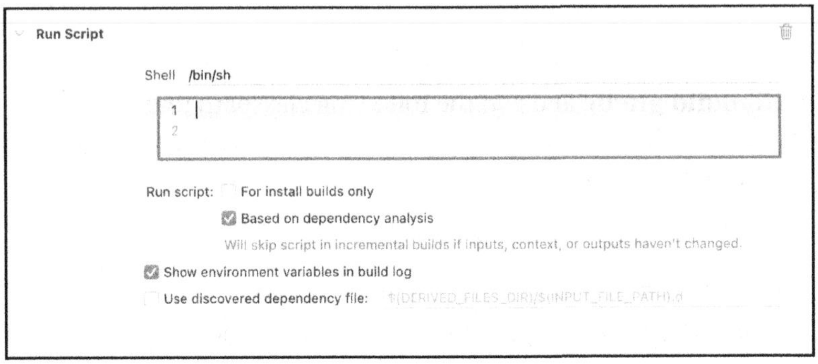


Add the following script in the text box:

```
$PODS_ROOT/FirebaseCrashlytics/upload-symbols --build-phase --
validate -ai <googleAppId>
$PODS_ROOT/FirebaseCrashlytics/upload-symbols --build-phase -ai
<googleAppId>
```

Lastly, in the script you just pasted, replace `<googleAppId>` with your **Google App ID**. Find it by navigating to **Project settings**, scrolling down, and selecting **iOS app**:

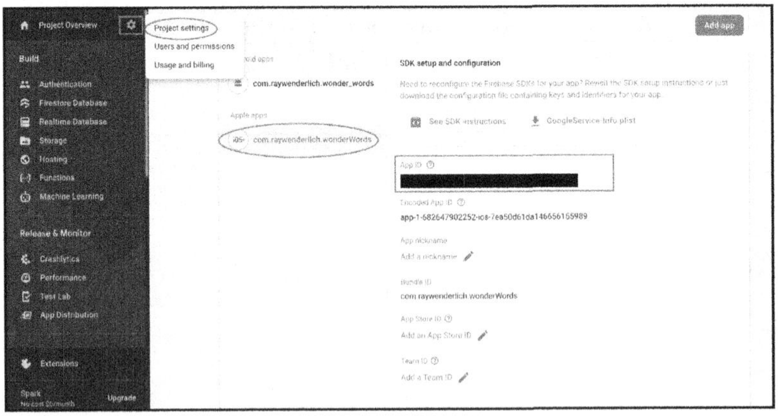


**Note**: iOS App ID is specific to every app; therefore, it's blacked out here.

# Initializing a Flutter App With Firebase Crashlytics

Before accessing the Firebase Crashlytics instance in the app, you need to initialize Firebase core services in the Flutter app. You do this by invoking `Firebase.initializeApp()` before the `runApp` statement. Open **lib/main.dart**, and look at the current implementation of the `main()` function:

```
void main() async {
  // 1
  WidgetsFlutterBinding.ensureInitialized();
  // 2
  await initializeMonitoringPackage();

  // TODO: Perform explicit crash

  // TODO: Add Error reporting

  // the following line of code will be relevant for next
chapter
  final remoteValueService = RemoteValueService();
  await remoteValueService.load();
  runApp(
    WonderWords(
      remoteValueService: remoteValueService,
    ),
  );
}
```

What the code above does is:

1. Ensures `WidgetsFlutterBinding` initialization. When initializing a Firebase app, the app interacts with its native layers through asynchronous operation. This happens via platform channels.
2. Initializes the Firebase core services, which are defined in **monitoring.dart** by calling `Future<void> initializeMonitoringPackage() => Firebase.initializeApp();`.

You can finally run the app again.

# Finalizing Firebase Crashlytics Installation

Now, as you have that settled, go back to your Firebase console and navigate to the **Crashlytics** tab. You may notice that something has changed. The button **Add SDK** has changed to a loading indicator saying that an app has been detected, as shown in the following image:

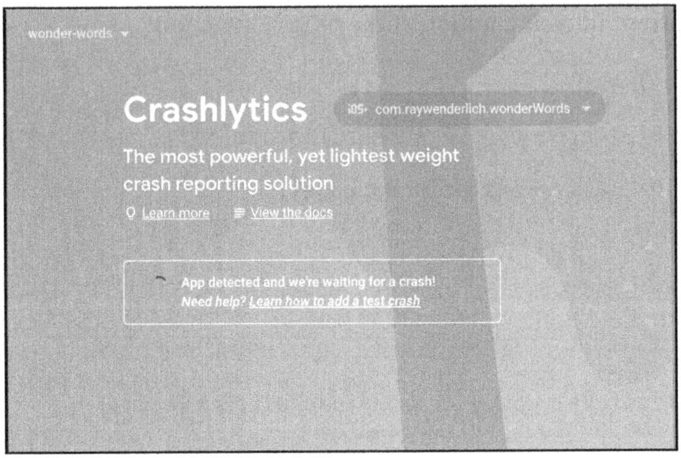


To proceed, you have to invoke an app crash. Hmm, how to crash an app on demand... Not a trivial task, right? Fortunately, the **flutter_crashlytics** package has your back.

Navigate to **explicit_crash.dart** located in **monitoring/lib/src/** and replace `// TODO: add implementation of explicit crash` with the following code:

```
import 'package:firebase_crashlytics/firebase_crashlytics.dart';
import 'package:flutter/foundation.dart';

class ExplicitCrash {
  ExplicitCrash({
    @visibleForTesting FirebaseCrashlytics? crashlytics,
  }) : _crashlytics = crashlytics ??
FirebaseCrashlytics.instance;

  // 1
  final FirebaseCrashlytics _crashlytics;

  // 2
  crashTheApp() {
    _crashlytics.crash();
  }
}
```

With the code above, you:

1. Define the instance of Firebase Crashlytics.
2. Add an implementation of an explicit crash.

In **main.dart**, replace `// TODO: Perform explicit crash` with the following code snippet:

```
final explicitCrash = ExplicitCrash();
explicitCrash.crashTheApp();
```

With the code above, you'll explicitly crash the app. Now, restart the app, and the app should crash.

> **Note**: Don't forget to remove the code above from your project when you're finished testing this feature. You won't need it anymore in the future, so you may delete the whole **explicit_crash.dart** file and its export in **monitoring.dart**.

Go back to the Firebase console, and notice that the UI of the Crashlytics tab has slightly changed again. Now, the button that says "Go to Crashlytics dashboard" has appeared, as you see in the following image:

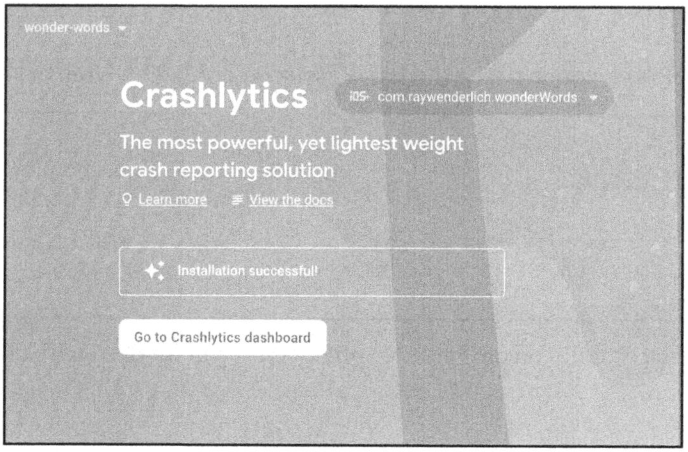

After pressing it, you'll navigate to the Crashlytics dashboard:

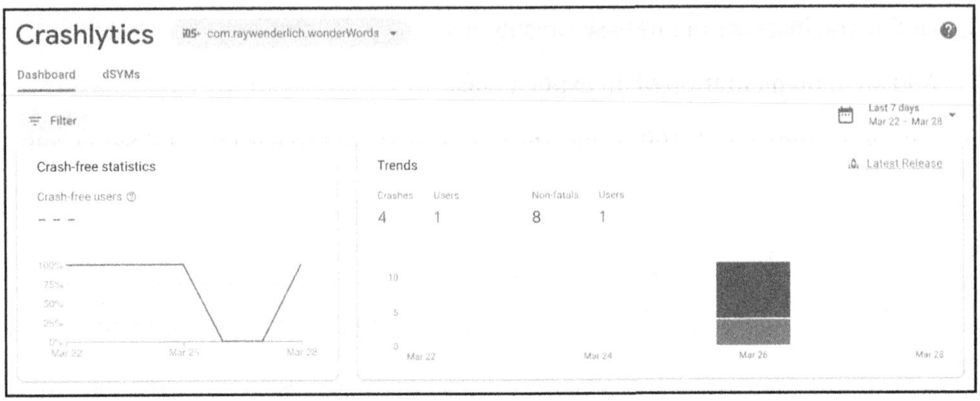


In the image above, you can see the overview of crashes in your app. The first panel shows the number of users without crashes over days represented in percentage. The second panel shows the number of crashes by type over time.

> **Note**: Your Crashlytics Dashboard should look very similar to the image above, except for the data displayed. In this case, a few crashes were performed over a few days, which is why the numbers on your console look a bit different.

# Analyzing Crashes

By navigating lower, you may see the list of issues recorded by Firebase Crashlytics:

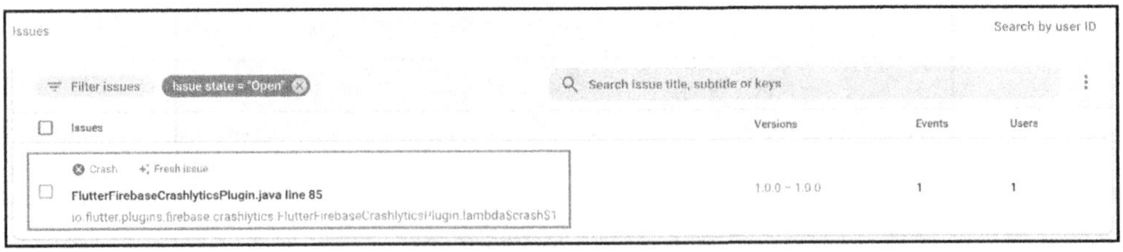


Firebase has successfully recorded the explicit crash you invoked with code from the previous section.

Diving deeper into this can uncover a lot of valuable information about how to reproduce — and eventually fix — the error that occurred:

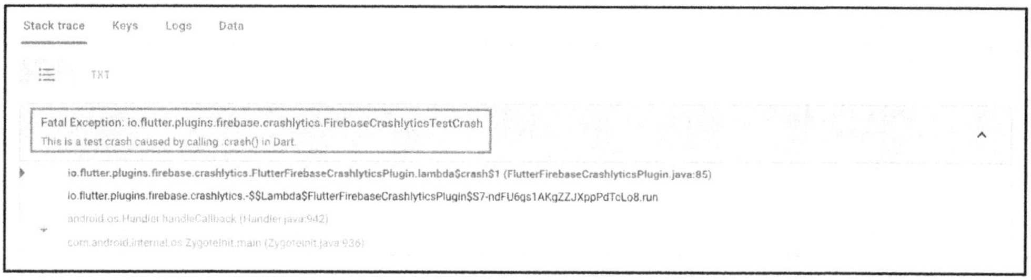


You can see the details of your first crash saying, "This is a test crash caused by calling .crash() in Dart". Now, you'll see how to record crash logs when the app crashes in real-time scenarios.

# Isolating Error-Catching Logic in a Single File

There are a few different types of errors. You'll dive deeper into the specifics of different error types in just a second, but before that, you have to prepare a few things.

Create a new file called **error_reporting_service.dart** in **packages/monitoring/lib/src**. Similar to what you did before, here you'll define an instance of Crashlytics Service and prepare a few functions that'll come in handy in the future.

Paste the following code snippet in the newly created file:

```
import 'package:firebase_crashlytics/firebase_crashlytics.dart';
import 'package:flutter/foundation.dart';

/// Wrapper around [FirebaseCrashlytics].
class ErrorReportingService {
  ErrorReportingService({
    @visibleForTesting FirebaseCrashlytics? crashlytics,
  }) : _crashlytics = crashlytics ??
FirebaseCrashlytics.instance;

  // 1
  final FirebaseCrashlytics _crashlytics;

  // 2
  Future<void> recordFlutterError(FlutterErrorDetails
flutterErrorDetails) {
    return _crashlytics.recordFlutterError(flutterErrorDetails);
  }

  // 3
```

```
  Future<void> recordError(
    dynamic exception,
    StackTrace? stack, {
    bool fatal = false,
  }) {
    return _crashlytics.recordError(
      exception,
      stack,
      fatal: fatal,
    );
  }
}
```

Here's what the code above does:

1. Declares an instance of Firebase Crashlytics.
2. Defines the method used for recording **Flutter framework errors**, a type of error you'll learn about in the next section.
3. Defines the method for recording other errors.

Don't forget to export the newly created file by replacing `// TODO: export error_reporting_service.dart file` in **packages/monitoring/lib/monitoring.dart**:

```
export 'src/error_reporting_service.dart';
```

## Handling Errors in a Flutter App

As already mentioned, there are a few different types of errors. Most of the time, when resolving the different types, you won't bother to distinguish between them. Nevertheless, for the sake of general knowledge, here are three types of errors that you may want to record:

- **Flutter framework errors** happen inside the Flutter framework. The most well-known example of this is `RenderFlex overflowed`.
- **Zoned errors** occur when running asynchronous code. An example of this error is one that happens during the execution of the `onPressed` method inside `FlatButton`.
- **Errors outside Flutter framework** are all the errors that happen outside of Flutter `context`.

The easiest way to handle them all is by replacing `// TODO: replace the implementation of main() function` with the following code snippet:

```
void main() async {
  // 1
  // Has to be late so it doesn't instantiate before the
  // `initializeMonitoringPackage()` call.
  late final errorReportingService = ErrorReportingService();
  // 2
  runZonedGuarded<Future<void>>(
    () async {
      // 3
      WidgetsFlutterBinding.ensureInitialized();
      await initializeMonitoringPackage();

      final remoteValueService = RemoteValueService();
      await remoteValueService.load();
      // 4
      FlutterError.onError =
errorReportingService.recordFlutterError;
      // 5
      Isolate.current.addErrorListener(
        RawReceivePort((pair) async {
          final List<dynamic> errorAndStacktrace = pair;
          await errorReportingService.recordError(
            errorAndStacktrace.first,
            errorAndStacktrace.last,
          );
        }).sendPort,
      );

      runApp(
```

```
        WonderWords(
          remoteValueService: remoteValueService,
        ),
      );
    },
    // 6
    (error, stack) => errorReportingService.recordError(
      error,
      stack,
      fatal: true,
    ),
  );
}
```

Here's what the code above does:

1. Initializes an instance of `ErrorReportingService`, which you defined in the previous section.
2. The whole content of the `main()` function is wrapped with the `runZonedGuarded()` function, which enables you to report zoned errors.
3. Similar to before, you have to ensure the binding of the widgets with the native layers and initialize Firebase Core services. To refresh your memory, jump back to the **Initializing a Flutter App With Firebase Crashlytics** section of this chapter.
4. This is a lambda expression that invokes the `recordFlutterError` method with the `FlutterErrorDetails` that holds the stack trace, exception details, etc. It records the Flutter framework errors.
5. This handles the errors outside of Flutter `context`.
6. This catches and reports the errors that happen asynchronously — zoned errors.

With that, you've covered the whole palette of errors that might occur in your project.

Now, you'll look at how to resolve the errors when they're recorded by Firebase Crashlytics. You'll learn about it with the example of the famous `RenderFlex overflowed`, which is a type of Flutter framework error. Dealing with other types of errors is very similar.

# Handling a Flutter Framework Error

First, you have to intentionally produce the `RenderFlex overflowed` error. To achieve that, open **packages/component_library/lib/src/count_indicator_icon_button.dart** and scroll to the end of file. Locate `// TODO: change the font size for invoking an error` and replace `small` with `xxLarge` so that it matches the following code:

```
// TODO: change font size back to FontSize.small
fontSize: FontSize.xxLarge,
```

This change increases the font size and invokes the `RenderFlex overflowed` error. Build and run the app, and when you navigate to the quote details screen, you'll notice the following changes in the UI:

In the image above, you can see a bottom overflow error for the two count indicators that have counts of 1 and 0.

Next, kill the app and re-run it so it can upload the crash details to Firebase. As soon as the app starts, refresh the Firebase Crashlytics console page. You'll find a new non-fatal error:

Click the crash to see more details:

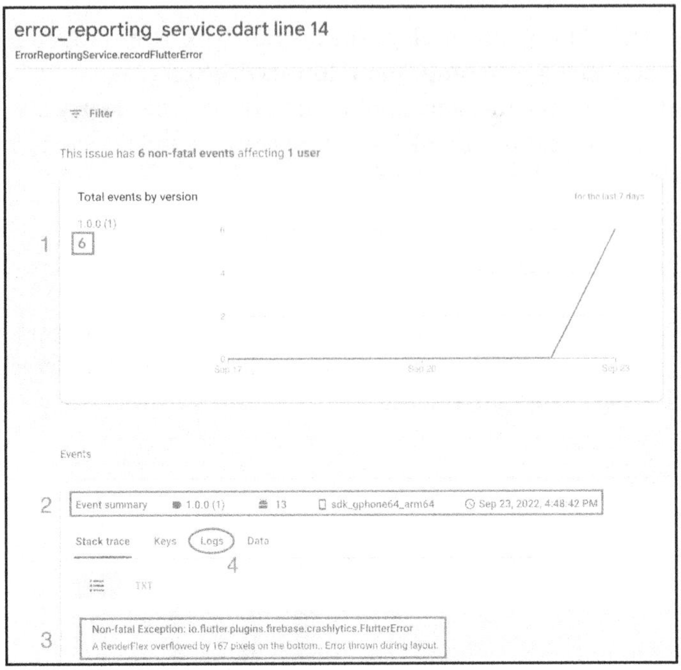


The image above resembles a typical error detail page in Firebase Crashlytics with the following details:

1. The **number of times** the event occurred.
2. A summary of the error that reveals **app version**, **operating system version**, **device model** and **time of occurrence**.
3. The **exception message** that you also see in the mobile app. Remember, when you run the app in Debug mode, the framework prints out the exception message in the app. But, when you run the app in Release mode, the framework hides that message and instead shows a gray box in place of the widget in question.
4. To fix the error, you need more details. The **Logs** tab will help you reproduce the error and pinpoint the exact line that caused it.

So, move to the **Logs** tab, and you'll see the entries below:

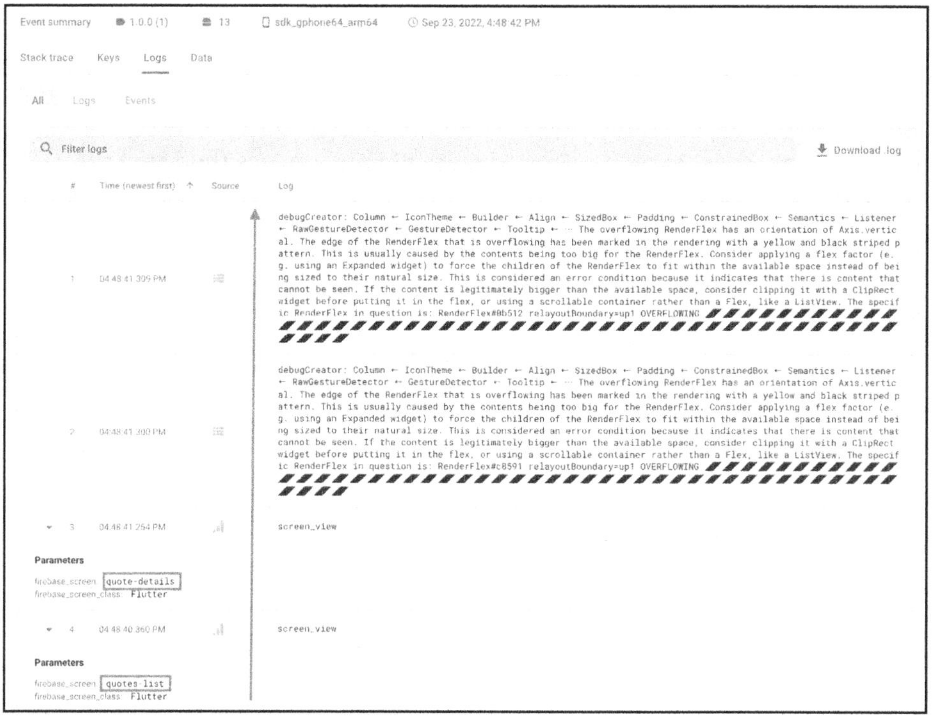


Try to get used to reading logs from the bottom to the top to reproduce the exact issue. So, as per the image above, the user navigated from the quote list screen to the quote detail screen and got the exception. This information helps, doesn't it? You can now easily reach the exact screen and fix the issue.

> **Note**: Hover on the icons under the **Source** header in the image above, and you'll notice that **screen_view** logs came from Analytics that you recorded initially in this chapter, and the top two logs are from Crashlytics. This allows you to get a clearer image of the crash.

With that, you've learned how to record and handle errors in real-life situations in Flutter. In the same way as above, you can solve all the error types that Firebase Crashlytics records for you.

> **Note**: Don't forget to remove the error you've caused above. Locate `// TODO: change font size back to FontSize.small` and replace the `fontSize` parameter with `FontSize.small`.

# Key Points

- Using **Firebase** services such as **Analytics** and **Crashlytics** is a must when supporting an app's lifecycle.
- Firebase Analytics offers valuable data on the structure of your audience as well as screen time, number of screen visits and custom event tracking.
- With the help of Firebase Crashlytics, you can record all the errors you might miss during the development process.

# Where to Go From Here

With this chapter, you've learned a very important lesson on how to track vital aspects of your app after finishing its initial development.

As only a limited amount of knowledge can fit in a book, there's plenty more to learn online at the respective doc sites for [Firebase Analytics](https://firebase.google.com/docs/analytics] as well as Firebase Crashlytics (https://firebase.google.com/docs/crashlytics).

# Chapter 13: Running Live Experiments With A/B Testing & Feature Flags

By Vid Palčar

In the previous chapter, you learned about two Firebase services — Firebase Analytics and Firebase Crashlytics. While browsing through your Firebase console, you might've noticed that it offers quite a few other interesting services. So, in this chapter, you'll look at two of those additional services — **Firebase A/B Testing** and **Firebase Remote Config**.

After thousands of hours spent learning good UX and UI practices, studying marketing and working on product development, there will always be situations when you won't be sure about a specific design decision, call-to-action strategy or advertising text. Even when you think you made the right choice based on your experience, there might be cases when taking a different approach would work better. You might think these differences are irrelevant to your app, but the truth is that an increase of only a few percentage points in user engagement might reflect enormous gains in your sales. The math behind that is quite simple: more sales = more money.

But now, you might be wondering how to determine which solution to a specific problem will work best for your users. That's where Firebase A/B Testing comes in handy. Publishing a new release of the app for every change required for your experiments would be very inconvenient. Firebase Remote Config has you covered there. With the help of a so-called feature tag, you can make changes to your app on the fly.

With Firebase A/B Testing, you can run experiments in marketing, advertising, politics, product development, design, etc. As mentioned already, you'll have to use Firebase Remote Config to implement those.

In this chapter, you'll learn how to:

- Add a feature flag to a specific feature.
- Perform changes in the app without rolling out a new version.
- Set up an experiment in Firebase.
- Perform and track experiments with Firebase.

While going through this chapter, you'll work on the starter project from this chapter's **assets** folder.

## A Deep Dive Into A/B Testing

The introduction already mentioned a few use cases of A/B testing. But before performing your first A/B test, you have to dive a little deeper into the theory behind it.

A/B testing is a simple experiment in which two different versions of a variable — A and B — are compared. The testing group is randomized and usually equally distributed between both samples. More complex cases might have more than just two versions of a specific variable. The use of A/B testing started far before the era of modern computers. Originally, A/B tests were used to figure out which advertising pamphlets worked best. Nowadays, A/B tests are standard procedure in product development as well as preparation of marketing materials — from small businesses to tech giants.

Here's how A/B testing works in the example of a simple call to action for a shoe store app. You start by preparing two versions of the call-to-action button text. The first one says: "Only five pairs left", and the second one says "Limited number of pairs left". After that, you have to clearly define the metrics you want to track for this experiment. You'll figure out why this is very important in that stage. For the sake of this example, say that you want to find out which text attracts more users to buy the product — this becomes the metric you want to track. Finally, you randomly distribute the two versions of the app amongst your users — 50% will use the first version of the app with the first text, and the other 50% will see the second one with the second text.

After performing the test for two weeks, you've noticed that 7% of the users with the first version of the app ended up buying the shoes. On the other hand, only 5% of users with the second version of the app made a purchase. The result makes quite a bit of sense. Users of the first version stress more about shoes going out of stock than the users of the second version; therefore, they're more motivated to buy. Based on that information, you clearly see that the first call-to-action text works better, and you can distribute it to all the users.

On the other hand, you might want to perform the same experiment and focus on slightly different metrics. If you want to measure the use time of your app, the result might be very different. Because the users of the second app version don't feel such an urgency to buy the product, they might spend a little bit more time scrolling through other products.

The example above was a very simple one, with only a slight difference between the two samples. But don't let this example fool you. In slightly more complex A/B tests, you could test the performance of two or even more completely different UIs and features, and measure multiple different metrics.

The last thing you need to understand before continuing with this chapter is the aspect of segmentation of the responses in a specific test. Even though, in the previous example, the first version of the variable — the call-to-action text — worked the best, this might not be the case for some subgroups of your testing group. For example, for a specific age group or gender, the second version of the variable might work significantly better. You must take this into account when you target your audience — you should distribute the second version of the call-to-action text to this specific subgroup once the test is finished.

# Logic Behind Remote Config and Feature Flags

As already mentioned, A/B testing and **Firebase Remote Config** go hand in hand. The second is normally used only as a tool to correctly distribute the different variables among the users when performing A/B tests. This will also be a case in the example for this chapter, although it's only fair to mention other use cases of Remote Config.

A **feature flag** defines a variable on which a variant of the specific feature is based. This can be a very simple variable, such as a string to define a button's text, as shown in the previous section, a Boolean to show or hide a specific feature, an integer to define the perfect size of items per pagination page, etc. On the other hand, it can be a very complex model to define, for example, the theme of the app.

Firebase Remote Config is a cloud service that allows you to perform remote changes to a feature flag in your app. With its help, you can change your app's appearance and behavior without rolling out the new version of the app. This can come in handy when you want to modify your app for a specific audience or when you want to roll out a new feature gradually. Pushing out a new feature can be a very stressful thing to do. You can't ever know how the users will react to a new feature; plus, there might still be a few bugs that you missed. Therefore, releasing a new feature only for a certain percentage of your users might be very useful.

# Installing Firebase Remote Config

Time to get your hands dirty. To add Firebase Remote Config, you'll use the firebase_remote_config (https://pub.dev/packages/firebase_remote_config) package. Locate **pubspec.yaml** in the **packages/monitoring** package:

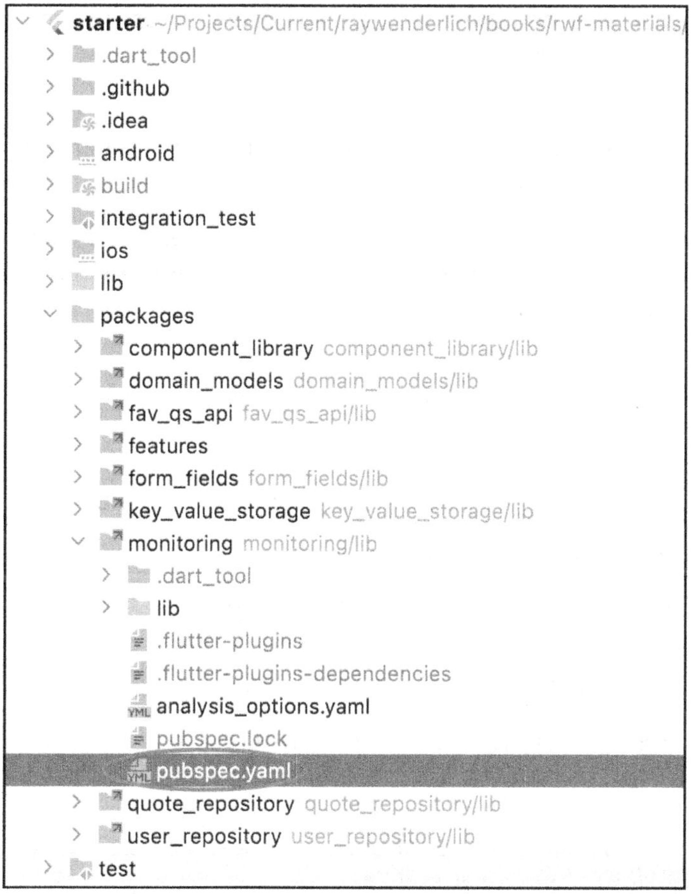

Replace `# TODO: add firebase_remote_config package` with the following line of code:

```
firebase_remote_config: ^2.0.11
```

> **Note**: **firebase_remote_config** also requires **firebase_core** to work, which you learned how to do in the previous chapter.

After you've added the required packages, run the `make get` command in the terminal to fetch the new packages.

In the **packages/monitoring/lib/src/** folder, locate `// TODO: add an implementation of RemoteValueService class` in **remote_value_service.dart**, and replace it with the following code:

```
static const _gridQuotesViewEnabledKey =
'grid_quotes_view_enabled';

// 1
RemoteValueService({
  @visibleForTesting FirebaseRemoteConfig? remoteConfig,
}) : _remoteConfig = remoteConfig ??
FirebaseRemoteConfig.instance;

final FirebaseRemoteConfig _remoteConfig;

// 2
Future<void> load() async {
  // TODO: add default values for your parameters
  await _remoteConfig.fetchAndActivate();
}

// 3
bool get isGridQuotesViewEnabled => _remoteConfig.getBool(
      _gridQuotesViewEnabledKey,
    );
```

This is what the code above does:

1. Initializes the instance of `FirebaseRemoteConfig`.
2. Fetches and activates the configuration that you'll set up on the Firebase Remote Config console.
3. Returns the value of the feature flag you defined.

Next, import the missing package by replacing `// TODO: import firebase_remote_config package` with the following line of code:

```
import 'package:firebase_remote_config/
firebase_remote_config.dart';
```

With that, you've successfully added the Firebase Remote Config package and created a wrapper around it.

# Creating New Parameters in Firebase Remote Config Console

Now that you've successfully added Firebase Remote Config into your app, you can start adding the parameters to change the app's appearance.

Go to your Firebase console and navigate to the **Remote Config** tab under the **Engage** section, as shown in the image below:

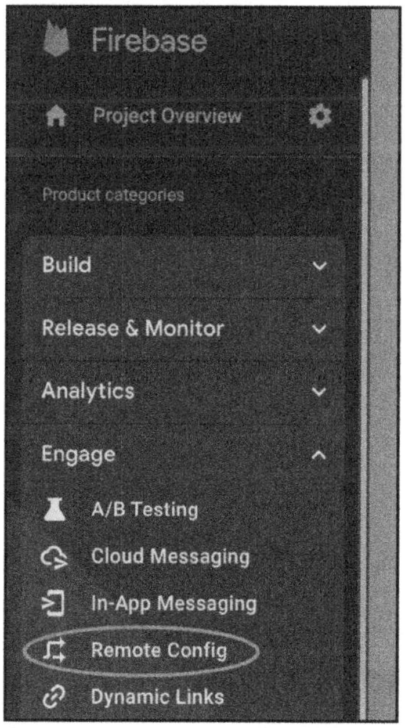

You may notice the **Create configuration** button on the screen:

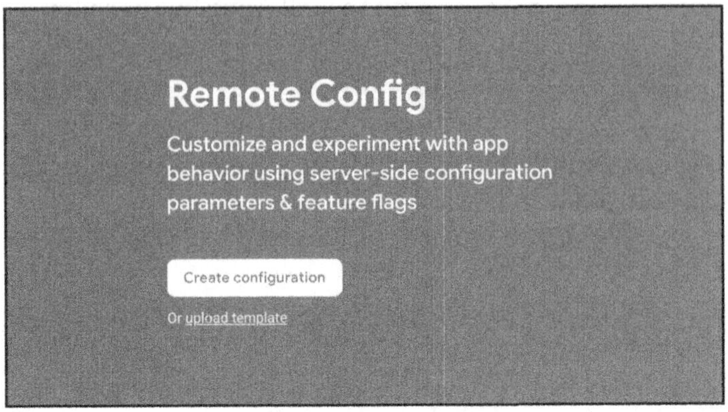


Clicking it will make the action window pop up, where you can configure your first parameter.

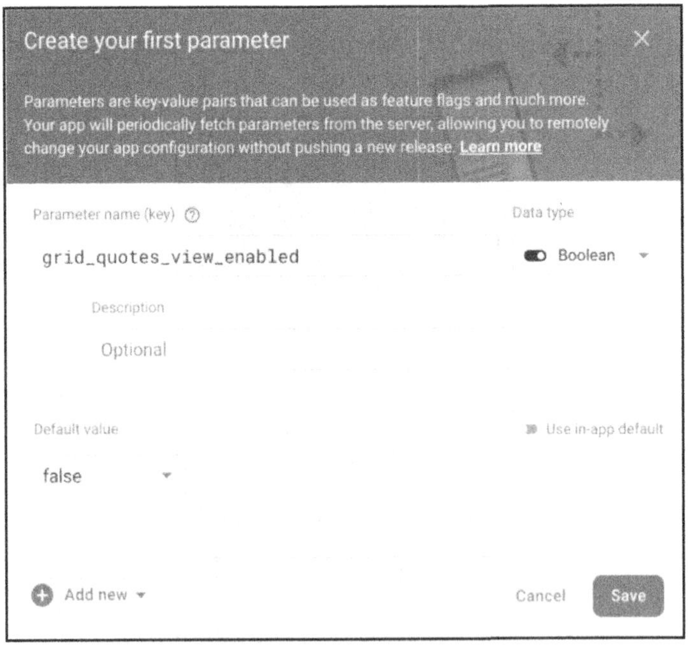

For this example, you'll manipulate the appearance of the quote list screen. You can see that the current layout of quotes is a staggered list. But you may want to change it to a normal list someday. To achieve this, create a new parameter called **grid_quotes_view_enabled** in the **Parameter name (key)** field, select **Boolean** as the **Data type** and set the **Default value** to **false**. For a better understanding, look at the picture above.

When you're done filling in all the required fields, click **Save** at the bottom of the window. With that, you'll be taken to the Remote Config console.

At the top of the screen, you'll have to click **Publish changes** to push the configuration that your apps can later use:

After you've clicked the button, scroll to the end of the screen and look at the **config panel**:

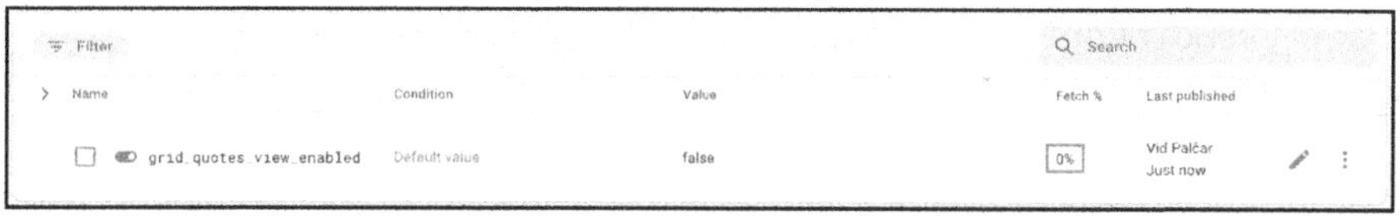


The config panel has a list of all the parameters that you've configured so far. For now, you've only configured one. Focus on the number in the **Fetch %** column. This shows the percentage of apps that have fetched this configuration and, consequently, updated the UI.

# Implementing UI Changes Based on Your Remote Config

First, navigate to the app's **main.dart** file located in the app-level **lib** folder. Find `// TODO: add loading feature flags from remote config`, and replace it with:

```
await remoteValueService.load();
```

With that, you always call the method responsible for fetching and activating the feature flags based on the remote configuration when launching the app. You may notice that the previous line of code comes just after the following line:

```
final remoteValueService = RemoteValueService();
```

The code above initializes the `RemoteValueService` object. Next, open **remote_value_service.dart** in the **monitoring** package, and replace `// TODO: add default values for your parameters` with the following code:

```
await _remoteConfig.setDefaults(<String, dynamic>{
  'grid_quotes_view_enabled': true,
});
```

This sets the default values of the parameters defined on your Firebase Remote Config console. In your case, this is the bool parameter `grid_quotes_view_enabled`. By default, you want to keep your quote's list screen layout as the grid. Therefore, you set the `grid_quotes_view_enabled` parameter to `true`. Remember, you've set the value of this same parameter to `false` in the Remote Config console, which means this will be overridden when you publish the changes.

In **quote_list_screen.dart** located in **packages/features/quote_list/lib/src**, find `// TODO: display different UI based on the value of grid_quotes_view_enabled parameter`. Replace the `QuoteSliverGrid` widget with the code below:

```
child: widget.remoteValueService.isGridQuotesViewEnabled
    ? QuotePagedGridView(
        pagingController: _pagingController,
        onQuoteSelected: widget.onQuoteSelected,
      )
    : QuotePagedListView(
        pagingController: _pagingController,
        onQuoteSelected: widget.onQuoteSelected,
      ),
```

With the code above, you'll display the quotes in the layout of either the grid or list. Build and run the app, and you'll see the following changes in the UI:

> **Note**: If you're having trouble running the app, you might have forgotten to propagate the configurations you did in the first chapter's starter project to the following chapters' materials. If that's the case, please revisit Chapter 1, "Setting up Your Environment".

Go back to your Remote Config Console and look at the value in the **Fetch %** column — you'll see that it changed to **100%**:

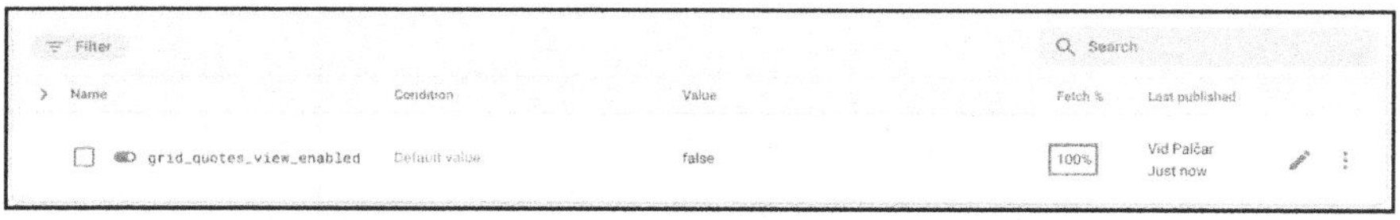


This means that the change has been applied to *all* of your app's users. If your UI didn't successfully update, delete the app and restart it.

Notice the **edit** button on the image above. By clicking it, you can change the value of a specific parameter. Try changing `grid_quotes_view_enabled` to **true** and refresh the app. You'll see that the appearance of the quote list screen changes back to the grid.

# Performing A/B Tests

By implementing Firebase Remote Config, you have control over the appearance and behavior of your app in the sense of predefined parameters. But now, your app has multiple different appearances, and you may be wondering which is the best for the end user.

In the case of the previous example, you have two variations of the quote list screen. You can find out which is better for your app's users with the help of A/B testing. Go back to your Firebase Remote Config console and click the **Create your first A/B Test** button on the **A/B Testing** panel:

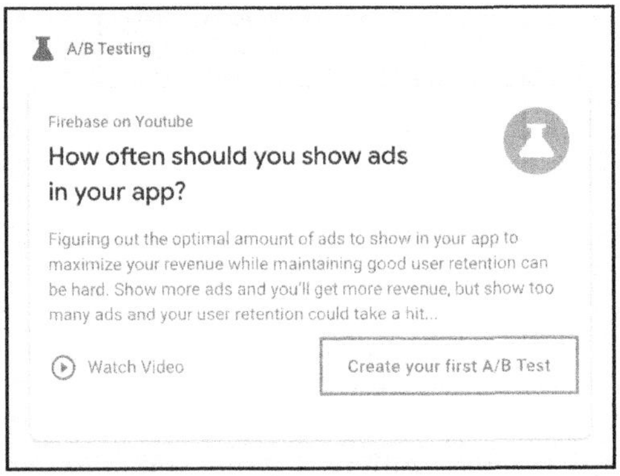


It will take you to the following screen:

By going through the following steps, you'll create a new A/B test. Set the **Experiment name** to **Quote List Retention** and click **Next** to continue. Then, select the app — iOS or Android — on which you want to perform tests. By clicking the **and** button, you may specify even more details on targeting.

Change the **Exposure** to **100%.** In real-life situations, you wouldn't want to perform the tests on *every* user, but for demonstrational purposes, this will work better for you:

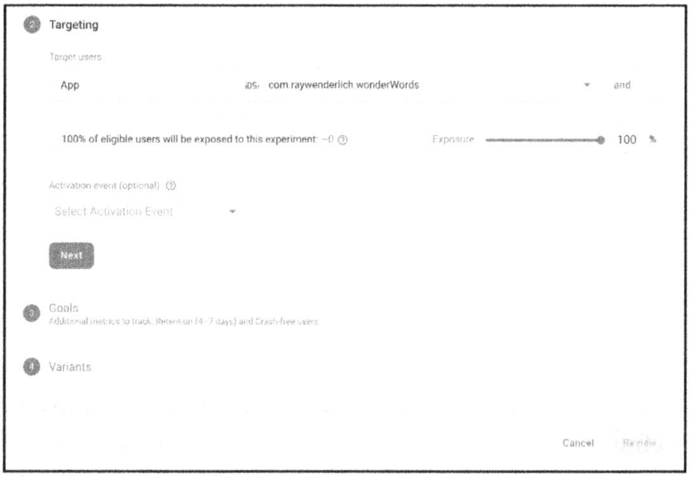


In the third step, **Goals**, set **Primary metric to track (determines leader)** to **Retention (1 day)**:

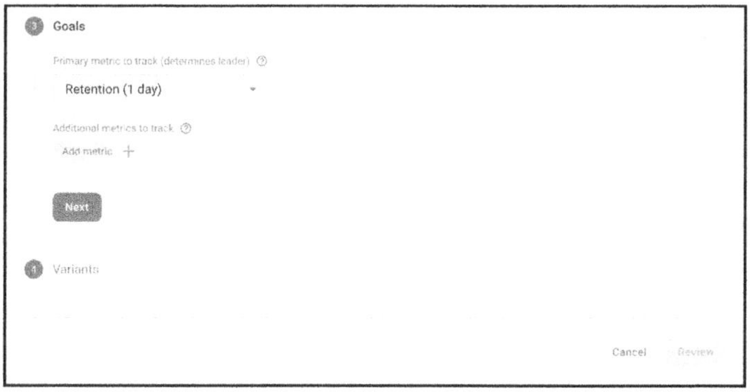

Finally, continue to the fourth step, **Variants**. Set the **Baseline Parameter** to `grid_quotes_view_enabled` with the value of **false**. Then, set the **Variant A Parameter** to `grid_quotes_view_enabled` with the **Value** of **true**:

When you've defined your first experiment, continue to the next screen by clicking **Review**. Then, start your first experiment by clicking **Start experiment**:

After starting the experiment, the parameters will be distributed to the users with the help of Firebase Remote Config, and the data on retention will be collected. Based on that data, deciding which appearance of the quote list screen works the best for the end user won't be such a difficult job anymore. After collecting some data, this is how your console will look:

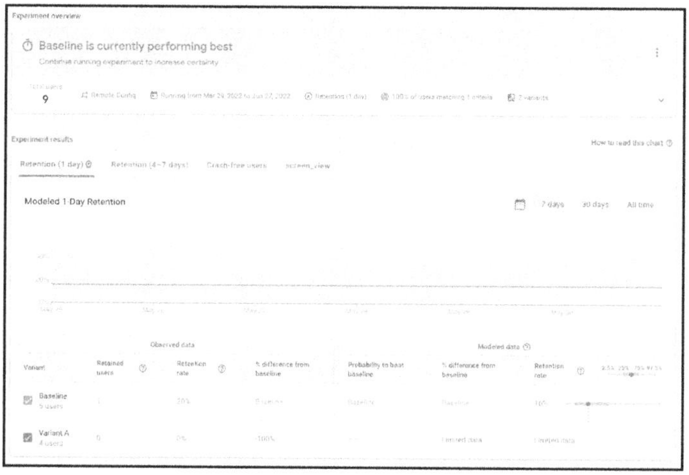


# Key Points

- **A/B tests** are crucial for making your app more suitable for its end users.
- **Firebase Remote Config** allows you to perform changes in the app without needing to release a new version.
- By performing different A/B tests on your app with the help of Remote Config, you may be able to make better decisions about your app's appearance and behavior.

# Chapter 14: Automated Testing

By Vid Palčar

In the previous chapter, you learned how to use Firebase Crashlytics to efficiently track errors in your app. This knowledge plays an enormous role when resolving the existing issues your users face. However, the experience for your users would be even better if the app *didn't have those issues* in the first place. It's delusional to believe your app will be bug-free with your first release, but you still try to get as close to this ideal scenario as possible. You can achieve this with the help of testing.

Your QA team — or you and your fellow developers, if you work in a smaller team — can only do so much to test your app manually. That's where **automated testing** can be a handy approach to make your work easier.

Besides being very limited with how much manual work you can perform — which relates directly to cost — performing automated tests also has other benefits. As people make mistakes, automated tests exclude the human error factor from app testing. With automated testing, you can get rid of repetitive work, perform the test with greater speed and consistency and test more frequently. All of these benefits result in a faster time to market.

Despite giving the impression that automated testing is this magical thing that will save you from all of the world's problems, in some cases, manual testing is actually better. You should choose manual testing over automated testing in instances when test criteria are constantly changing, cases that aren't routine and generally in situations when manual tests haven't been executed yet.

You can use a few different types of automated tests for different parts of your app. To ensure that your app is well-tested, you have to provide high **test coverage**. This is the percentage of your app's executed code covered by automated tests. In other words, an app with high test coverage is less likely to run into undetected bugs.

In this chapter, you'll learn about:

- **Unit tests**.
- **Widget tests**.
- **Integration tests**.
- Using **mocking** and **stubbing**.
- Writing and executing examples of each test type.

Throughout this chapter, you'll work on the starter project from this chapter's **assets** folder.

> **Note**: If you're having trouble running the app or the tests, you might have forgotten to propagate the configurations you did in the first chapter's starter project to the following chapters' materials. If that's the case, please revisit Chapter 1, "Setting up Your Environment".

# Types of Tests

As already mentioned, there are quite a few different types of automation tests. In this chapter, you'll mainly deal with three test types — unit tests, widget tests and integration tests. You'll get deeper into those in just a moment.

For general knowledge purposes, it's also worth mentioning some other types, though they're not as important in testing mobile apps. They are:

- **Smoke testing**, also known as **confidence testing**, is a set of tests designed to assess the stability of a deployed build.
- **Golden file testing** is a special type of testing in which you compare specific behavior to the golden file. In the case of API testing, this golden file can be the response you expect from the API. On the other hand, when testing your mobile app's UI, the golden file would be the screenshot of the UI you expect to see on your mobile device.
- **Performance testing** tests the software's speed, responsiveness and stability under the workload.

# Unit Testing

Unit testing ensures that a specific unit of software behaves as intended. The term "unit" isn't very clearly defined. It can be a complete chunk of the software but usually represents a smaller part of code, like a function or class.

By writing unit tests for smaller units and later combining them, you can gradually provide high test coverage for very complex applications.

The unit test's purpose is to ensure the correct behavior of more primitive isolated units. To imitate interactions of this specific unit with other parts of software, **mocks** and **stubs** are often used — but more on that later. The biggest advantage of the unit test is that it can detect issues very early in the development cycle. These issues can be bugs caused by wrong implementations or flaws in the design of a specific unit. When writing unit tests, you're often more conscious of the inputs the specific unit receives, the outputs it returns and the error conditions the unit might run into.

On the other hand, unit testing can only catch the errors that might happen in the scope of this specific unit. Therefore, you should always perform unit tests in parallel with other test types, such as widget tests.

Before diving deep into the next type of test, look at two already mentioned concepts that have a significant role in unit testing — mocking and stubbing.

### Mocking and Stubbing

When performing unit tests, you must focus on the pure functionality of a specific unit. This means you should try to prevent any uncontrolled influence of other internal or external units/services with which your unit interacts. This is where you'll use mocking and stubbing.

Mocking is the process in which you create a fake version of an internal or external service. During the process of testing, it replaces the actual service.

The purpose of stubbing is very similar to the purpose of mocking, which is why people usually have a hard time distinguishing between them. Stubbing — like mocking — creates a stand-in but only simulates a behavior rather than the whole object or service.

When you're testing your Flutter apps, you'll use a few different libraries for mocking and stubbing, which will make the process of testing easier.

## Widget Testing

Widget testing is a special term used specifically in testing Flutter apps. The general developer community usually refers to them as **component testing**.

As you've probably already figured out, widget testing ensures that a specific widget or portion of the user interface looks and works as intended without needing a physical device or simulator. This last advantage results in low execution time, allowing you to perform hundreds of tests per minute.

The principles you'll learn about widget testing can also apply to integration testing.

## Integration Testing

If you jump back to the section on unit testing, there was one disadvantage mentioned at the end of the section. This is where integration testing saves the day. Integration testing is a process in which you test interactions among different units and components — in this case, widgets.

It's usually performed after unit and widget testing, as it doesn't work well for detecting issues happening inside a specific unit or component. Nevertheless, it plays a crucial role when providing high test coverage for your project.

To perform integration tests, you'd use different integration-testing tools. You might be aware of one such tool — **Selenium**. Selenium is an open-source program that facilitates automation testing for web-based applications. You might remember YouTube videos on web scraping that were quite popular in the past. Although this isn't its sole purpose, you can get a good idea of what such a program does. With the help of Selenium, the web scraping program navigated through pages of a specific website and eventually got to the point where it took specific data from the site and stored it in the database.

Integration testing isn't much different from this. You use integration-testing software to execute interactions with the different units and eventually compare the output with your expected result. In Flutter integration testing, you won't use any third-party software, as Flutter SDK has you covered.

In addition to integration-testing tools, you'll also use mocks and stubs when performing integration tests.

# Writing Tests for Flutter Apps

Open the starter project in your preferred IDE. If you quickly run through the folder structure of either the Flutter app or package, you may notice the folder called **test**. This is where your tests will live:

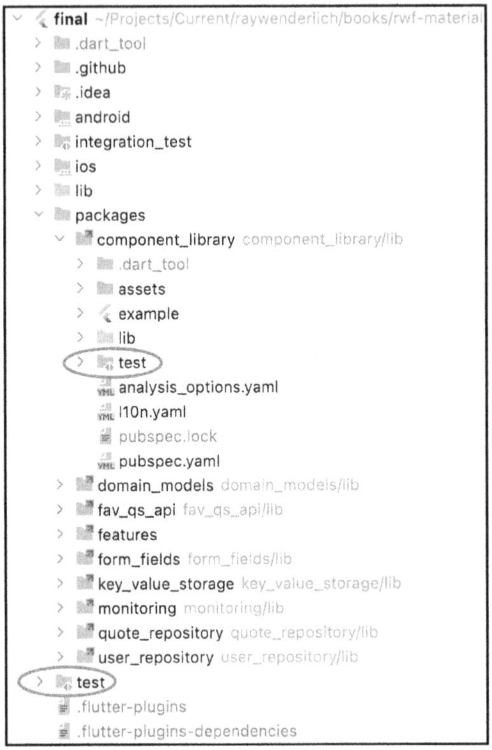

In the image above, you can see test folders for your WonderWords app and **component_library** internal package. Expand the other **packages** folder, and you'll see that it also contains a **test** folder.

Next, open **example_test.dart** located in the root-level **test** folder, and look at the example implementation of very basic tests:

```
import 'package:flutter_test/flutter_test.dart';

// 1
void main() {
  // 2
  group('Group description', () {
    // 3
    setUp(() {});
```

```
    // 4
    test('Test 1 description', () {
      // 5
      expect(1, 1);
    });
    test('Test 2 description', () {
      expect(1, 1);
    });
    // 6
    tearDown(() {});
  });
  // 7
  test('Test 3 description', () {
      expect(1, 1);
    });
}
```

Here's what the code above does:

1. This is the entry point of your test program. Your code for performing tests will live inside the `main()` function.
2. With a group, you can join multiple tests together. It takes two required parameters — description, which will be included in descriptions of the tests inside the group, and function parameter, inside which you'll define your tests.
3. `setUp()` is used as a part of code, which will always run before the tests.
4. This is a top-level test function in which you'll write an implementation of a specific test.
5. This function compares your test result with your expected value and checks if the test was successful.
6. `tearDown()` works very similarly to the `setUp()` function, but this function executes code after tests.
7. This is the same function as `test()` after comment `// 4` but is outside the group, which shows that `test()` can run outside the group.

## Running Flutter Tests

You can run your tests in multiple different ways. Here, you'll explore using both your IDE and your terminal to run your tests.

When looking at your file editor, notice the green arrows along the left side of your code. One is parallel to the implementation of the `main()` function, one is parallel to the `group()` function and one is parallel to the `test()` function:

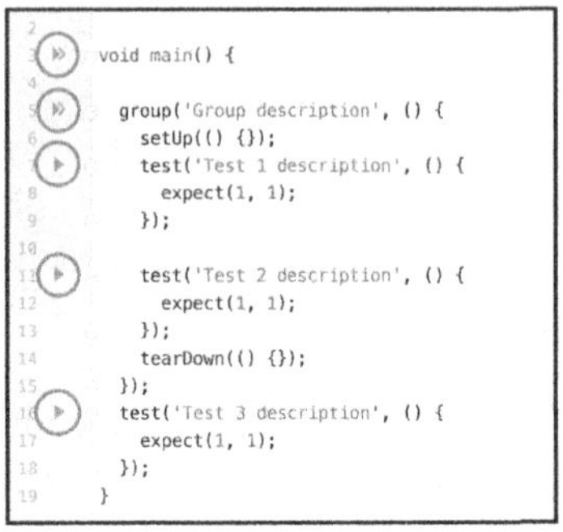


In the image above, you can see what the interface will look like in Android Studio. If you open the same file in Visual Studio Code, the logic behind testing is very similar.

To test this, click the double arrow next to the `main()` function, and all the tests inside it should be executed. The same goes for running the `group()` function. You can also run an individual test by clicking the green arrow next to that test.

After tests run — either successfully or unsuccessfully — the design of the arrows changes slightly, and the console shows the test results:

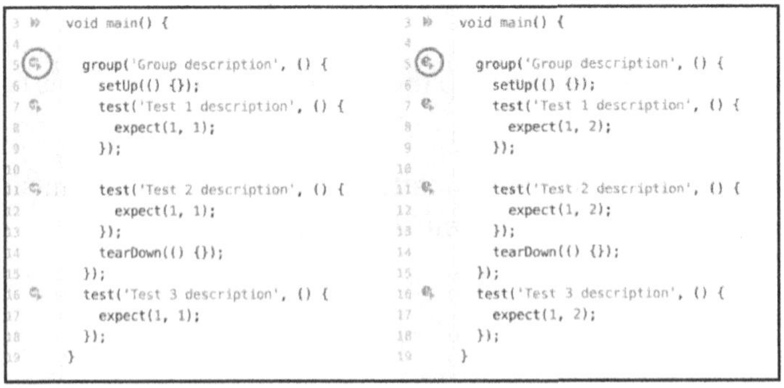

The left image shows the tests that ran successfully, and the right image shows tests that failed.

To better understand why the tests fail, you have to look at the console:

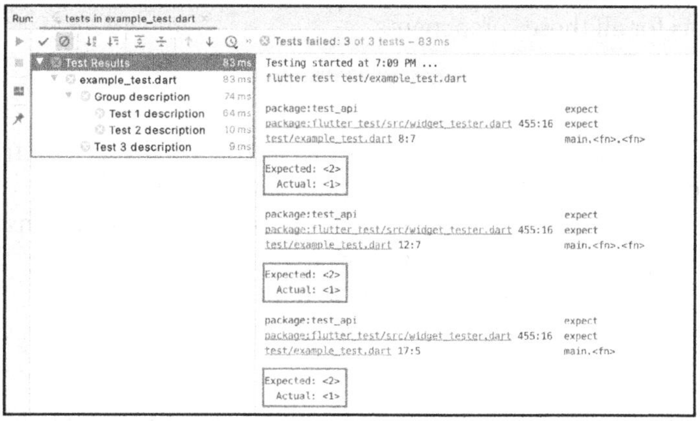


On the left side of the image above, you see that all the tests failed. You'll check the right side of the console to see what went wrong. While the expected value was 2, the actual result was 1. Return to the previous picture, and you'll see that, for the sake of example, the values `expect(1, 2)` function was changed.

On the other hand, you can also run tests in the terminal. Navigate to the root of the package for which you want to run the test, and use the following command to run all the tests in a specific file:

```
flutter test test/example_test.dart
```

If you want to run only a specific test or group of tests, use an additional flag `--plain-name` with the description of the group or test. For your example of a group with the description "Group description":

```
flutter test --plain-name "Group description" test/
example_test.dart
```

> **Note**: The command above won't work if you try to run it outside the package you want to test. This is because all the important packages you use for testing are added as **dev dependencies**. So, it means they won't be fetched in the app that uses these packages.

Now, you're ready to write your first actual tests.

# Writing Unit Tests

If you think about the past chapters, you've learned about **repositories**, **mappers**, **remote APIs**, **BLoC** business logic, etc. In the following sections, you'll learn how to write unit tests for all these components.

## Writing Unit Tests for Mappers

Before you start writing the code, it's worth visualizing what you want to achieve with it. In the first test, you'll create a test for a mapper that maps `DarkModePreferenceCM` into `DarkModePreference`. So, from the extension that defines this mapper, you'd expect that in the case of `DarkModePreferenceCM.alwaysDark`, it would return `DarkModePreference.alwaysDark`. This is exactly what you'll write in your first test.

Open **mappers_test.dart** located at **packages/user_repository/test**. In it, replace `// TODO: add unit test for DarkModePreferenceCM to domain mapper` with the following code snippet:

```
//1
test('When mapping DarkModePreferenceCM.alwaysDark to domain,
return DarkModePreference.alwaysDark',
    () {
  //2
  final preference = DarkModePreferenceCM.alwaysDark;
  //3
  expect(preference.toDomainModel(),
DarkModePreference.alwaysDark);
});
```

This is a very simple example of a unit test but is a great example to get started. Here's what the code above does:

1. As already mentioned, this is the top-level function that will execute when you run the test. As the first required parameter, it takes the description of the test, and the second required attribute takes an implementation of the test.
2. Here, you store the instance of `DarkModePreferenceCM` in a variable.
3. Here, you compare the output of the testing mapper with your expected result.

Before running this test, you only have one thing left to do — add the missing imports by replacing `// TODO: add missing imports` with the following code:

```
import 'package:domain_models/domain_models.dart';
```

```
import 'package:key_value_storage/key_value_storage.dart';
import 'package:test/test.dart';
import 'package:user_repository/src/mappers/mappers.dart';
```

Now, you're ready to run the tests and check if your implementation of `DarkModePreferenceCMToDomain` mapper is correct. Use one of the previously explained methods to run the tests. By running it in the terminal, this is the output:

```
00:01 +1: All tests passed!
```

Congratulations, you've written your first unit test!

## Writing a Unit Test for Your Repository

Next, you'll write a test for your `UserRepository` focusing on only one function — `getUserToken()`. Think of the situation when the previously mentioned function will be invoked, when a successful authentication happened sometime in the past, and the token was saved in the secure storage. In this case, you'd expect from the function that it returns a valid token.

Start by opening **user_repository_test.dart** located in the **packages/user_repository/test**. Replace `// TODO: add an implementation for UserRepository.getUserToken() test` with the following code snippet:

```
test('When calling getUserToken after successful authentication,
return authentication token',
    () async {

  // TODO: add initialization of _userRepository

  expect(await _userRepository.getUserToken(), 'token');
});
```

The code above is a standard skeleton for performing automated tests in Flutter with the already completed `expect()` function with the logic from before. For now, ignore the missing imports — you'll add them later — and focus on the instance `_userRepository` of `UserRepository`, which has yet to be initialized. To do so, replace `// TODO: add initialization of _userRepository` with the following:

```
// TODO: add initialization of _userSecureStorage

final _userRepository = UserRepository(
  secureStorage: _userSecureStorage,
  noSqlStorage: KeyValueStorage(),
  remoteApi: FavQsApi(
    userTokenSupplier: () => Future.value(),
```

```
    ),
  );

  // TODO: add stubbing for fetching token from secure storage
```

UserRepository's constructor requires two parameters — noSqlStorage and remoteApi. These don't play any role when executing getUserToken(). But if you go to the implementation of this class, you'll see that you can also provide the secureStorage attribute when testing this repository. This one, on the other hand, plays a huge role when executing getUserToken(). As mentioned before, it's crucial when performing unit tests to prevent any unexpected behavior of other units with which the testing component interacts. To take control over the behavior of this object, you'll make a mock for UserSecureStorage.

To make things easier, you'll use the Flutter community library **mockito**. First, add the library to the **pubspec.yaml** file of the **user_repository** package by replacing # TODO: add mockito library with the following code:

```
  mockito: ^5.2.0
```

Make sure to use correct indentation, and don't forget to fetch packages by running the flutter pub get command in the root of the current package. Next, replace // TODO: add missing packages and an annotation to generate the mock with the following code:

```
import 'package:fav_qs_api/fav_qs_api.dart';
import 'package:key_value_storage/key_value_storage.dart';
import 'package:mockito/annotations.dart';
import 'package:mockito/mockito.dart';
import 'package:test/test.dart';
import 'package:user_repository/src/user_secure_storage.dart';
import 'package:user_repository/user_repository.dart';
// TODO: add missing import

@GenerateMocks([UserSecureStorage])
```

You can generate a mock class for UserSecureStorage with the annotation you just added. For now, ignore the unnecessary import that was added among other imports — you'll need it in just a moment. Run the following command in the terminal under **package/user_repository directory** to generate a mock class:

```
flutter pub run build_runner build --delete-conflicting-outputs
```

You may notice that a new file was generated in the same folder where your current file is located. This is where the definition of your mock test was generated. Now, you have to initialize the missing variable by replacing `// TODO: add initialization of _userSecureStorage` with the following line of code:

```
final _userSecureStorage = MockUserSecureStorage();
```

Don't forget to add the missing import by replacing `// TODO: add missing import` with:

```
import 'user_repository_test.mocks.dart';
```

If you look at the code you just wrote, it looks like it might be ready to perform a test. Run the test in the terminal, and you'll quickly notice that something went wrong with the following output:

```
00:01 +0 -1: When calling getUserToken after successful
authentication, return authentication token[E]
MissingStubError: 'getUserToken'
No stub was found which matches the arguments of this method
call: getUserToken()

...

00:01 +0 -1: Some tests failed.
```

From the output above, you can see that you forgot to implement stubbing of specific behavior. So, when your mock object executes `getUserToken()` on secure storage, you have to stub a behavior in which the token is returned. You can achieve this by replacing `// TODO: add stubbing for fetching token from secure storage` with the following line of code:

```
when(_userSecureStorage.getUserToken()).thenAnswer((_) async =>
'token');
```

The function you just wrote is quite intuitive. When you call `getUserToken()` inside your mock object, it returns the token you hardcoded to `token`. Run the test again, and it'll work like a charm.

## Writing a Unit Test for API

In the following section, you'll write a unit test for your `signIn()` function for `FavQsApi`. Imagine the most common scenario when the user enters the correct credentials, and the remote API returns the correct response. In this case, you expect `signIn()` to return an instance of the `UserRM` object. Again, you'll have to stub the behavior of the remote API returning a success response. You could use the **mockito** package for mocking again, but this is a bit tricky when performing HTTP requests with the help of the **dio** package. Therefore, you'll use the **http_mock_adapter** package, which makes things easier for you. First, replace `# TODO add http_mock_adapter`, located in **packages/fav_qs_api/pubspec.yaml**, with the following line, and fetch the missing packages:

```
http_mock_adapter: ^0.3.3
```

Don't forget to run `flutter pub get` in the terminal inside the **fav_qs_api** package or `make get` at the root of the project. Next, navigate to **sign_in_test.dart** located in the packages' **test** folder, where a few things have been prepared for you in advance.

```
import 'package:dio/dio.dart';
import 'package:fav_qs_api/src/fav_qs_api.dart';
import 'package:fav_qs_api/src/models/models.dart';
import 'package:fav_qs_api/src/url_builder.dart';
// TODO: add missing import
import 'package:test/test.dart';

void main() {
  test(
      'When sign in call completes successfully, returns an
instance of UserRM',
      () async {
    // 1
    final dio = Dio(BaseOptions());

    // TODO: add dioAdapter which will stub the expected
response of remote API

    // 2
    final remoteApi =
        FavQsApi(userTokenSupplier: () => Future.value(), dio:
dio);

    // 3
    const email = 'email';
    const password = 'password';

    final url = const UrlBuilder().buildSignInUrl();
```

```
    final requestJsonBody = const SignInRequestRM(
      credentials: UserCredentialsRM(
        email: email,
        password: password,
      ),
    ).toJson();

    // TODO: add an implementation of request stubbing

    // 4
    expect(await remoteApi.signIn(email, password),
isA<UserRM>());
  });
}
```

This is what the code above does:

1. Initializes an instance of the `Dio` object, which is required to perform HTTP requests.
2. Initializes the remote API and provides the required testing attributes.
3. Initializes all the required variables, which are used when performing the sign-in request.
4. Evaluates if the tested function returns the correct output.

Next, replace `// TODO: add dioAdapter which will stub the expected response of remote API` with:

```
final dioAdapter = DioAdapter(dio: dio);
```

And `// TODO: add missing import` with:

```
import 'package:http_mock_adapter/http_mock_adapter.dart';
```

This initializes the `DioAdapter` object, which will be used later to stub the behavior of a successful response. Finally, replace `// TODO: add an implementation of request stubbing` with the following code snippet:

```
dioAdapter.onPost(
  url,
  (server) => server.reply(
    200,
    {"User-Token": "token", "login": "login", "email": "email"},
    delay: const Duration(seconds: 1),
  ),
  data: requestJsonBody,
);
```

The implementation of the code above is again quite intuitive. When performing the POST request using prespecified parameters, after a one-second delay, `dioAdapter` will stub — imitate the successful response. Check the FavQs API (https://favqs.com/api) under the "Create session" section, and you may see that the response body of the stubbed response perfectly matches the response body of the API definition. The only thing left is to run the test.

Again, as expected, everything worked fine:

```
00:02 +0: Sign in: When sign in call completes successfully,
returns an instance of UserRM
*** Request ***
uri: https://favqs.com/api/session
method: POST
responseType: ResponseType.json
followRedirects: true
connectTimeout: 0
sendTimeout: 0
receiveTimeout: 0
receiveDataWhenStatusError: true
extra: {}
headers:
 Authorization: Token token=
 content-type: application/json; charset=utf-8

*** Response ***
uri: https://favqs.com/api/session
statusCode: 200
headers:
 content-type: application/json; charset=utf-8

00:02 +1: All tests passed!
```

This is how the output looks. Notice that it's a bit different from previous outputs. Additionally, it prints out the log for `Request`.

## Writing a BLoC Unit Test

The final unit test you'll write in this chapter is the BLoC test. It's very important to also test your business logic. Again, there's a very useful library that makes testing BLoC business logic much easier: the **bloc_test** library. The package is already added to the **pubspec.yaml** folder of the **sign_in** package located in the **packages/features** folder. Now, open **sign_in_cubit_test.dart**, located in the packages' **test** folder. In it, replace `// TODO: add an implementation of BLoC test` with the following code snippet:

```
blocTest<SignInCubit, SignInState>(
  'Emits SignInState with unvalidated email when email is
changed for the first time',
  // 1
  build: () => SignInCubit(userRepository:
MockUserRepository()),
  // 2
  act: (cubit) => cubit.onEmailChanged('email@gmail.com'),
  // 3
  expect: () => <SignInState>[
    const SignInState(
        email: Email.unvalidated(
      'email@gmail.com',
    ))
  ],
);
```

Here's what's going on in the `blocTest` function:

1. Initialize the `SignInCubit` object.
2. Act on the cubit. This is what happens when the user enters the email address in the text field.
3. Evaluate the new state and compare it with your expected result.

Next, replace `// TODO: add missing imports and a mock class for UserRepository` with the following line of code. This creates a mock for `UserRepository`:

```
import 'package:bloc_test/bloc_test.dart';
import 'package:form_fields/form_fields.dart';
import 'package:mockito/mockito.dart';
import 'package:sign_in/src/sign_in_cubit.dart';
import 'package:user_repository/user_repository.dart';

class MockUserRepository extends Mock implements UserRepository
{}
```

The last thing you have to do is run the test and check if it works correctly.

# Writing a Widget Test

In the following section, you'll write a widget test. To perform it, you'll use the `widgetTest()` function, which is also implemented as a part of the **flutter_test** package. You'll start with the implementation of the widget test. You'll test if the `FavoriteIconButton` recognizes the `onTap` gesture. Open **favorite_icon_button_widget_test.dart**, located in the **test** folder of the same package **component_library**. In it, replace `// TODO: add an implementation of widgetTest` with the following code:

```
testWidgets('onTap() callback is executed when tapping on
button',
    (tester) async {

  // 1
  bool value = false;

  // 2
  await tester.pumpWidget(MaterialApp(
    locale: const Locale('en'),
    localizationsDelegates: const
[ComponentLibraryLocalizations.delegate],
    home: Scaffold(
      body: FavoriteIconButton(
        isFavorite: false,
        // 3
        onTap: () {
          value = !value;
        }),
      ),
  ));

  // 4
```

```
    await tester.tap(find.byType(FavoriteIconButton));
    // 5
    expect(value, true);
  });
```

Here's what's going on in the code above:

1. The variable that will be manipulated on the tap gesture is initialized.
2. The `pumpWidget` function helps build the widget. Notice that the function it tests is wrapped in a few additional widgets. This is required for multiple reasons, one being that you're using internationalization inside `FavoriteIconButton`.
3. You define the action triggered on tap.
4. In this step, the button is being pressed. Notice the parameter provided inside the `tap()` function. You have to tell which widget has to be tapped. You can achieve that by searching for the correct type of widget through the widget tree. The other option would be adding a key attribute to the `FavoriteIconButton` widget and searching by key. There are multiple different ways of searching the widget.
5. You evaluate if the test was successful by comparing the value of `value` that changed with the tap gesture with the expected value.

After running the just-implemented test, you can see that the widget was correctly implemented.

# Writing an Integration Test

There's only one more test type that you should write to make sure that your app potentially runs without bugs — the integration test. This test is a bit different from the ones you've run so far, as it requires a physical device or emulator to execute. For performing integration tests for a Flutter app, you need the **integration_test** package.

First, open the **pubspec.yaml** file located at the root of the project, and replace `# TODO: add missing package` with the following code snippet:

```
  integration_test:
    sdk: flutter
```

Don't forget to fetch missing dependencies. Here, you'll test the flow from starting the app, entering the search key "life" into the search field and checking if any results are returned for this search key.

> **Note**: There might be situations when this integration test fails because you won't mock the remote API. Such instances might be when your device or emulator isn't connected to the internet or if something's wrong with the remote API. This is the decision you'll make in this specific example. As this is only an example test implementing stubbing for requests would take the focus of the topic. Feel free to test your knowledge by adding mocking for remote API, as shown in the **Writing a Unit Test for API** section.

Next, open **app_test** located in the **integration_test** folder at the root of the project. Before continuing to the integration test's implementation, add the required import for this test by replacing `// TODO: add missing package` with the following line of code:

```
import 'package:integration_test/integration_test.dart';
```

Replace `// TODO: add an implementation of integration test` with the following code:

```
// 1
IntegrationTestWidgetsFlutterBinding.ensureInitialized();
testWidgets('search for life quotes', (tester) async {
  // 2
  app.main();
  // 3
  await tester.pumpAndSettle(const Duration(seconds: 1));
  // 4
  final searchBarFinder = find.byType(SearchBar);
  // 5
  expect(searchBarFinder, findsOneWidget);
  // 6
  await tester.enterText(searchBarFinder, 'life');
  // 7
  await tester.pumpAndSettle();
  // 8
  expect(find.byType(QuoteCard), findsWidgets);
  });
```

Here's what this code does:

1. Enables executing tests on a physical device.
2. Runs the app.
3. Rebuilds the frames every second as long as their frames are scheduled.
4. Searches for the `SearchBar` with the help of searching by type.
5. Evaluates that exactly one `SearchBar` widget is present on the screen. Look at the UI design of the app — this is what the app should look like.
6. Enters the search key "life" into the text field of the `SearchBar` widget.
7. Again, rebuilds the frames until the new quote list is loaded.
8. Checks that your request was successful by making sure that the UI returns widgets `QuoteCard`. If that request fails, no `QuoteCard` widgets will be available on the screen.

Before running the test, make sure to run the app as you normally would. Doing so will ensure that all the packages are fetched, all pods are installed, etc. Because you aren't stubbing the API requests in this specific example, run it using the following command — just make sure to replace `YOUR_TOKEN` in the command with the token you registered for the FavQs API:

```
flutter test integration_test/app_test.dart --dart-define=fav-
qs-app-token=YOUR_TOKEN
```

When you run the test, you'll notice that the app automatically starts on your connected device or emulator, performs all the previously mentioned steps, and successfully exits.

# Challenges

To test your understanding of the topic, try to write a few automated tests on your own. There are a few examples ready for you:

1. Write a unit test for mapper defined by the extension `DarkModePreferenceDomainToCM` — for example, of `DarkModePreference.alwaysDark`.
2. Write a unit test for `UserRepository`'s `getUserToken()` function — for instance, when the user isn't authenticated yet.
3. Write a unit test for `FavQsApi`'s `signIn` function — for instance, when a user enters incorrect credentials.
4. Write a widget test to check if `FavoriteIconButton` really shows `Icons.favorite_border_outlined` when the `isFavorite` is set to `false`.

Try to optimize the examples by joining them into groups with already existing tests. If you get stuck, check the solution in the **Challenge** project.

# Key Points

- **Automation testing** is a crucial part of software development, as it helps you provide a bugless app to your users.
- A well-tested app has high test coverage.
- Three types of tests are important when testing a Flutter app — unit tests, widget tests and integration tests.
- **Unit tests** are mainly used to test smaller chunks of code, such as functions or objects.
- **Widget tests**, also known as component tests, are used to test the behavior and appearance of a single widget or tree of widgets.
- **Integration tests** play a significant role when testing interactions among different widgets and units.

# Chapter 15: Automating Test Executions & Build Distributions

By Vid Palčar

Software development is always an iterative process. You'll always need to update your app with bug fixes to your existing features and new features to improve your project. Mobile development in Flutter is no different. Quite a few repetitive tasks are connected to both bug fixes and feature development. You have to test the code by running automated tests, create a build for all the supported platforms and upload just-created builds to some platform where other team members, the QA team and end-users can test and use them. This can be very time-consuming. Therefore, in this chapter, you'll learn how to automate these tests.

In software development, **CI/CD** are practices dealing with automating operating activities so you can focus on development activities. **CI** stands for **continuous integration** and covers automated test execution and building code artifacts such as Android builds. On the other hand, **CD** stands for **continuous delivery**, which primarily focuses on deploying code artifacts.

Automating all repetitive processes sounds great, but one important question must be answered to make it happen: How will the system know when to execute automated tests and build and deploy the apps? Keep reading to find out.

In this chapter, you'll:

- Learn how to use **GitHub Actions** to set up and execute CI/CD for your Flutter project.
- Learn how to automate test execution.
- Learn how to automate building mobile apps for both iOS and Android.
- Become familiar with different development workflows and dive deeper into **Gitflow**.

Throughout this chapter, you'll work on the starter project from this chapter's **assets** folder. This chapter requires basic knowledge of **Git**. Therefore, if you don't have experience using it, check out the Git Apprentice (https://www.raywenderlich.com/books/git-apprentice) book.

> **Note**: If you're having trouble running the app, you might have forgotten to propagate the configurations you did in the first chapter's starter project to the following chapters' materials. If that's the case, please revisit Chapter 1, "Setting up Your Environment".

If you want to use the final project for this app, you still have to follow along with this chapter, as it requires a few additional steps to work. These include creating a GitHub repository, adding GitHub secrets, and generating access tokens and certificates for GitHub.

# Software Development Workflows

The debate over the best way to accomplish something never ends. Therefore, this section will cover the software development workflows that are most commonly used in the developer community. When working on a project alone, it often feels like you don't need strictly defined workflows. But when more people join your team or you try to automate some parts of your work, sticking to a workflow becomes much more important.

When developing software, you most often encounter two development workflows — **Gitflow** and **trunk-based development**.

# Gitflow

The Gitflow development workflow uses multiple long-lived branches. To better understand the following explanation, look at the scheme below:

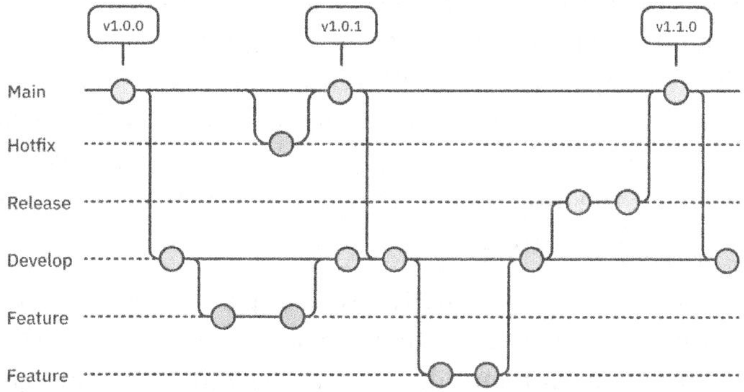


When the project starts, the **main** branch is created. Alternatively, it can also be called the **master** branch. From this branch, the **develop** branch is created and used as the stable source of code. This is a starting point for any **feature** branch. Feature branches are created from the develop branch and are used as long as a specific feature is in development. When the work is done, the feature branch is merged back to the develop branch, usually with the help of the **pull request**.

When a sufficient number of features are created, or a new release is scheduled, the **release** branch is created from the develop branch. From this point on, no new features should be added to this branch. The purpose of this branch is to prepare the necessary documentation for the new features, create release notes and resolve smaller bug fixes. When this is completed, you merge this branch to the main branch, where the code for the new release will live. To ensure that you have the latest stable version of your codebase on your develop branch, you have to merge the main branch back to develop.

You'll deal with one more type of branch if you choose Gitflow as your software development workflow — **hotfix** branches. These branches are created directly from the main branch. When you detect a bug in your latest release, you'll create a hotfix branch, where you'll resolve the issue. This will be merged directly back to the main branch, where a new release will be created. Once again, the main branch will be merged back to develop.

You may notice that this isn't an ideal methodology if you want to achieve efficient continuous integration and delivery. Some feature or release branches might exist for a longer period. Meanwhile, other developers might merge the features they're working on back to the develop branch. Therefore, you'll have to deal with issues such as merge conflicts. On the other hand, it requires quite some synchronizing between your team members to find the right time to create a release. As releases aren't made very often, the internal testers won't be able to provide efficient feedback on the work that's been done since the last release.

To get rid of this issue, developers usually also set up a custom CI/CD for the develop branch. Here, all the newly created features are built and deployed to the development environment for internal testing immediately after merging. You'll create one such automation in the following sections.

# Trunk-based Development

A trunk-based development workflow, on the other hand, keeps the stable code on the main branch. Work is divided into very small batches, which are developed on short-lived branches. Those branches are merged back to the main branch quickly, ensuring the building of code on a daily basis. This allows internal testers to provide developers with regular feedback, which contributes to more agile work. Despite merging often, this doesn't solve the problems that occur due to merge conflicts, which occur during the phases of code reviews.

The graphical representation looks more like this:

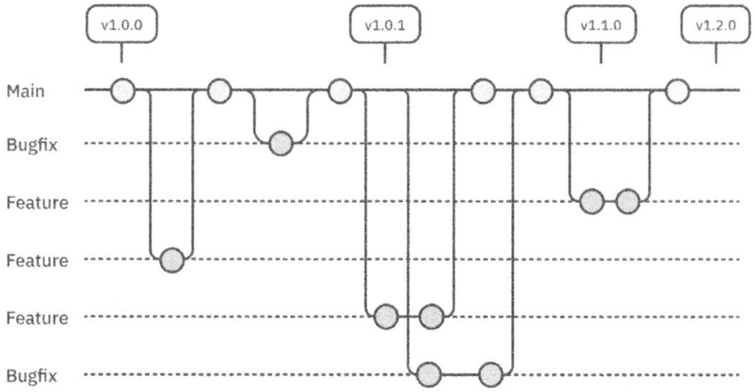


This methodology gives developers more freedom when scheduling the rollout of the new version, as the code on the main branch is always stable and ready for deployment.

# Setting up CI/CD for a Flutter App

The workflow you choose for your app's development will definitely affect the CI/CD pipeline, despite the general concepts always staying the same. With that being said, you'll start by creating a new repository on GitHub (https://github.com/) named **wonder_words**:

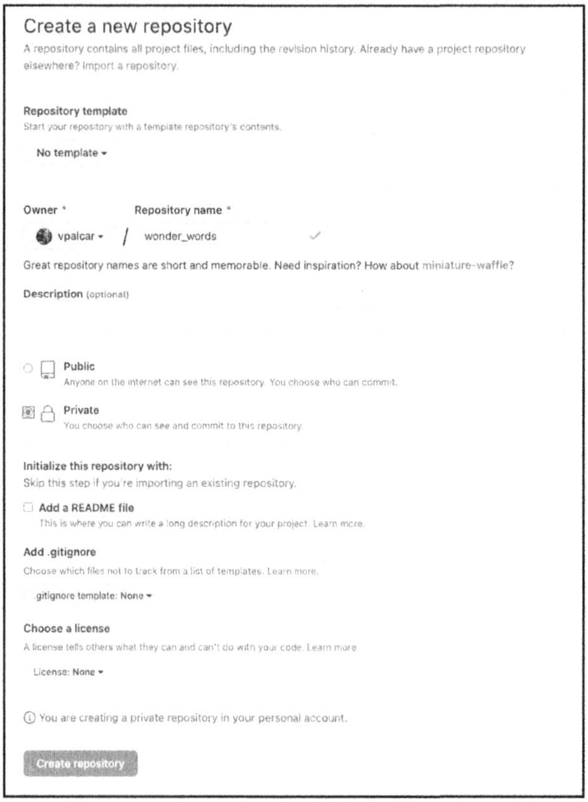


To do so, you need a GitHub account. For this specific project, it doesn't make much difference whether you choose the private or public option. It's worth mentioning that a free private account offers a limited number of build minutes per month, whereas a public account is unlimited. Still, it's suggested that you create a private repository, as the number of build minutes provided for it will be sufficient for this example. You also don't need to create any of the suggested files, as your starter project already contains them.

When you've successfully created a new repository, this is what you'll see:

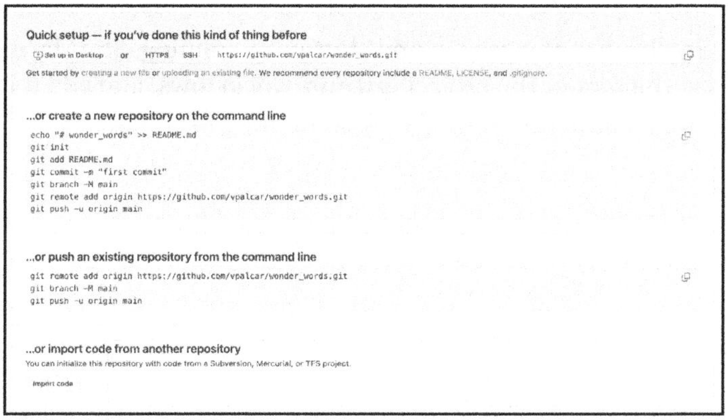


As you can see in the image above, you have quite a few options to add a project to your GitHub repository. For this example, use the following commands in the terminal at the root of the starter project:

```
git init
git remote add origin <REPOSITORY_URL>
git branch -M main
git add -f *
git commit -m 'Initial commit'
git push -u origin main
```

**Note**: Make sure to replace **<REPOSITORY_URL>** from the first command with the actual URL address to the repository you just created. This should push the whole starter project to your remote repository.

Next, create and push a new branch named **develop** using the following commands in the terminal:

```
git checkout -b develop
git push -u origin develop
```

With that, you set the base structure of the Gitflow software development workflow.

# Creating Your First GitHub Action Job

Now, you can finally open the project and start programming. Start by creating two nested folders at the root of the project **.github/workflows**, and add the file named **cicd.yml**. Your folder structure should look something like this:

> **Note**: If you're following the chapter using Android Studio, it might ask if you want to add the newly created file to the **.gitignore**. You must *not* do that.

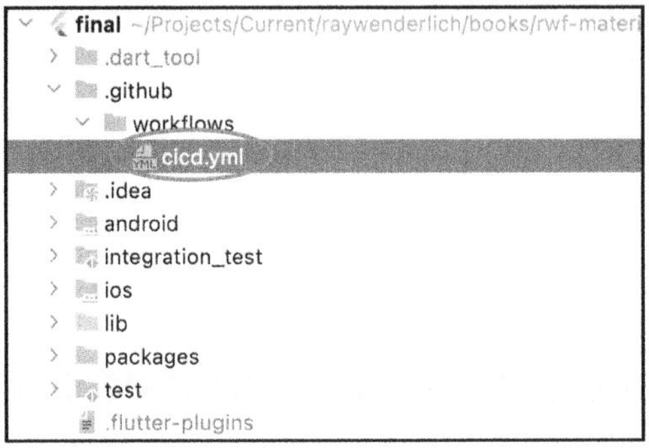


Open the file, and paste the following code into it:

```
# 1
name: Test, build and deploy
# 2
on:
  pull_request:
    branches:
      - develop
  push:
    branches:
      - develop

# 3
permissions: read-all

# 4
jobs:
  # TODO: Remove the example job after testing
  # 5
  example:
    name: Example of a job
    # 6
    runs-on: ubuntu-latest
    # 7
    steps:
```

```
# 8
- name: Echo text
  run: echo This\ is\ my\ first\ Github\ actions\ job
```

> **Note**: Make sure to use the correct indentation for the code above. Otherwise, it might not work correctly.

Here's what the code above does:

1. Defines the name for this specific workflow.
2. Specifies the events on which to execute this workflow. In this case, it will run when the pull request is merged to the develop branch as well as when new code is pushed to the develop branch.
3. Defines the permission scope.
4. Lists the jobs that will run in this workflow.
5. Defines the unique identifier for the job. Jobs from a single workflow run in parallel unless you define that one job is a prerequisite for another one. This is where those unique identifiers come in handy.
6. Specifies the OS for the machine on which the job will run.
7. Lists the steps that will run in a predefined order.
8. Defines the name of the step and command that will be executed.

To see this in action, commit the changes done using the "Example GitHub actions job added" commit message and push it.

> **Note**: Make sure the authorization you're using for this Git repository has a "workflow" scope. If it doesn't, GitHub won't let you push the changes.

Go back to the GitHub page. Under the **Actions** tab, this is what you'll see:

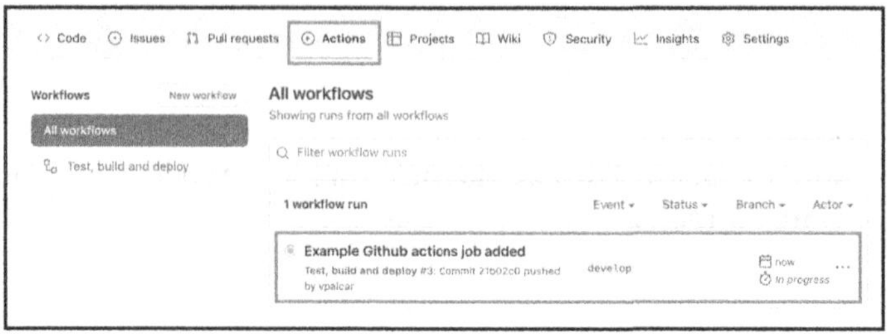


When the workflow completes, this is how the tab will look:

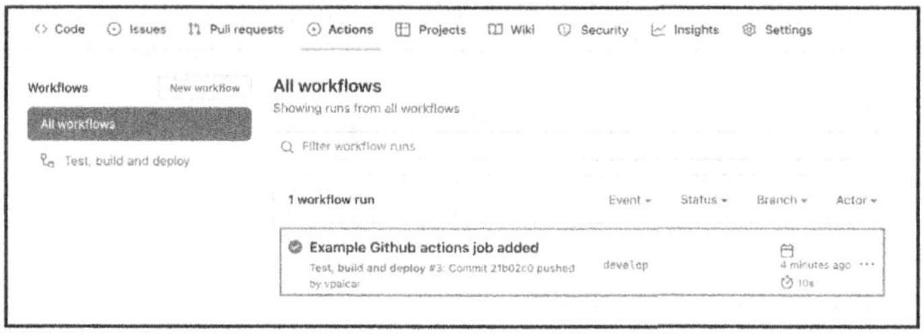


If you click the workflow that just completed, you'll see a list with the jobs run as a part of this workflow:

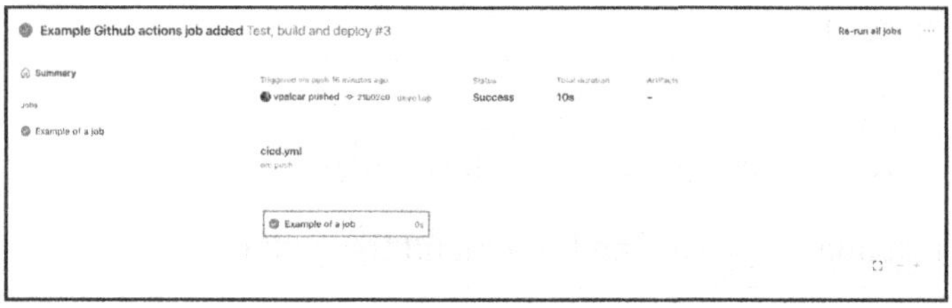


By selecting a specific job, you can check the details of what's been going on:

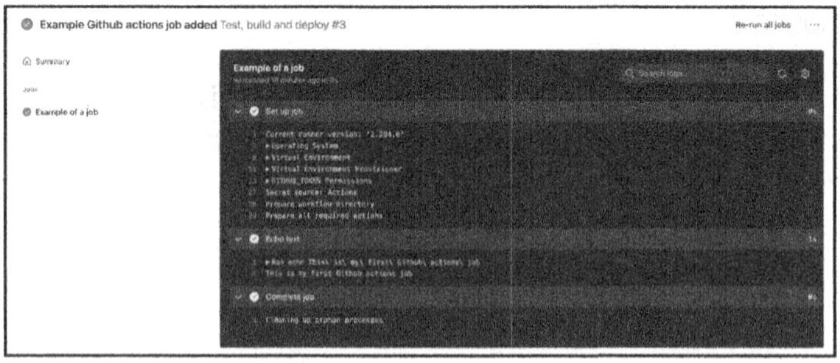

This might feel useless at the moment but is crucial when the job fails. You may notice that, despite the fact that you defined only one step for this specific job, it executed multiple steps. This is because a few steps run before and after the steps you've defined. They set up and clean the machine on which the job is running.

# Automating Test Execution

Now, as you understand the basics, you can start to move to the real deal. Locate `# TODO: Remove the example job after testing`, and replace the code below it with the following:

```
test:
  name: Test
  runs-on: ubuntu-latest
  steps:
    # 1
    - name: Clone flutter repository with master channel
      uses: subosito/flutter-action@v2
      with:
        channel: master

    # 2
    - name: Run flutter doctor
      run: flutter doctor -v

    # 3
    - name: Checkout code
      uses: actions/checkout@v2

    # 4
    - name: Get all packages and test
      run: make get && make testing
# TODO: add a job for building Android app
```

The code above:

1. Clones the Flutter, which is necessary to execute the tests.

2. Runs Flutter doctor, which will install all the necessary development tools.

3. Checks out the code.

4. Fetches the missing packages and runs make test, which will run tests in all packages.

When you commit and push the changes, you should see output very similar to before. By checking the details of this job, you should be able to see whether any tests weren't successful.

# Automating Android Builds

As your tests have run through successfully, you may proceed with building the apps. You'll start with the Android app. To do so, replace `# TODO: add a job for building Android app` with the following code snippet:

```
android:
  name: Build Android
  runs-on: ubuntu-latest
  steps:
    # 1
    - name: Clone flutter repository with master channel
      uses: subosito/flutter-action@v2
      with:
        channel: master
    - name: Run flutter doctor
      run: flutter doctor -v
    - name: Checkout code
      uses: actions/checkout@v2
    # 2
    - name: Set up JDK 1.8
      uses: actions/setup-java@v1
      with:
        java-version: 1.8
    # 3
    - name: Clean and fetch packages
      run: make clean && make get
    #4
    - name: Build apk
      run: flutter build apk
    # TODO: add deployment logic
```

Very similarly to the previous job, you:

1. Clone Flutter, run Flutter doctor and check out the code.
2. Install Java JDK, which is required to build your app.
3. Clean the repository and fetch packages. Additionally, you could add `make lint` and `make format` commands here. They would throw an error and cancel the build in cases where the app doesn't obey the rules of linting or is incorrectly formatted. But the better option would be to use Git hooks with Flutter Lefthook, which would run those two commands before committing. In the case of any issues, it wouldn't let the developer push the changes to the remote. This is a good practice, as it resolves formatting and linting issues before the build.
4. Finally, builds the Android APK.

Having built the APK doesn't help you much if you aren't able to access it. To do so, you need to deploy the app.

To deploy both apps, you'll use Firebase App Distribution.

# Deploying Android App to Firebase App Distribution

Before continuing with coding, you need to take care of a few things. Go to your Firebase console, and locate the App Distribution tab in the left-hand sidebar. When opening it, this is what you should see:

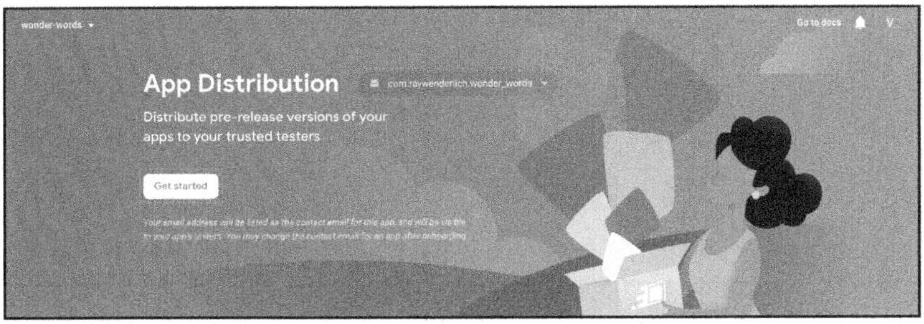


In the drop-down menu, choose the Android app and click **Get started.** It'll take you to the screen where you can upload your Android app and distribute it to your testers:

Continue to the **Testers & Groups** tab. Add the testers who'll test your app, and add them into groups. For now, just create one group that you'll use primarily for Android testing:

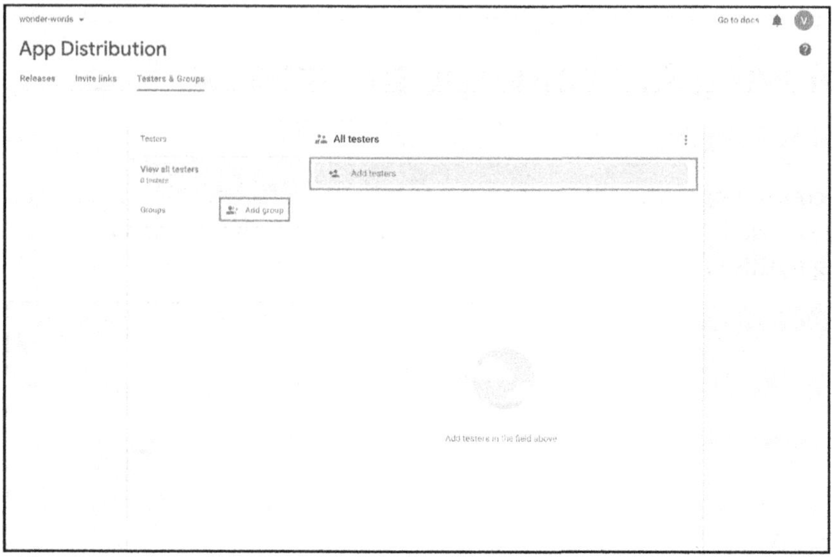


Next, install Firebase tools by running the following command in the home directory:

```
npm install -g firebase-tools
```

> **Note**: Using **npm** to install Firebase tools is the easiest approach. If you don't have npm installed on your computer, see alternative options in Firebase's documentation (https://firebase.google.com/docs/cli).

By running the following command, you can log in to your Firebase account and receive the Firebase CLI token, which you'll need in the next step:

```
firebase login:ci
```

Quite a bit of vulnerable information is connected with the deployment of your app, which shouldn't just be hardcoded in your sources, especially if you use a public repository. But there's a good workaround for securely saving your secrets — you have to set them as environment variables. To achieve that, go back to your repository on the GitHub website, and go to the **Settings** tab:

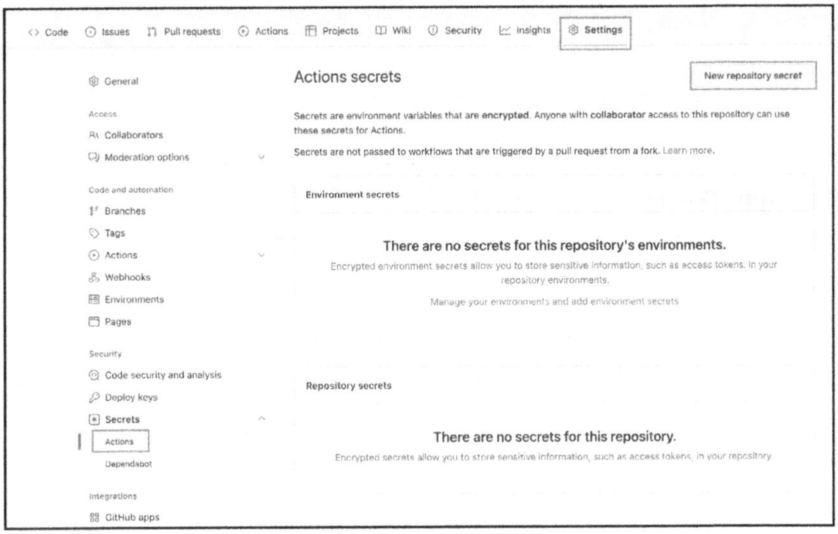


In the sidebar, locate the **Secrets / Actions** tab, and click **New repository secret**. It'll take you to the next screen, where you'll define **FIREBASE_CLI_TOKEN** as a secret name and add the token you received in the previous step after running the `firebase login:ci` command as a value:

You'll repeat the process two more times to store the **TESTERS_GROUPS** variable of the comma-separated list of groups you defined as testers group before and **FIREBASE_APP_ID_ANDROID**, which you can find in the Android settings of the Firebase console:

Under the **App ID** name:

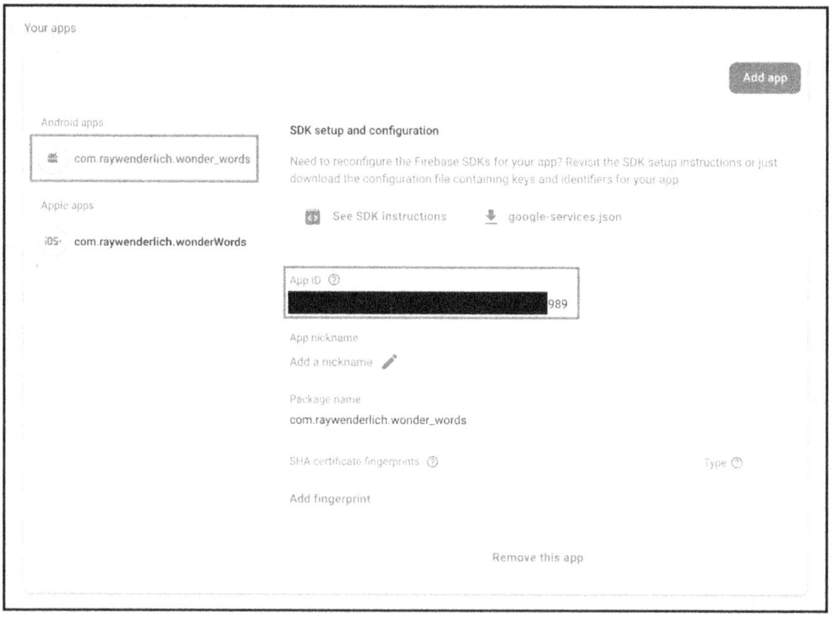

When you add all the missing secrets, this is what the list of secrets should look like:

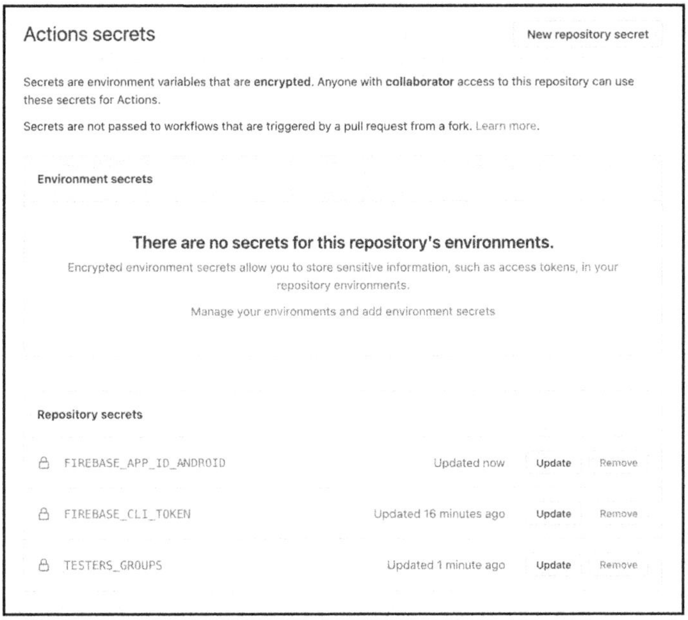


Now, you can finally complete the Android deployment by replacing `# TODO: add deployment logic` with:

```
- name: Firebase App Distribution
  uses: wzieba/Firebase-Distribution-Github-Action@v1
  with:
    appId: ${{ secrets.FIREBASE_APP_ID_ANDROID }}
    token: ${{ secrets.FIREBASE_CLI_TOKEN }}
    groups: ${{ secrets.TESTERS_GROUPS }}
    file: build/app/outputs/flutter-apk/app-release.apk
```

The previous code sets the secrets as well as the Android file path as parameters; everything else is handled by the action on its own. After the deployment successfully completes and after committing and pushing the changes, an app is added in the Firebase App Distribution and mail is sent to the testers:

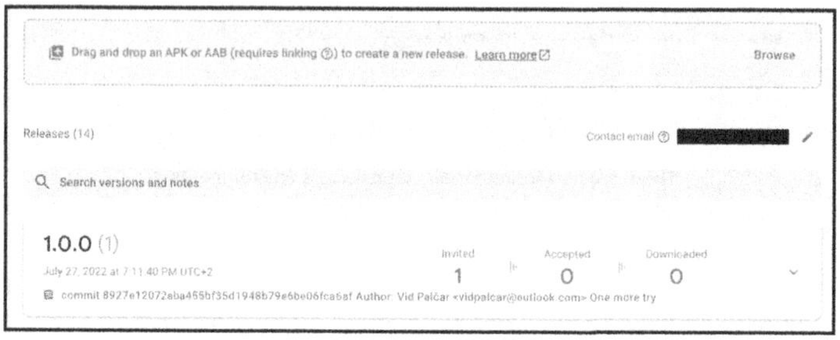


# Automating iOS Builds and Deployment

Unfortunately, iOS build and deployment automation is much more complicated than Android. To build the app, you're required to sign it with Apple developer certificates. The process is very time-consuming and requires installing the whole set of tools. Because this topic is almost broad enough for its own book, check the following video course (https://www.raywenderlich.com/1259223-fastlane-for-ios) covering building and deploying iOS apps using fastlane.

# Key Points

- By automating test execution, software building and deployment, you can save a lot of time by avoiding repetitive work.
- The practice of automating operational tasks is called **CI/CD**, which stands for **continuous integration** and **continuous delivery**.
- Multiple workflows make continuous integration and delivery more efficient. The most common are **Gitflow** and **trunk-based development**.
- **GitHub Actions** is a great tool to help you execute automated testing, software building and deployment.
- To make your life easier, use **fastlane** when implementing a pipeline for iOS app building. Check this video course (https://www.raywenderlich.com/1259223-fastlane-for-ios) to see what fastlane offers.

# Where to Go From Here?

CI/CD is a very big topic; therefore, it's worth exploring a bit deeper than was explained in this chapter. Take a look at how you can use fastlane to deploy both Android and iOS to Google Play and the App Store. Nevertheless, your end users will download your app from the stores, not from the Firebase App Distribution, which can be very convenient for an internal testing team. Also, the current implementation of the pipeline for Android has a smaller flaw; therefore, think about how you could implement an automatic build number incrementation for Android too.

On the other hand, you should look at what can be done when the jobs or workflows are completed. No information is reported if any issues appeared or any tests failed. Think of how to efficiently add build reports to your CI/CD.

# 16 Conclusion

What a ride! You covered many real-world Flutter examples, such as managing state with Cubits and dynamic theming. We hope you enjoyed this ride and that you learned a lot along the way. We encourage you to use these new techniques and knowledge in your projects. Go out there and create your own real-world apps, and come back here if you need help.

If you have any questions or comments as you work through this book, please stop by our forums at https://forums.raywenderlich.com/c/books/real-world-flutter-by-tutorials.

Thank you again for purchasing this book. Your continued support is what makes the tutorials, books, videos, conferences and other things we do at https://www.raywenderlich.com possible, and we truly appreciate it!

— Edson, Vid, Girish, Emily and Matt

The *Real-World Flutter by Tutorials* team

Made in the USA
Monee, IL
08 November 2026

67811062R20223